Pashtun Tales

Aisha Ahmad and Roger Boase

Pashtun Tales

from the
Pakistan-Afghan Frontier

Saqi Books

British Library Cataloguing-in-Publication Data
A catalogue for this book is available from the
British Library

ISBN 0 86356 438 0

copyright © 2003 Aisha Ahmad and Roger Boase

All illustrations, courtesy of the British Library
copyright © the British Library

this edition first published 2003

*The right of Aisha Ahmad and Roger Boase to be identified as the authors of
this work has been asserted by them in accordance with the Copyright, Designs
and Patents Act of 1988*

Saqi Books
26 Westbourne Grove
London W2 5RH
www.saqibooks.com

For my mother
who represents the best in the Pashtun tradition
And in memory
of my beloved father

Aisha

It is not the running around but that which is written on the forehead.

Pashtun proverb

Think in this batter'd Caravanserai
Whose Doorways are alternate Night and Day,
How Sultan after Sultan with his Pomp
Abode his Hour or two, and went his way.

Omar Khayyam

Contents

Contents

Plates

Preface

Peshawar, capital of the North-West Frontier Province of Pakistan, has always been renowned for its folktales. This small city is about twenty miles from the Khyber Pass, the main pass linking Afghanistan with the Indian subcontinent. The name itself, *pesh awar,* means 'frontier town'. In the olden days it was an important stopping-place for traders, because here the caravan routes from China, India, Persia, and Turkestan converged. It is said that travellers used to meet in the famous Qissa Khwani, or Storytellers' Bazaar, where they would exchange stories learnt on their travels.

Despite Peshawar's reputation as a meeting place for storytellers, in 1977, when I asked a friend to find me a professional reciter of tales, he was unable to find one anywhere in the city or in the neighbouring villages. Even after months of searching, he had only found people who knew one or two stories. He mentioned this to a friend of his, a schoolmaster in one of the Mohmand villages, who said that he knew just the person we were looking for. In his village, when he was a boy, all the menfolk used to gather in the *hujra,* or guest-house, during the long winter nights to listen to thetales of Saeed Khan Baba. In his youth Saeed Baba, like most storytellers, had been in the service of a wealthy landowner, but he had later moved to the common village *hujra.*

11

It was in this way that Saeed Khan Baba entered our lives. He was a tall dark Mohmand Pashtun,[1] whom the villagers nicknamed Qissa Khwan (Story Teller) or Qissa Mar (Story Maker). He was illiterate, but claimed to know five hundred stories by heart, some of which, he said, could fill volumes. He was able to recite these stories in either rhymed verse or prose. So in the heat of the summer afternoons, when Peshawar slept, we sat under the large revolving fan, drinking cold water and listening to Saeed Khan Baba, as he brought the room alive with princes and princesses, *jinn* (spirits) and fairies and far-off mountains, fabulous lands where birds and beasts talk and possess more wisdom than wise men.

The storyteller, like the barber, the carpenter, the weaver, or any other craftsman, has his specific place in Pashtun society. He is often a figure of fun and is ridiculed by the villagers. The Pashtun peasant earns his livelihood from the land by sweat and toil, whereas the storyteller makes his living by the ingenuity of his tongue. Since he is obliged by his profession to utter falsehoods to please or flatter his audience, he is often regarded as a sycophant or even a liar. As the princes and landowners grew tired of hearing the old stories, the storyteller had to invent new ones, more fantastic and extraordinary than the last, often using the same folk types and motifs. If he failed to comply, he would lose an audience and be banished from the *hujra*.

Today people in the villages prefer to listen to the radio, and the art of storytelling is beginning to die out in the rural areas as well as in the towns. If these tales had not been recorded and translated, some of them might have vanished without trace and this would have been a great loss.

The traditional Pashtun way of life was seriously disrupted by the social consequences of the Soviet intervention in Afghanistan, the mass exodus of refugees to Pakistan, Iran, and elsewhere, and many years of civil strife. Before 1978 the Pashtuns were much the largest of the many ethnic groups in Afghanistan, constituting more than 51 per cent of the population. But the Soviet invasion and the subsequent civil war greatly altered the ethnic composition of Afghanistan because over 80 per cent of the 6.2 million Afghan refugees who emigrated at that time were Pashtun. By the mid-1990s the Pashtuns formed 45 per cent of the Afghan population. The further destruction and displacement of people, caused by four years of drought, the US military campaign in Afghanistan, and the fall of the Taliban government, reduced that percentage to about 38 per cent, making them still nevertheless the largest of the ethnic groups in Afghanistan.[2]

The Pashtuns form the largest Muslim tribal society in the world. The majority of them live near the Pakistan–Afghan border. In fact far more Pashtuns now live in Pakistan than in Afghanistan – 12 million compared with 7 million. They trace their descent to Qays bin Rashid of Gor, a tribal chieftain of the seventh century AD, whom they claim was the thirty-fifth lineal descendant of Afghana, son of Jeremiah, whom they say was son of Saul, the first king of Israel. However, modern historians believe that they are descendants of the Aryan horde that had moved down from Central Asia a millennium before Alexander the Great crossed the Hindu Kush in 327 BC and whose blood was mixed with that of later invaders.[3]

The stories reflect the Pashtun code of honour, known as *Pakhtunwali*. This code is based on three obligations: revenge, hospitality, and forgiveness.

Revenge. The first duty is to avenge a wrong, *badal*, a word that means 'exchange' or 'retaliation'. According to a well-known Pashto proverb, 'The Pashtun who took revenge after a hundred years said, "I took it too quickly".'[4] In another proverb, it is said: 'Feuds ate up the mountain, taxes the plain.'[5] Tribal feuds over *zar, zan,* and *zamin* (gold, women, and land) are a constant drain on the economy. In the story of 'Musa Khan Deo' (no. 14), when the princess plucks the magic flower from Musa Khan's garden and cuts off his moustache, the demon swears by the honour of his tribe that he will not rest until he has drunk the princess's blood. Similarly, in 'The Barber and the Peasant's Wife' (no. 35), when the barber cuts off the peasant's moustache, the wife disguises herself as a man to avenge the insult.

Hospitality. The second duty is to treat guests with great hospitality, *melmastia*, and to guarantee their security. A debt for hospitality received takes precedence over all other claims,[6] including the duty of retaliation. This is exemplified in the story of 'Prince Bahram' (no. 26) when the prince spares the lives of the six *jinn* whom he has defeated in single combat, because their sister had shown him hospitality by offering him food. At the risk of his own life, he unties the *jinn*, feeling that it would be wrong to refuse the sister's request.

Forgiveness and submission. The third duty is to grant asylum to a person, even an enemy, who comes as a supplicant and sues for peace. This is called *nanawati,* which means 'submission' or 'forgiveness'. This is illustrated in a Baluch folktale: an old *Khan* killed his own son who had brought dishonour on his clan by murdering their guest Badshah Gul in order to avenge his brother's death (Dupree, pp. 127–8). An example of *nanawati* is when four demons, who have been ordered to stand guard over the prince and the princess, fall at the feet of the merchant's demon and ask for his forgiveness because they are his tenants and owe him allegiance (no. 25).

The tales also illustrate many other features of Pashtun society:

Belief in fate or destiny. The Pashtun believes that man is impotent in the face of destiny. 'It is not the running around,' says the proverb, 'but that which is written on the forehead.'[7] This is exemplified in the story of 'Fate and Intelligence' (no. 1; AT 945).[8] If a man is destined to succeed, he will do so despite his blunders, whereas if a man is destined to die, his intelligence will not save him.

Debt among peasants. Poverty and debt are the harsh facts with which the peasant farmer constantly has to contend. As a result of crop failure, or because of extra expenses on such family events as weddings and funerals, or medicine for an ailing relative, he is forced to mortgage his land to a moneylender, to whom he may have to sell his crop before it is harvested. It is for this reason that the vizier, in 'The King and the Clever Vizier' (no. 2), tells his travelling companion to ask the farmer whether he has eaten his stack of wheat, or whether he will eat it. If the farmer had grown the wheat on borrowed money, he might, quite literally, have to starve. In 'The Woodcutter' (no. 29) a poor man is offered a piece of land and some melon seeds by a wealthy landlord, but he does not realize that, in return for the seeds and the lease of the land, he is expected to give the landlord half his crop.

The importance of male heirs. In all peasant societies male children are important. They continue the family line and provide help on the land. If a man dies without leaving behind male heirs, the brother of the deceased may seize his property, thus leaving his family destitute. This is why the vizier, in 'The King and the Clever Vizier' (no. 2), says that a man is not dead if he has male heirs. Three stories are obviously concerned with the desire for male heirs: 'Musa Khan Deo' (no. 14), 'The Sin of Pride' (no. 8), and 'Prince Bahram (no. 26). In each case a king, or rich man, has all that he could wish for, except a son. While he is seated outside in the courtyard, lost in thought, a fakir, or mendicant dervish, notices his troubled expression and provides him with the means of obtaining a male heir.

The stupidity and disloyalty of the menial tribes. The weaver and the barber are both treated with condescension because they belong by their profession to menial tribes. They are considered stupid and are said to be entirely lacking in a sense of honour. They thus provide a butt for humour. In the story of 'The Weavers' (no. 33), the weaver, after falling into a well while fleeing from a sheep, curses his own friend and tries to bribe the sheep with gifts of cloth in order to save his own skin. Similarly, the barber's son (no. 31) repays his generous helper by leaving him prostrate on the ground with a broken leg. Even birds, *jinn*, and fairies belong to tribes. The starling (no. 18), who is from a menial tribe, dishonours her husband, the parrot, by leaving her house in search of worms, thereby breaking her purdah (see *pardah* in the Glossary) and her marriage vow.

The attitude to women. Women are either considered fickle or virtuous. The theme of the adulterous wife, whose black action (*tor*) can only be atoned for by exile or death, occurs in several stories. The black lover embodies the threat of exogamy in a society where people rarely marry outside their clan. In 'Gul and Sanobar' (no. 22) and 'The Three Friends' (no. 23), the wife has a black lover who lives in the jungle. After failing to kill the black man, Sanobar takes his wife to an island, knowing that he will face dishonour if he returns to his father's kingdom. In 'The Three Friends', the king relates how his wife had turned him into a dog upon learning that he had killed her black lover, and how he was eventually able to retaliate by turning her into a donkey (AT 449). In 'The Parrot and the Starling' (no. 18), the parrot recounts how a peasant and a prince both catch their wives with black men. The peasant kills his wife and the prince's wife, and the two men vow never to remarry. In 'The Prince and the Fakir' (no. 19), the prince's low opinion of women is confirmed, although he had tried to guarantee that his wife would always be faithful to him by bringing her up in isolation from society.[9]

It cannot be said that the tales, as a whole, are misogynistic. The virtuous woman, who knows how to preserve her honour, possesses more wisdom and courage than a man. The vizier's wife, in 'The Clever Princess' (no. 6), serves eggs in different colours in order to teach the lecherous king that one woman is much like another (AT 983). But it is worth noting that when the virtuous woman leaves home to engage in heroic deeds, as in the case of the gardener's daughter (no. 4), who faces all kinds of hazards in the search for her lost husband (AT 425), she dresses as a man.

Riddles. Many of the stories contain riddles or enigmatic statements. The solution to these riddles may be the motive for a quest, or the condition imposed for releasing a prisoner or winning the hand of a princess. In 'The King and the Clever Vizier' (no. 2; AT 875D) and 'The Clever Princess' (no. 6), the king sends his vizier in search of an answer to a question, and in both cases it is a clever peasant girl,[10] or her son, who provides the answer. Sometimes the answers to questions are expressed by means of gestures. By pointing to a pool of donkey's urine, by setting fire to a turban-cloth, and by exchanging clothes with the vizier, a woodcutter is able to solve some difficult problems about God and the nature of the world, earning for himself the right to keep the king's gold (no. 29). Another test of wit, involving the use of sign language, is found in the story of 'Sass Begum' (no. 5; AT 516A).

Belief in miracles. Extraordinary feats are performed by fakirs, saints, and persons skilled in sorcery. A *pir*, or saint, turns his begging-bowl upside down, and prays to God that the night will continue until the fakir withdraws the curse that he has put upon one of his disciples (no. 11). In another tale (no. 12), there is a similar test of miraculous power between a saint of Baghdad and a *deo*, or demon, which ends in the demon's conversion to Islam. Many deeds of this kind are related in the story of 'Hazrat Ali Sahib' (no. 27), an exciting apocryphal account of the heroic adventures of Ali, the Prophet Muhammad's son-in-law, and his son Muhammad Hanafiyah, or Hanifah. The most sensational episode is when Hazrat Ali discovers his long-lost son and his wife's head splits open with jealousy, and he then presses the two halves of the head together again. It is in remembrance of this event, says the storyteller, that women part their hair in the middle. Another miracle is the resurrection of the two men in the story of 'The Fakir and the Princess' (no. 13). The princess, in her confusion, places the severed heads on the wrong bodies and is told by the spirit of the dead saint to cut off the heads and repeat the operation. *Jinn* are summoned by the burning of a hair,[11] human beings are kidnapped by fairies and *deo*s, and a friendly *deo* takes Prince Bahram in search of the Princess of the

17

Tower at such speed that his eyes have to be bandaged (no. 26). In 'Gul and Sanobar' (no. 22), the Simurgh,[12] a fabulous bird of Persian mythology, deposits the merchant on the island where the young couple live.

Humour. The majority of the comic tales in this collection concern fools and their absurdities, persons with some physical handicap or affliction, such as baldness or deafness, and impostures of one kind or another. In addition, there is a tale in which two swindlers attempt to swindle each other (no. 30). One swindler pretends to be dead in order to be rid of his companion, who claims a share of the money that they have acquired through perjury. Some robbers, who come across the sham dead swindler, abandon their stolen goods and flee in terror when they hear the voice of his companion concealed in a nearby grave (AT 1532). Perhaps the funniest tale is about the misunderstandings arising from deafness (no. 32). Although the comic tales form the most clearly defined category, humour is not confined to these tales alone. To cite one example, a Hindu vizier is punished for falsely accusing a Muslim vizier of accepting a valuable and exotic bird as a bribe by being made to appear like such a bird (no. 9).

Popular wisdom. In all the tales, even the most fantastic, there is a vein of down-to-earth realism and popular wisdom characteristic of a peasant tribal society. For example, in 'The Dancing Dolls' (no. 20), the peasant sits down and eats the *paratha*s, or pancakes, intended for his wife's lover before putting his wife and her lover to death. In 'The Parrot and the Starling' (no. 18), a woman pulls out the beard of her late husband so that he resembles the thief whose body has disappeared (AT 1510), and the storyteller adds: 'It is an easy matter to remove the hairs from a dead man.' The tales abound in observations of this kind: one way of distinguishing between a man and a woman is that women leap with the left leg forward (no. 14); a parrot dropped from a height can break its fall by landing on its beak;[13] smoke from a fire can be seen a long way off at dawn, just as light from a fire can be seen a long way off at night (no. 26). Even some of the details about exorcism and sorcery are accurately reported. For example, the special prayers which the mullah is asked to perform to exorcize evil spirits in 'The Barber and the Peasant's Wife' (no. 35) would be familiar to a Pashtun audience, as would the use of a charm, or *taweez*, such as is described in 'The Shy Prince' (no. 24).

The style of the tales is always stark and economical. Descriptive adjectives and metaphors are comparatively rare. Often a seemingly irrelevant detail is introduced at the beginning of a tale that later proves to be of vital significance. It has not been my purpose to embellish the tales in any way, but to remain as faithful as possible to the original. However, unnecessary repetition has been avoided and foreign words have been eliminated as far as possible.

Despite the typically Pashtun character of these tales, it should be emphasized that many themes occur which transcend geographical and linguistic boundaries, as will be apparent from the Folkloristic Analysis, the Index of Tale Types, and the Index of Folk Motifs. For example, 'The Lion of the Jungle' (no. 10) is a version of 'Androcles and the Lion', which was recorded by Apion in Greek nearly two thousand years ago, and 'Sweeter Than Salt' (no. 3; AT 923) has been found in many parts of the world and forms the basis of the plot of Shakespeare's *King Lear*. Other tales contain elements from Persian romance and the *Arabian Nights*.

The stories have been divided into six sections: Wit and Intelligence, Virtues and Vices, Miracles and Magic, Courtship and Infidelity, Epic and Romance, and Comedy and Farce. This is merely a convenient system of division since most of these tales contain a blend of wit, fantasy, comedy, and romance. Rhymed ballads and modern epics about local Pashtun heroes have been excluded as extraneous.

I would like to thank Saeed Khan Baba for relating most of the stories in this collection; Misal Khan for introducing me to

Saeed Baba; Feroz Shah, Master Sahib, and Fazle Hadi for helping me to collect the remainder of the tales and for assisting in the oral translation into Urdu.

I am indebted to Tariq and Sikander Ahmed for their generous help and to the late Professor William Brass who encouraged me to undertake my Ph.D. research on Pashtun women[14] and indirectly made this collection possible. I am also indebted to the great English poet John Heath-Stubbs and Professor Akbar Ahmed, the leading authority on Pashtun society, for their valuable advice.

I wish to thank André Gaspard of Saqi Books for agreeing to publish the tales, the Folklore Society for the use of their exhaustive library of folktales, and the British Library for granting permission to reproduce plates from James Atkinson, *Sketches in Afghanistan* (X614), Emily Eden, *Portraits of the Princes and People of Afghanistan* (X43), and James Rattray, *Costumes and Scenery of Afghaunistaun* (X562).

I would also like to mention Moti Ayah, now long dead, who told me my first folktale before I could even walk.

I am grateful to Dr Roger Boase for editing the text and compiling the notes and glossary, to Professor Alan Deyermond for checking the bibliography, and to Kathy, Mansur, and Muin for their critical comments.

However, it is to my parents that I owe my greatest debt, to my mother Nafees Jhan Begum and to my father, the late Mohammed Salahuddin Ahmad, and it is to them that I dedicate this book.

Aisha Ahmad, London, April 2002

I

Wit and Intelligence

1

Luck and Intelligence

Once upon a time Intelligence and Luck were talking to one another. 'If I enter a person, I can make him famous overnight,' said Intelligence.

'Yes perhaps,' replied Luck, 'but if I bestow my favour on a common man, I can raise him from his lowly status to that of a king.'

Intelligence was not convinced. 'I am better and more important than you,' he said proudly.

'No,' retorted Luck, 'I am better than you.'

Each refused to listen to the other. Thus they began to argue. Finally Intelligence had an idea: 'It's no use arguing. Let us have a competition to decide which of us is superior. You will first enter a man, and afterwards I shall enter him, and whichever of us can make him famous will be the winner.'

Now it so happened that at that very moment a poor peasant was returning home after a hard day's work in the fields. 'Look how poor he is,' said Luck, pointing to him. 'Give me three days and I'll show you what I can make of him.'

Intelligence did not believe him: 'All right, let's see what you can do.'

Thus Luck entered the poor peasant as he was returning to his hut in the mountains.

Early next morning the king of that country went out hunting in the same mountains, and by noon he felt very thirsty. Seeing the peasant's hut, he approached and knocked on the door. The peasant came out. 'My good man,' said the king, 'I am extremely thirsty. Give me something to drink.'

The man went indoors and returned promptly with a bowl of cold milk. Now this man had no intelligence, so he did not greet the king or show him any sign of respect. Instead he said brusquely, 'Take this, drink it, and go on your way.' The king was annoyed by the peasant's lack of courtesy, but once his thirst had been quenched he felt better disposed towards him.

'What work do you do?' asked the king politely.

'I'm an honest labourer, not a thief,' replied the peasant, as though he had been accused of stealing.

'Since you claim to be honest, I shall make you my servant,' said the king.

'I am willing to be your servant, but on one condition,' said the stupid peasant, 'and that is that my salary should be equal to that of the vizier.'

To his surprise, the king agreed, and so the poor peasant travelled to the royal palace with his new master.

Now when the courtiers heard that the peasant was to receive the same salary as the vizier, the king's chief minister, they were astonished, and wondered why the king was being so generous to such a stupid and uncouth man. And they ridiculed the newcomer whenever they were given the opportunity.

The vizier was indignant that someone else should receive a salary equal to his own. So he began to plot the peasant's downfall. One day, he called the peasant to one side. 'The king loves you very dearly,' he said. 'Tomorrow, when he is seated on his throne, you must take him by one leg and drag him to the middle of the court room.'

Since the peasant had no intelligence, he agreed to follow the vizier's advice. Next day, when the king was seated on his throne and holding court, the peasant ran into the room, caught hold of one of the king's legs, and dragged him to the middle of the room. The king was shocked and speechless with anger. The conduct of his new servant seemed incomprehensible to him until he heard a crash. He looked round and saw that the roof under which he had been sitting had collapsed, killing everyone who had been standing or sitting beneath it. Luck had come to the peasant's rescue. The king was very pleased. He summoned the peasant and thanked him for saving his life, and bestowed many honours upon him.

The vizier was puzzled by this unexpected turn of events and became even more jealous. He had wished to bring discredit upon the peasant, but instead he had only helped to bring him more success. For many days he was lost in thought, hatching plots to discredit and ruin the peasant. But all his efforts came to naught. Luck was on the side of the poor peasant: whatever he did turned out well, and the king was delighted with him and showered him with gifts and gold coins.

Now, although his efforts to bring about the peasant's downfall had repeatedly failed, the vizier continued to devise new schemes. One day, he again called the peasant aside and said, 'In the past you have greatly benefited from following my advice. The king is very pleased with you and you have been well rewarded. Listen and I shall tell you how to gain even more rewards. Tomorrow, when the king arrives and sits down on his throne, you must knock the turban off his head with a hard blow.'

'It is true,' the peasant said to himself. 'In the past the kind vizier has given me good advice, so I had better do what he suggests.'

Next day, when the king arrived and seated himself on his throne, the peasant knocked the turban off his head with a hard blow. The king was furious and stamped his feet in rage. But, lo and behold, when he looked at his turban, he saw, to his astonishment, that there was a large scorpion inside it. One of his courtiers then boldly stepped forward and killed it. The king realized that his life had been saved once again and that now he was doubly indebted to his new servant, so he called for the servant and offered him his daughter's hand in marriage.

'There!' said Luck to Intelligence. 'Now what do you think? Should I make him a king, or is this sufficient proof of my power?'

'No, wait,' answered Intelligence. 'Let me show you what miracles I can perform.'

So Luck abandoned the man and Intelligence entered him. From that moment onwards the peasant became cautious and pondered deeply before taking any action.

One day, the king was taking an afternoon nap in the garden when a pigeon flew by and let fall its droppings on his collar. The peasant happened to be passing. He saw this, and thought to himself: 'If the king wakes up and sees this dirt on his collar, he will be very angry.' So he took out his dagger and, as quickly and as quietly as he could, he tried to remove the droppings. But suddenly, with a start, the king awoke. 'You ungrateful wretch!' he cried in anger when he saw the dagger in his servant's hand. 'So now you want to murder me and sit on my throne.' Without waiting for an explanation, he ordered his guards to cut off the man's head. And, without delay, the executioner cut off his head with one stroke of the sword.

Intelligence said nothing. 'Now do you admit that I am superior!' said Luck triumphantly.

2

The King and the Clever Vizier

here was once a king who was widely renowned for his wisdom. Yet certain questions about the world continued to trouble him. One day, he called his vizier, and said to him, 'I want you to find the answer to a question to which I have given much thought and to which I can find no solution: Are there more intelligent than unintelligent people in the world?'

The vizier agreed to search for the answer to this question, although he did not know where to begin, or which route to take, or whom to ask. But since he was accustomed to dealing with problems of this nature, this particular question did not seem insoluble. So he decided to go into the world in search of the answer. He left the palace and took the first path that he came to.

After walking for many miles, the vizier noticed a man walking in front of him who was heading in the same direction. He quickened his pace and caught up with him.

'My good man, where are you going?' asked the vizier, when the two men had exchanged greetings.

'I am going to my village,' replied the man.

The vizier decided to accompany him. On the way to the village they passed a graveyard. There they saw some men digging a grave.

The vizier stopped and turned to his companion: 'Go to the gravediggers and do as I say. First greet them with the customary words, "May you never feel tired." Then you must inquire whether they are burying the living or the dead, and see what they say.'

So the man approached the gravediggers. First, he greeted them with the words, 'May you never feel tired,' to which they replied, 'You are welcome.' Then he asked them, 'Are you burying the living or the dead?'

'O foolish man!' they cried, beating him on the head with their spades. 'How can you bury the living?'

The man did not stay in that place for long. He hurried back to his travelling companion.

'What was their answer?' asked the vizier.

'You got me into trouble for no good reason,' replied the man in annoyance. 'When I asked them, "Are you burying the living or the dead?" they thought me a fool and beat me on the head with their spades, and said, "How can you bury the living?"'

'It is they who are the fools,' said the vizier, shaking his head. 'Let us go on our way.'

They travelled in silence for some time until they met a farmer. This man had just finished harvesting his wheat, and had built a large stack in one of his fields. He had sent one of his sons home to fetch sacks for the grain. He had a satisfied smile on his face as he tidied the stack with his pitchfork. After some time his son appeared with the sacks and a pair of scales.

The vizier turned to his companion, and said, 'Go and greet the farmer. Then ask him whether he has eaten the wheat he has harvested, or whether he is going to eat it.'

The man approached the farmer and repeated the vizier's question, 'Brother, have you eaten the wheat, or are you going to eat it?'

On hearing this, the smile disappeared from the farmer's face, and he struck the man with his pitchfork, saying, 'O foolish man, I am just stacking the wheat. How could I have eaten it?' So once again the man returned to the vizier with a look of accusation.

'What did the farmer say?' asked the vizier, before his companion had time to say anything.

'He struck me with his pitchfork, and said, "O foolish man, I am just stacking the wheat. How could I have eaten it?"'

'It is he who is foolish,' said the vizier, shaking his head again. 'He does not understand.'

They left the farmer with his stack of wheat and continued on their way until they came to a river. When they reached the bank of the river, the vizier said to his companion, 'You be my bridge to cross the river, or I shall be your bridge.'

The man looked at the river, and replied, 'The river is very wide. Even if I were to lie down, I wouldn't be able to span it. It would be best,' he suggested, 'if we both hitched up our trousers and attempted to cross the river on foot.'

So they hitched up their trousers, took off their shoes, and waded across the river. After reaching the far bank, they walked on until they came to the village where the vizier's companion lived. 'Look!' he said, pointing. 'We have reached my village. You are welcome to come and eat and stay the night in my house.'

The vizier declined the invitation. 'No,' he said, 'the only place in the village where I intend to spend the night is a place where there are no dogs.'

The man was puzzled. 'There is no such place in the village,' he said.

The two men bade each other farewell and prepared to go their separate ways. Before parting, the vizier offered some advice: 'When you approach your house, you shouldclear your throat. Then, when you reach the door of your house, you should clear your throat a second time. Then, when you enter the house, you should clear your throat a third time.'

Now this man had a young daughter. And it so happened that, on account of the heat, she had come out into the courtyard to have a bath. When she heard the first cough, she knew that her father had returned home, so she quickly put on her blouse; when she hea rd the second cough, she put on her *shalwar* trousers; and when she heard the third cough, she covered her head with a veil. So when her father entered, she was ready to greet him. 'Father,' she said, 'who were you with today who made you so wise?'

'I was with the biggest fool in the world,' he replied, and he recounted what had happened: 'We were walking together when we saw some men digging a grave, and he told me to ask them whether they were burying the living or the dead. I went up to them and asked them this question, and they beat me with their spades, saying, "How can you bury the living?" I returned to the vizier and reported what they had said, and he answered, "They are foolish."'

'Your companion was right,' said his daughter, who had been frowning with concentration. 'If he has heirs and his heirs are alive, he is not dead but living.'

The man cor.tinued with his story: 'Then we met a farmer who had just finished harvesting his wheat. He had built a large stack, which he was tidying with his pitchfork. The vizier told me to ask him whether he had already eaten his wheat, or whether he was going to eat it. When I repeated the vizier's question, the farmer struck me with his pitchfork, and said, "I am just stacking the wheat. How could I have eaten it?"'

The daughter, who had been listening carefully, said, 'It is the farmer who is stupid, not your companion. Your companion wanted to know whether the farmer had already eaten his wheat, because he had borrowed money to grow it, or whether he had no debts to settle and was going to sell it.'

The man continued with his story: 'We walked and walked until we came to the bank of a river. At this point the vizier said that I could be his bridge or he could be my bridge. I naturally told him that the river was too wide for me to lie across, and I suggested that we hitch up our trousers and wade across on foot.'

When the daughter heard this she said, 'He was right, because if he had crossed the river on your shoulders, or you on his, one of you would have crossed without getting his feet wet.' Then she asked, 'Where is this man?'

'I invited him to spend the night in our house,' replied the father, 'but he said that he would spend the night in a place where there are no dogs. So I told him that there was no such place in the village.'

'Hurry!' exclaimed the daughter, 'He must be in the mosque where no dogs are allowed to enter.'

The father went to the mosque, and to his great surprise, he found the vizier sitting there.

'How did you find me?' asked the vizier.

The man explained: 'When I coughed three times before entering my house, my daughter asked me who had taught me to be so intelligent. So I told her how we had met, and gave her an account of the day's events, and she told me where to find you, for she wishes to invite you to spend the night in our house.'

The vizier accepted the invitation. He was delighted that he had discovered one intelligent person among all the unintelligent people whom he had met that day.

3

Sweeter than Salt

here was a rich and powerful king who had seven daughters. One day he summoned all his daughters and told them to sit with him. They sat down and started to talk among themselves.

Then the king suddenly turned to his eldest daughter. 'How much do you love me?' he asked.

'Dear father, to me you are sweeter than sugar,' she answered, without hesitation.

The king was very pleased, and put the same question to each of his daughters in turn. The second daughter answered, 'As sweet as honey.' The third, 'As sweet as molasses.' The fourth, 'As sweet as brown sugar.' The fifth, 'As sweet as sherbet.' And the sixth, 'As sweet as the sweetest *halwa* sweet.'

The king, much flattered by these replies, now turned to his youngest daughter. 'And how sweet am I to you?' he asked.

The youngest daughter thought for a while, then answered, 'Respected father, you are sweeter to me than salt.'

The king was furious with his youngest daughter, and all her sisters reproached her. 'You should be ashamed of yourself for

1. Interior of the Palace of Shah Shujan, King of Kabul (Rattray, pl. 3)

2. Dost Muhammad Khan Barakzai (Rattray, pl. 2)

3. Mirza Fayz, an Usbek Ambassador (Rattray, pl. 22)

4. Lady of Kabul (Rattray, pl. 24)

5.   Mosque and Tomb of the Emperor Sultan Mahmud of Ghazni (Rattray, pl. 10)

6.   The Avenue at Babur's Tomb (Atkinson, pl. 23)

insulting our father,' they said. 'Couldn't you have compared your love to something other than salt? Ask for his forgiveness immediately,' they advised her, 'and apologize for what you have said.'

'But what I said is true,' replied the innocent little princess. 'To me my father is sweeter than salt.'

Hearing this, the king grew even more annoyed. He stamped his foot and ordered his youngest daughter to leave the palace at once, vowing never to set eyes on her again.

When the princess left the palace she had nowhere to go. She wandered sadly through the city, but was unable to find a place to lie down and rest. So she continued to walk until she came to a forest. Tired and lonely, she lay down to sleep on a bed of leaves, and here in the forest she made her home, livingon fruit that she picked from the trees.

Time passed, and one day, as the princess was walking through the forest, she came upon an old woman who was sitting on the bank of a river grinding corn. The princess sat down quietly beside her.

'Who are you, my child?' asked the old woman, surprised to find a stranger sitting beside her.

Hearing these kind words, the princess was reminded of her sorrow and began to weep. The old woman stopped grinding the corn and embraced the young girl. 'Who are you?' she asked once again. 'Where have you come from? And where are you going?'

'Mother,' replied the princess, 'I'm a poor defenceless girl with no one in the world to help me except God. As I was wandering through the forest I saw you, so I came and sat down beside you. I have nowhere to go,' she added, 'so if you will allow me, I shall be your servant.'

'My child,' answered the old woman, 'I have only one son in this world. We are poor, but content. He cuts wood in the forest, loads it on a donkey, and takes it to the city. There he sells it in the bazaar. With the money he receives, he buys corn, and I grind the corn to make bread for our two daily meals. You are welcome to stay with us and be my daughter.'

That evening, when the old woman's son returned home, he was surprised to see a young girl sitting with his mother. 'Who is she?' he asked.

'She is a stranger to these parts,' replied the mother, 'and has no one in the world to care for her, so I have made her my daughter.'

The young man was delighted to have such a beautiful companion. 'God-willing,[1] you will live with us in comfort,' he said, addressing the princess. 'The only difficult work is chopping wood and I do that myself. You can stay at home with my mother and help her with the housework.'

'Of course I shall help in the house,' replied the princess, 'but I shall also go with you to the forest every day to chop wood.'

'Chopping wood isn't easy,' protested the young man.

'If I am to stay here,' she insisted, 'I must be given my fair share of work.'

So the princess settled down to her new life with the old woman and her son. Every morning she would accompany the young man to the forest to chop wood. The son was very happy because he could not have found a more beautiful young companion. The princess had also grown very fond of him. They would talk together for hours, and the days passed quickly.

One day the princess had gone to the forest as usual and was attempting to cut one of the lower branches of an old knotted tree when she noticed on the topmost branch two black snakes. The two snakes were sitting talking to one another. She stopped cutting and hid so that she could listen to their conversation.

'My friend,' said one snake to the other, 'tell me something unusual.'

'What could be more unusual than this very tree on which we are sitting,' replied the other snake. 'Underneath this tree is buried the biggest treasure in the world. There is so much gold, and there are so many precious stones, that even the wealth of two kings would seem small by comparison.'

The first snake was amazed. 'Is this really true?' he said, and then added thoughtfully, 'But as long as we are alive no one will ever be able to cut down the tree and dig up its roots to lay their hands on the treasure.'

'You are right,' whispered his friend, 'but there is just one way of destroying us. If someone sets fire to the tree, we shall be helpless, because we ourselves will be burnt to death as well as the tree.'

When the princess heard this conversation she crept away and then ran to her companion. 'Make haste,' she said, 'we must return home.'

'But we haven't cut any wood as yet,' objected the young man.

'Don't worry. We shan't be needing any wood. I'll explain it all to you later.'

They ran home as fast as their legs would carry them and looked for some matches. Once they had found some, they went back to the forest and stealthily made their way to the old knotted tree. Then the princess asked the young man to place some dry sticks round the tree and to kindle a fire. He did not argue, but did exactly as he was told. When the fire began to blaze and bright orange flames licked all the branches, the snakes wriggled from one side to the other in an effort to escape.

The snakes begged the princess to save them. 'We promise never to harm you,' they pleaded. But the princess did not listen, for she knew that they could not be trusted, and soon the flames enveloped them.

'We deserve to die, it is our fault,' said one snake to the other. 'If we had guarded our secret, instead of opening our mouths, we would still be alive today.' With these words, the two black snakes were burnt to death, and in next to no time the tree was reduced to cinders.

When the ashes had cooled, the princess and the woodcutter started digging. They first pulled up the roots of the tree, and then dug deeper. After digging for a long time, they discovered twenty chests.

'What are these?' asked the young man.

'Be quiet, and load them on the donkey,' replied the princess.

The chests were so heavy that they had to make several trips to transport them to the house. The princess took some of the chests, while the woodcutter stayed behind to guard the others and wait for her return. In this way they managed to take them all home.

'Daughter, what are these?' asked the old woman.

'Open the m,' replied the princess, 'and you will see for yourself.'

When they opened the chests, they were astonished to see gold, diamonds, and all kinds of precious stones. The princess took a large diamond from one of the chests and said to the woodcutter, 'Go to the bazaar in the city, sell this diamond, and buy food for us all.'

The woodcutter set off happily for the city. When he reached the city, he went to the first jeweller in the bazaar and showed him the diamond. The jeweller looked at it, then shook his head regretfully and gave it back. 'I cannot buy this,' he said, 'it is too valuable. Go to the biggest jeweller in the city; perhaps he may be able to help you.'

The woodcutter visited many jewellers' shops in the bazaar, but no one could afford to buy his diamond. Finally, he entered the last shop, which was the biggest of them all. The jeweller gasped when he saw the sparkling stone. 'I'm afraid I cannot afford to pay for this beautiful diamond,' he said, 'but you can take my entire shop and all its contents in exchange for it.' The woodcutter agreed. So the jeweller took the diamond and handed over the keys of his shop.

After collecting some money from the till, the woodcutter locked up the shop, bought a plentiful supply of food, and returned home.

'How much did you sell the diamond for?' asked the princess, when he arrived home laden with food. Whereupon the young man recounted what had happened and how he had acquired a jeweller's shop in exchange for the diamond.

Next morning the princess gave the woodcutter more instructions. 'Go to the bazaar,' she said, 'and buy a fine horse for yourself and fine clothes for all of us.'

The young man went to the city again and bought the finest thoroughbred horse that he could find. Then he bought some expensive cloth for his mother and the princess, and also some cloth for himself. He waited at the tailor's shop until the clothes were ready and then rode home with them.

Next day the princess sent the young man in search of forty labourers to build her a magnificent palace in the middle of the forest. The labourers arrived and work startedon the palace. It was such a splendid building that it took two years to complete. In the meantime, the old woman arranged the marriage of the young princess and her son. The young man's business had prospered in the city and his name had become well known all over the kingdom. He was renowned for his wealth and honesty and for his generosity to the poor and needy.

Many years passed. One day it so happened that the king went out hunting with his vizier and his guards in that same forest. They had spent the whole day hunting, buthad failed to shoot any game. They had lost their way and were feeling hungry and exhausted when they came across a magnificent palace.

'Who owns this palace?' inquired the king, turning to his companions.

'I've heard of this palace,' replied one of the king's guards. 'It belongs to the biggest jeweller in the city, a man renowned for his wealth and generosity.'

Hearing this, the king called aside his vizier. 'Go and inform them that I shall be their guest tonight. We shall see for ourselves how generous he is and how he entertains his guests.'

The vizier took the message to the palace. When the princess heard that her father would be their guest that night, she sent word to her husband to return home at once, and she ordered her servants to prepare a huge banquet.

The jeweller hurried home to greet his new guests. The king and the vizier were ushered into the banqueting hall; the other members of the king's retinue were lavishly entertained in the *hujra* (guest-quarters).

As soon as the king and the vizier were seated, the dinner was served. On one tray the servants brought *pilau* rice, sweet saffron rice, chicken, lamb, *halwa*, and sherbet. On a separate tray they brought maize bread, spinach, and yoghurt. The princess had ordered that all the rich dishes should be excellently cooked, but she had given instructions that they should contain no salt. Salt was only to be used in the simple dishes of spinach and maize bread.

After tasting the various dishes, the king and the vizier pushed aside the rich dishes and ate only the food containing salt.

When they had finished eating the jeweller asked them politely, 'Did you enjoy your meal in our humble house?'

'The food was excellent,' they both replied. 'But it had one serious fault,' added the king. 'There was no salt in it, and without salt, food has no taste. Therefore we both preferred eating the simple spinach and maize bread, which contained salt.'

At that moment the young princess entered the room. 'Respected father,' she said, 'you are sweeter to me than salt is to food.' The king was astonished to see his daughter, and both the jeweller and the vizier were puzzled by the princess's words. 'Tell me, daughter, how did you come here?' asked the king. The princess gave the king a full account of everything that had happened to her since she had left the royal palace. Then she explained: 'I gave special orders that salt should not be put in your food, because you don't like salt.'

The king bent his head in shame. 'My daughter, I beg you not to reproach me. What you said about your love being sweeter than salt is absolutely true and I ask for your forgiveness.'

The king told his daughter to rise and embraced her. After escorting the princess and her husband back to his kingdom, the king entrusted the care of his realm to his new son-in-law, and they lived happily ever after.

4

The Gardener's Daughter

here was once a good king who had only one son. This son was so fond of women that he had forty wives.

One day the prince and the vizier had gone out hunting on horseback, and had wandered far afield, when they came to a garden. In the middle of the garden there was a *charpoy* bed, and on the bed sat the gardener's daughter. Her friends were bringing her flowers from the garden, and she was making garlands. They say that this girl was exceedingly beautiful and when the prince saw her, he fell in love with her. 'Let us go home at once and make the necessary arrangements,' he said to the vizier, 'because I have fallen in love with the gardener's daughter.'

The vizier accompanied the prince to the palace and informed the king, 'Your son wishes to marry the gardener's daughter.'

When the king heard this, he summoned his advisers, and they agreed that a message should be sent to the gardener, requesting that he allow the young prince to marry his daughter. But the gardener was not happy to receive this message. 'I do not wish to marry my daughter to the prince. I would prefer that she marry a poor man like myself.'

The envoys returned to the king and gave him the gardener's reply. Undeterred, the king sent his vizier. He too, however, returned empty-handed. So the king himself, accompanied by his vizier and his guards, went to visit the gardener. 'My son likes your daughter,' he said, 'therefore I command that you give your consent to the marriage.'

The gardener invited the king and his companions to be seated. 'I'll call all my relatives together,' he said, 'and if one of them is willing to marry my daughter, then I cannot give her to you; but if none of them wishes to have her, then you may take her.'[1]

Once the king had agreed to this proposal the gardener sent for all his male relatives. When they had gathered together he asked them, 'Would any of you like to marry my daughter?' There was no answer. The gardener then turned to the king. 'I am now ready to give my daughter to you,' he said.

The king was very pleased. 'Tell me what you would like in return?' he asked.

'Three thousand rupees as a bride-price,' replied the gardener.[2]

When the price was agreed, and the wedding date was fixed, the king returned to the palace and ordered that preparations for his son's marriage should begin immediately.

On the appointed day the wedding procession made its way to the gardener's house. The marriage ceremony was performed, and the bride was placed in a palanquin and carried to the prince's palace. When the prince approached the palanquin, the gardener's daughter called out from behind the curtain, 'You approach me with such deference that one would think that you had married the daughter of King Rustam, and not the daughter of a poor gardener.'

Hearing this, the prince stopped and turned to one of the men in the procession. 'Where is the kingdom of King Rustam?' he inquired.

The man pointed to the east. 'In that direction,' he replied. The prince did not waste another moment, but set out eastwards.

After travelling for three days, he met five swindlers. One of them was a woman. They had made a comfortable resting-place by the roadside, and whenever a traveller passed they would invite him to sit down and rest. Then, while their guest was resting, they would produce some cards and say, 'Come, let's play.' In this manner they cheated many an innocent wayfarer.

When the prince reached this spot, the swindlers invited him to join them, and while he was resting, they placed some cards before him and urged him to play. The prince agreed, and began to gamble with the swindlers. By the end of the day he had lost all his money.

Then one of the swindlers said, 'You haven't any money left. You cannot gamble empty-handed, but you can always play for the clothes you are wearing.'

'Do you want to strip me naked?' asked the prince.

'If you lose the game, we will give you some old clothes to wear in exchange for your new ones,' the swindlers replied.

The prince agreed, and he and the swindlers gambled together. Once again he lost the game and had to forfeit his new clothes. The swindlers gave him some old clothes, which he put on, and then he continued on his way.

After travelling for many days, he finally reached the kingdom of King Rustam. 'I must make a proposal of marriage to King Rustam's daughter,' he said to himself. So he asked the citizens, 'What is the custom in this country for those who wish to ask for the princess's hand in marriage?'

They replied: 'In the courtyard of the palace you will find a drum, and near it sits a watchman. If you go and beat the drum, you will be taken into the king's presence. Then you can ask the king whatever you want.'

The prince went to the royal courtyard and began to beat the drum. No sooner had he done so than the watchman stepped forward and took him into the king's presence.

'What brings you here?' inquired the king.

'You have a daughter and I have come to marry her,' said the prince.

'Before I give my daughter to you,' said the king, 'you will have to answer three simple questions. If you fail to answer these questions, I shall order your head to be cut off.'

'What is the first?' asked the prince.

'First, what, in this world, brings man the greatest happiness?'

'Land and wealth,' replied the prince.

'No,' said the king. 'You have failed the first test.' Then he asked, 'What is the most useful thing in the world which is moist?'

'Butter,' replied the prince.

'No,' said the king. 'You have failed the second test.' Then he asked, 'What plant produces the best flower in the world?'

'The rose-bush produces the best flower in the world,' replied the prince.

'You have failed all three tests,' said the king, and he ordered the executioner to cut off his head.

When the princess heard the news, she approached her father, and said, 'Please don't cut off his head. Give him a water-bag and he can water my plants for me.' So the prince was given a leather water-bag and became King Rustam's water-carrier.

Meanwhile, the gardener's daughter had just arrived at her husband's palace. There she met the prince's other wives. 'Where is the prince and how does he spend his time?' they all inquired.

'Since the day of my marriage I haven't set eyes on him,' she replied. 'I'm so worried about him. Whenever I eat bread, I wonder to myself, "Has the prince eaten or not?" Whenever I lie down on my bed, I wonder, "Has he found a place to rest?" God alone knows what trouble he may be in.' Then she appealed to the other wives, 'If one of you is prepared to rescue him from King Rustam, I shall accept her as my leader and I shall become her faithful servant; but if no one volunteers, you must accept me as your leader and we shall set out to rescue him.'

The wives unanimously agreed to appoint the gardener's daughter as their leader, and she issued them with instructions: 'You must keep whatever money you receive until this coming Friday, and by the following Friday every woman must obtain men's clothing and a sword.'

By the second Friday each of the prince's wives had managed to obtain men's clothing and a sword. They all met in the gardener's daughter's room, and she led them to the king's stables. She summoned the groom. 'We are the forty-one wives of the prince,' she announced, 'and we require forty-one horses because we wish to go out for a ride.'

Having procured the horses, they put on men's clothes and rode off. Next morning the people of the kingdom began whispering among themselves. There was a rumour that the prince's wives had run away.

After travelling for three days, the prince's wives met the five swindlers. The wives greeted them. 'Peace be upon you,' they said. 'And peace be upon you also' came the reply. The swindlers then invited the wives to come and rest for a while. As soon as the wives had sat down the gardener's daughter noticed the prince's clothes lying in a corner. She thought to herself: 'They probably won those clothes from him at cards; they must have given him other clothes or sent him away naked.' While these thoughts were running through her head, one of the swindlers showed her some cards, and said, 'Place a bet on the king and whoever picks that card is the winner.'

The gardener's daughter placed a bet of a thousand rupees on the king. The swindler lost. So she placed a bet of two thousand rupees on the king and the swindler did the same. Once again the gardener's daughter won. The swindlers wanted her to continue the game, but she hid the cards.

'What are you betting now?' they inquired.

'Nothing,' she replied, rising to her feet.

They pleaded and begged, but she refused to continue the game. The swindlers thought to themselves: 'If she spends the night with us here, we can easily recover the money.' So they said to her and her companions: 'Please, we invite you to spend the night here as our guests.'

Since the gardener's daughter was determined to win back her husband's clothes, and thus take revenge on her husband's behalf, she agreed. She called all the wives together and gave them instructions: 'Four of you must keep watch during the first hour of the night; four of you during the second hour of the night; four of you during the third hour of the night; four of you during the fourth hour of the night, and so on. Observe very carefully the eyes of the female swindler. When she is fast asleep, hide my shoes somewhere.'

During the third hour of the night, the female swindler fell asleep. So the four wives who were keeping watch took the gardener's daughter's shoes and hid them, and then they themselves went to sleep.

They all awoke soon after daybreak. The gardener's daughter pretended to look for her shoes, which her companions had hidden at her own request. She turned to the female swindler and complained: 'You have acted dishonestly: you have stolen my shoes. If you had asked me, I would have given them to you.'

The female swindler denied that she had stolen the shoes.

'If you haven't stolen my shoes, then your companions have,' retorted the gardener's daughter.

The female swindler turned to her companions. 'If you have stolen the shoes without my knowledge, I ask you to return them at once,' she said.

The four male swindlers pleaded innocence.

'All right,' said the gardener's daughter, 'I shall search through your belongings, and if I find my shoes hidden among them, I shall take everything you possess save the clothes you are wearing.'

The swindlers quickly agreed to this condition, because the gardener's daughter and her companions outnumbered them and surpassed them in strength. The gardener's daughter and her companion numbered forty-one, whereas the swindlers only numbered five. The gardener's daughter ordered her companions to make a thorough search of the swindlers' belongings. Of course the wives knew exactly where to find the shoes because they themselves had hidden them. When they returned with the shoes, the gardener's daughter said to them, 'Gather together all the swindlers' belongings and let us go on our way.'

The female swindler fell at the feet of the gardener's daughter. 'Take me with you,' she begged. The gardener's daughter agreed. Then, believing that they were all men, the female swindler made a proposal of marriage: 'Either you can marry me yourself, or else you can marry me to one of your followers.'

'We'll decide about that later,' replied the gardener's daughter.

So the gardener's daughter, her forty companions, and the female swindler continued on their way. After travelling for many days, they reached the kingdom of King Rustam. They pitched their tents outside the city gates and began to prepare a meal. 'You sit down and eat and drink,' instructed the gardener's daughter, 'while I go into the city to find out what King Rustam has done to the prince.'

She entered the city and inquired: 'What did King Rustam do to the last man who came seeking his daughter's hand in marriage?'

The people answered: 'The king asked him to answer three questions, but he could not answer them, so he ordered his executioner to cut off his head. But the princess persuaded her father to spare the man's life and to give him a water-bag with which to water her plants.'

The gardener's daughter was happy and relieved to learn that her husband was still alive. 'I shall spend the night in the city,' she thought. She accosted some people in the street. 'I am a traveller,' she explained. 'Where can I spend the night?'

'There is a wise old woman in the city. You can spend the night on her house,' they told her.

She went to the old woman's house and knocked on the door. 'I am a traveller,' she said. 'Will you allow me to spend the night here?'

'Do come in,' replied the old woman. 'You are welcome to make this your home as long as you stay in our city.'

Then the gardener's daughter gave the old woman three rupees. 'Please,' she said, 'go and buy the necessary food and prepare something for my dinner.'

In those days things were cheap. So the old woman was able to buy a chicken for one rupee, lentils for eight annas, and rice for eight annas. And she saved the third rupee for herself.

In the evening the gardener's daughter asked, 'Do you have a bed for me?'

'Yes,' answered the old woman. 'If you give me one rupee, I shall give you a bed.'

The gardener's daughter gave her another rupee, and then inquired, 'Is it true that King Rustam has a beautiful daughter?'

'Yes,' replied the old woman, 'she is very beautiful.'

'If she is so beautiful, why doesn't she marry?'

The old woman explained: 'There are three conditions attached to her marriage. The king is only willing to marry her to the man who can give the correct answer to three questions.'

'What are these three questions which no one has succeeded in answering?'

'They are really very simple,' said the old woman. 'The first question is: What, in this world, brings man the greatest happiness? The answer is obvious: children – for if God blesses a man with children, this is the greatest source of joy. The second question is: What is the most useful thing in the world that is moist? The answer of course is rainwater, for without it the crops would die. The third and final question is: What plant produces the best flower in the world? The cotton flower is the best and most beautiful flower in the world, because, by means of this flower, decency is everywhere preserved, since from it comes the cotton out of which our clothes are made.'

Next morning the gardener's daughter took leave of the old woman. Then she went straight to the courtyard in the royal palace where the drum was kept, and she started to beat on it. Whereas all previous suitors had barely touched the drum for fear that they would make too much noise, she beat it so hard that it broke.

'Why did you break the drum?' asked the watchman.

'It has served its purpose,' she replied. 'From now on it will be of no use to anyone.'

The watchman led the girl into the king's presence. 'This youth has broken the drum.'

'What is the purpose of your visit?' inquired the king.

'You have a daughter and I would like to win her hand,' she answered.

'In order to do that,' said the king, 'you will first have to answer three questions. If you answer them correctly, my daughter is yours; if not, I shall order my executioner to cut off your head.'

The gardener's daughter was confident. 'All right, I'm ready for your questions.'

'What, in this world, brings man the greatest happiness?'

'Children, if God grants them to a man,' she answered.

The king smiled and said, 'This youth has answered the first question correctly.' The judges nodded their heads. Then he asked the second question: 'What is the most useful thing in the world that is moist?'

'Rainwater,' she answered.

'Correct,' said the king, and he turned to the judges and exclaimed, 'He has passed the second test.' Then he asked the third question: 'What plant produces the best flower in the world?'

'The cotton-flower is the best flower in the world,' she replied without hesitation.

The judges were united in their verdict: 'This youth has answered your three questions correctly. Now you must allow him to marry your daughter.'

The king invited the gardener's daughter to be seated. 'I am willing to allow you to marry my daughter,' he said, 'but do you have a house and a village of your own?'

'Do not be deceived by my appearance,' she replied. 'My tents and my attendants are outside the city gates.'

Hearing this, the king guessed that this youth must be of royal birth and he was very pleased.

'Put your daughter in a palanquin,' said the gardener's daughter, 'and send her to my tent.' When the king had done this, she made a second request: 'My attendants and I have had trouble obtaining water, and we need a water-carrier.'

The king summoned all his water-carriers. 'Choose the man you want,' he said.

The gardener's daughter chose the prince, her husband, and took him back to her tent. There, without revealing her true identity, she gave him instructions: 'Go and fetch a mullah from the city.'

'Why a mullah?' asked the prince.

'Because I shall have you married to the daughter of King Rustam.'

The prince could hardly believe his ears. 'I shall go and fetch the mullah at once,' he said, 'but I have no money.' She gave him some money and he went to fetch the mullah. And thus it came about that the prince married King Rustam's daughter.

Next morning the prince picked up his water-bag to go and fetch water from the city. 'Wait,' shouted the gardener's daughter, 'we don't need water, and we are now returning to our kingdom.' Then she asked him: 'Do you have a house and a village of your own?'

'Yes,' he replied, 'and in my country I am a prince.'

'Will you come with me?' she asked; 'or would you prefer to return to your country?'

'Please give me a horse and a thousand rupees for expenses so that I can return to my country,' he replied.

'I shall grant your two requests,' she said, 'if you will give me your leather water-bag and your metal drinking-bowl.'

The prince agreed. He gave her the water-bag and the drinking-bowl, and she gave him a horse and a thousand rupees for expenses. Then she and her companions mounted their horses and rode home as fast as they could.

When the prince reached his kingdom some days later, he was in a bad temper. 'Where is the gardener's daughter?' he asked. 'She has been the source of all my troubles.'

Hearing these words, the gardener's daughter brought him the water-bag and the drinking-bowl that he had given her outside the gates of King Rustam's city. 'Don't be so proud of having married King Rustam's daughter, for it was I who arranged the marriage,' she said.

'You have won and I have lost,' conceded the prince, and from that day onwards the prince lived happily ever after with his forty-two wives.

5

Sass Begum

There was once a king who had only one son. He loved him more than anything in the world and gave him whatever he desired. The wisest men in the land were in the service of his son, and they were charged with educating him from an early age. The prince's favourite companion was the vizier's son; they were always together both by day and by night.

When the prince and the vizier's son became young men, they spent much of their time hunting. One day they had gone out hunting as usual and had failed to shoot any game. Feeling tired, they sat down to rest on the bank of a river that flowed through the forest.

While they were gazing at the scenery they saw a boat glide past. In the boat sat a beautiful girl with a bowl in her hand. When she saw the two young men sitting on the river-bank, she filled the bowl half full of water and then threw the water back into the river. Then she removed her veil and hid her face in the long tresses of her hair. Then she lifted the five fingers of her right hand and one finger of her left hand. Whereupon the boat drifted out of sight.

The young man was perplexed and turned to the vizier's son. 'Can you explain? The girl in the boat made signs to us, but I understood nothing.'

'What else am I a servant for?' replied the vizier's son. 'I will explain everything. She filled her bowl half full of water and then emptied it to indicate that her father's name is King Neemjam: *neem*, meaning half, *jam*, meaning bowl. She hid her face in the long tresses of her hair to indicate that Zulfan, hair, is the name of the town where she comes from. And she lifted up six fingers to indicate that her name is Sass Begum, or Lady Six. Now what do you propose we should do?'

'We must find her,' replied the prince.

They returned home and made preparations for a journey. When they were ready they chose the two best horses in the king's stables and set out in search of the girl. After several days, they reached the city of Zulfan and took up lodgings with an old widow. The vizier's son spent a good deal of time with the old woman, asking her questions about King Neejam. She told him that the king had a daughter who was renowned for her beauty and intelligence. 'They say,' she said, 'that she is beyond compare.'

When the vizier's son repeated the old woman's words to the prince, the young man grew impatient. 'We have waited long enough. We must arrange to meet her as soon as possible.'

So the vizier's son went to the old woman, and said: 'Go to the princess and tell her that two young men whom she saw on the river-bank have come to meet her.'

The old woman began to grumble. 'My son,' she said, 'already I'm nearing the grave; the king would have me put to death for suggesting such things.'

The vizier's son was not deterred; he knew how to persuade her. 'If you agree to deliver this message to the princess, I shall give you as much gold as you desire.'

As soon as the old woman heard about the gold she ceased grumbling and agreed to take the message that very day. She went to the palace and asked to see the princess. She was directed to the girl's bedchamber. There the princess was sitting with some of her companions. The old woman gave her salaams and then came straight to the point: 'The two young men whom you saw on the river-bank would like to meet you.'

Hearing this, the princess became angry. 'Let us beat this cunning old woman to teach her a lesson. There are some sticks lying in the garden,' she said to her companions.

The old woman did not delay a moment longer, but ran home as fast as she could. The prince and the vizier's son saw her hurrying into her house. 'What happened? Why did you return in such a hurry?' they asked her.

'Go away and leave me alone,' she shouted angrily. 'You want the princess to break my old bones.'

'Mother,' said the vizier's son, 'did you deliver our message?'

'Yes,' she replied, 'but when the princess heard the message, she told her companions to beat me with sticks. I ran for my life and was lucky to escape alive.'

The vizier's son did his best to comfort and console her. 'Don't worry,' he said, 'no one can harm you.' Then he called the prince aside. 'Tonight you must go to the palace garden. There you must lie down and wait for the princess, but whatever happens don't fall asleep.'

The prince went to the garden and waited for the princess, but when half the night had passed, he fell asleep. When the princess came and saw that the prince was sleeping, she took his handkerchief out of his pocket and placed one ripe and one unripe berry in it. Having done this, she slipped the handkerchief back into his pocket and went away. At dawn the prince awoke and, seeing nobody, he returned to the old woman's house and said to the vizier's son, 'I saw nothing.'

'I don't believe you,' said the vizier's son. 'You must have fallen asleep and the princess must have come while you were sleeping.' Then, noticing a bulge in the prince's pocket, he put his hand in and took out the handkerchief, and in it he found the two berries, one ripe and the other unripe. He showed them to the prince: 'This proves that the princess did come last night.'

The prince looked puzzled. 'What does this sign mean?' he asked.

The vizier's son explained: 'By means of these berries, she wishes to say that your teacher is as mature as the ripe berry and that you are as green as the unripe berry. You must return to the garden tonight and try not to fall asleep.'

The prince returned to the garden that evening, but again, when half the night had passed, he fell asleep. When the princess came and saw that he was sleeping, she put some walnuts in his pocket. The prince woke up early next morning and, finding his pocket full of walnuts, he returned to the old woman's house and asked what the walnuts could mean.

The vizier's son explained: 'She wishes to say that you are like a child who still plays with walnuts.' He then informed the prince that he had to go to the bazaar to buy some meat. He went out and shortly returned. 'I must cut the meat,' he said to the prince. 'Please hold it while I chop it into little pieces.' So saying, he placed the meat in the prince's hand and began cutting it with a sharp knife. When he had almost finished, he intentionally cut the prince's finger. The prince screamed in pain. His friend apologized. 'I shall put some medicine on it and bandage it,' he said. But instead of medicine, he put salt on the wound, and then bandaged the finger.

In the evening the vizier's son accompanied the prince to the garden. He told the prince to enter, but he himself remained outside. That night the prince was unable to sleep, because the wound in his finger caused him such pain. He was therefore awake when the princess entered the garden. She came and sat down beside him.

But it so happened that one of the gardeners was returning home late, and when he saw the princess and the stranger sitting together, he immediately went and reported what he had seen to the king. The king ordered his army to surround the garden and to wait until daybreak, so that they might seize the stranger and find out who he was.

The vizier's son was filled with dismay when he saw the king's army surrounding the garden. While he was plotting some method of helping the prince to escape, he saw a Hindu woman approaching. She was carrying some flowers in her hand and was chanting 'Ram, Ram' in praise of Rama Krishna. The vizier's son ran up to her. 'Mother, where are you going?' he asked.

'I am going to a grave in the garden to place these flowers there,' she answered.

'I will give you a bag of gold,' he said, 'if you will give me your flowers and your clothes.'

She agreed. He gave her a bag of gold, and took her flowers and clothes, and disguised himself. Then he walked to the garden gate, chanting 'Ram, Ram.' Believing that he was the Hindu woman who often used to visit the grave in the garden, the sentry allowed him to enter. He went straight to where the prince and princess were sitting. They were both quite taken aback by his strange appearance.

'Make haste,' he said to the princess. 'Put on these clothes and return to the palace immediately. The king's army has surrounded the garden.'

The princess quickly put on the clothes that had once belonged to the Hindu woman and returned to the palace without being discovered.

At daybreak the king's army entered the garden, arrested the prince and the vizier's son, and took them to the king.

'What were you doing in my garden at night?' asked the king. 'We are both travellers,' answered the vizier's son. 'We reached the city late, and we are strangers to the place. So we went to the garden, and since we were both exhausted after our long journey, we fell asleep. When we woke up in the morning, your guards arrested us and brought us to you; we don't know why.'

'Let them go,' ordered the king to his soldiers. 'They are travellers.'[1]

The prince and the vizier's son returned to their kingdom and recounted their adventures. The young prince asked his father to arrange his marriage to Sass Begum. The vizier carried magnificent gifts from the prince's father to the princess's father, with a request for the girl's hand in marriage. Sass Begum's father was pleased and accepted the proposal. The young prince married Sass Begum and they lived happily ever after. The vizier's son continued to act as the prince's adviser.

6

The Clever Princess

here was once a king who had only one daughter, and she was a very intelligent girl. One day, after returning home from court, his daughter approached him as he sat on his bed, and greeted him. 'My daughter has never greeted me before,' he thought to himself. 'I must ask her what this means.'

'Do you wish to say something?' he asked.

'Yes,' she answered, 'I want to ask you a question. If you can give me the answer, then you are my father. If not, I cannot disown you, but you must provide me with a separate house to live in, and we shall have nothing more to do with one another.'

'What is your question?' asked the king.

The daughter replied: 'There is a tray. On it there is a melon and a knife. The knife cannot cut the melon, and if it does, the melon cannot fill the tray. What does this mean?'

The king bowed his head in thought, but could make nothing of it, so he said to his daughter, 'Go and rest. This time tomorrow I shall give you the answer.'

Next day the king called his vizier and repeated his daughter's question, but the vizier could not solve the riddle. 'I cannot tell you what it means, but I shall go and meet other kings and find out the answer for you.'

'You are trying to evade the question,' said the king. He then turned to his military commander and put the same question to him.

'If there is an enemy to be defeated and put to death, I will willingly do it,' replied the commander, 'but this a problem for the intellect, so you should ask the vizier.'

The king then turned to his chief magistrate and asked him if he could answer the question.

'If it were a question to be decided by the Muslim Shariah law, I could have settled it,' replied the magistrate, 'but this a problem demanding wit and intelligence, and it is therefore the duty of the vizier to find the answer.'

The king held court all day, but he and his advisers could not solve the riddle. In the evening, when he returned to his room, he said to his daughter, 'There were too many law-suits to be dealt with and I forgot about your question. This time tomorrow I shall give you the answer.'

On the following morning, he again asked the vizier and his other ministers to consider the question, but the day passed in discussion and they were unable to find the solution. On the third day, he ordered his vizier to go and not return until he had found the answer. That evening, on his way home from court, he ordered one of his tenants to vacate his house and move elsewhere so that his daughter could go and live there. And when he returned home, his daughter greeted him and repeated the same question.

'I am trying to find an answer to your question,' replied the king. 'In the meantime, I have evicted one of my tenantsso that you can move into his house.'

That very night, the princess left the palace with her old maidservant, taking with her the few belongings that she required: two *charpoy* beds, some furniture, and a small quantity of food.

As the proverb says, 'It takes a short time to ask a question, but a long time to answer it.' Because this is a story, it has been quickly recounted, but a full year had elapsed since the princess had left her father's palace, and during that time the vizier had travelled from one place to another in search of an answer to the question. One day, feeling depressed and tired, he returned home and lay on his bed. His wife thought to herself: 'I must ask why, for one whole year, he has been running around, and why he has been so worried.'

'What is the cause of your worry?' she asked.

'The king has asked me to solve this question. There is a tray. On it there is a melon and a knife. The knife cannot cut the melon, and if it does, the melon cannot fill the tray.'

'And don't you know the answer?'

'No,' replied the vizier.

The vizier's wife was surprised. 'The salary which you have received all these years from the king has been unlawfully earned. What work have you done for him if you don't even understand the meaning of this?'

'For over a year now this question has puzzled me,' he said. 'If you know the answer, let me have it.'

'I cannot give you the answer,' replied his wife, 'because you are the king's servant for a hundred rupees a day, and if I give you the answer, we shall both become his servants for the same wage: whenever you have a problem which you cannot resolve, the king will send you to me and I too will be troubled and unable to do any other work.'

Whereupon they began to quarrel. The night passed and it was already daybreak. The vizier lost his patience and picked up a stick. 'Tell me quickly,' he said.

'I will not give you the answer myself,' she replied, 'but I can tell you where you can go and find it. There is a man called Gul

Deen who has a daughter. She is a friend of mine. Go to his house and you will find her. When you meet her, tell her who you are and what you have come for. She will explain what your question means.'

The vizier went to a village called Spirsang in search of Gul Deen. When he reached the village he asked for him. One of the villagers pointed to the Persian water-wheel and said that it belonged to him, and that the house beside it was where he lived. Before he arrived at the house, he saw the girl whom he had come to meet working in the fields. She was very beautiful. 'I had better not ask her where to find Gul Deen,' he thought to himself as he approached her, 'because she is young and beautiful, and it would be improper to ask her a direct question.' So he decided to greet her and then ask her to fetch her father.

'Peace be upon you,' he said.

'And peace be upon you also' came the reply.

Having dismounted, the vizier left his horse to graze and sat down on a *charpoy* bed that he found by the roadside. His lips were parched with thirst, so he asked the girl for some water. She took the metal drinking-bowl from the earthenware jar and went to fetch some water from the well. She filled it up and brought it back.

The vizier was so tired and thirsty and so captivated by the girl's beauty that, had he drunk the whole bowl of water, he could easily have died. When the girl read the expression on his face and realized the truth of his condition, she moved away without handing him the bowl. The vizier was puzzled: 'I asked her for water. She brought it, yet she did not give it to me. Why?'

The girl went nearby where some bundles of straw lay on the ground. She picked up a few pieces of straw and put them in the bowl to prevent the vizier from drinking all the water in one gulp, and gave him the bowl. The vizier was baffled. 'I wonder why she put straw in the water. Perhaps there is a reason for this,' he reflected. 'It is better to drink the water than throw it away. I shall drink it slowly so as to avoidthe straw, and then I can drink more later.' So he drank slowly so as to avoid the straw, and thus, with difficulty, he drank a quarter of the water in the bowl and his thirst was quenched. The girl had been standing in front of him, and when she stretched out her hand to take the bowl, he caught her hand.

'Please let go of my hand,' said the girl.

But the vizier refused to let go. 'Tell me first why, when I asked you for water, you very willingly brought it; then you went and put straw in it. Why did you do this?'

'Didn't you understand?' said the girl.

'No,' he replied.

'Who are you?' she then asked.

'I am the king's vizier.'

'The salary which the king gives you is unmerited,' said the girl, 'because you didn't even understand why I put straw in your water.' She explained: 'I did this because, when I brought the water to you, you were so thirsty that, had you drunk all the water in one gulp, you would have died. So I decided to put straw in it to prevent you from drinking it quickly.'

The vizier was amazed, and said to himself: 'By God, what an intelligent girl! From the expression of the face she can understand matters of the heart.'

The vizier forgot that he had come in search of an answer to the king's question, and began thinking about the girl. Meanwhile, the girl drove the bullocks round in a circular path so that the Persian wheel watered the fields. Time passed, and when evening came, she untied the bullocks from the wheel and went home. The vizier took his horse and followed her. When she reached home, she tied up the bullocks, washed her hands, and started kneading flour. The vizier entered the house. There was a *charpoy* bed in the courtyard and the vizier sat down on it.

'Where is your father?' asked the vizier, when the girl began to bake bread in the clay oven.

'He is mixing earth with earth,' replied the girl.

'Where is your mother?' he asked.

'She is separating earth from earth.'

'Where are your brothers?' he asked.

'They are trying to bring the dead to life.'

After some time the girl's father returned home. When he saw the vizier sitting there, he thought: 'Perhaps it is one of our guests.' So he shook hands and greeted him politely.

The vizier realized that this must be the girl's father, so he returned his greetings, and said: 'I asked your daughter where you were, and she said that you were mixing earth with earth.'

'Yes I was,' replied the father. 'I dig graves for the dead in this village. A man died recently and I dug a grave for him. When I had finished, I put the dead man in it. To prepare the grave, I used earth, and when a man dies, he becomes earth, so that is how I was mixing earth with earth.'

When the mother returned, she saw the vizier sitting with her husband. She thought that he must be one of her husband's relatives, so she welcomed him.

'Where were you?' asked the vizier, when she had sat down. 'When I asked your daughter where you were, she told me that you were separating earth from earth.'

'She was right,' replied the woman. 'I am the village midwife. A woman has just given birth and I attended the birth, then took my payment and returned home. So I was separating earth from earth.'

The girl's three brothers arrived. Their clothes were wet. They changed their clothes, and then came and sat down.

'Where have you been?' the vizier asked them. 'When I asked your sister, she said that you had gone to try to bring the dead to life.'

'She was right,' they replied. 'We have a garden which was parched dry, and we were thinking how to bring the dead trees to life. A villager suggested that we should dig a well in the middle of the garden and give the plants and trees water from it. We have been doing this for eight days, and now the plants and trees have revived. They were dead and we brought them to life.'

'This also makes sense,' thought the vizier.

He spent the night there, and at daybreak the father, mother, and the three brothers left the house, and the girl took her bullocks and went to the Persian wheel to water the fields. The vizier followed her.

'You still haven't asked me why I came here,' he said to her.

'What right have I to ask you?' said the girl. 'If you wish to tell me the purpose of your visit, do so quickly, or else I shall acquire a bad reputation. People will say, "She is a young girl and has no shame: she has been seen more than once talking with a stranger."'[1]

The vizier mentioned the name of his wife, without saying that she was his wife. 'Do you know her?' he asked.

'I know her very well,' replied the girl. 'How is she? Is she well?'

'Yes, she is well,' he said. 'The king has asked me a question which I cannot answer. Your friend told me that you would know the answer. There is a tray. On it there is a melon and a knife. The knife cannot cut the melon, and if it does, the melon cannot fill the tray.'

The girl thought for a moment, then said: 'I shall tell you the answer on one condition, namely that you marry me. I shall also explain the meaning of any question that the king may ask. Even if he does not ask a question in words, you have only to describe the expression on his face and I shall tell you what is in his heart.'

The vizier was very pleased. 'If you wish to marry me, I will do so immediately.'

The girl said that she was ready to go with him there and then. So they both mounted his horse and travelled to his village. When the vizier entered his house with the girl, his first wife picked up her veil.

'You brought me here, but your first wife is leaving,' said the girl to the vizier.

'How can you tell?' he asked.

'Did I not tell you that I understand matters of the heart. She is leaving because she is angry that you brought me. If you want to stop her, then try to do so now.'

'Let her go,' said the vizier.

The first wife left the house, and the vizier sent for the mullah to perform the marriage ceremony.

One day passed, and then another, and so on, and the vizier failed to attend the court. During his long absence, the king had appointed another vizier to fulfil his duties. The king now called this new vizier, and asked him: 'Why does my vizier never attend the court? He must have married a beautiful woman. Perhaps he cannot drag himself away from her. She must indeed be beautiful to have caused him to neglect his duties for so long. How can I catch a glimpse of her?'

'What you say is not right,' said this vizier, 'but since I am your vizier, I advise you to summon him to court. If he wants to retain his position, he will come, and if not, he will not come. As soon as he comes you can put the question to him: "Do you want to be my vizier?" If he answers yes, then tell him: "You have just married. Do you intend to invite us to dinner in honour of your recent marriage?" If he agrees, he will take you to his house, and his wife will not be veiled in your presence, because the king's servant's wife does not observe purdah in front of her husband's master. Once you have seen her, and if you like her, you can take her at any price, even if it means killing the vizier. If you do not like her, you can have dinner and then come away.'

So the king sent a man to his old vizier to ask him if he wished to retain his position as vizier. The vizier said yes and hurried to the palace. When he entered the king's presence, the king said, 'Congratulations! I hear that you have just married.' Then he added, 'Have you any intention of inviting us to dinner to celebrate the wedding?'

'Yes, if you command,' replied the vizier.

'You may now leave and make preparations for our dinner,' said the king.

The vizier returned home and told his wife to make preparations for the king's dinner. The wife spent the whole day cooking many different dishes. In the evening, she asked her husband, 'Is there anything else that I should prepare?'

'No,' replied her husband.

Then the wife told him to go and fetch the king. The vizier went to the door, deep in thought, and returned. After he had done this several times, she said to him: 'You have spent a lot of money on this dinner. Why don't you call the king?'

'I am on my way to call the king,' said the vizier. He left the house, but instead of going to call the king, he went and spent the night with one of his friends.

The vizier's wife knew that her husband was running away and was unwilling to call the king because the king had such a bad reputation with women. She said to herself: 'I shall invite the king myself and teach him a lesson, so that in future he leaves other people in peace.' So she sent one of her servants to fetch the king.

When the king arrived, accompanied by his new vizier, his military commander, his chief magistrate, and four other men, she asked the servants to serve the dinner that she had prepared. Meanwhile, she herself remained in the next room. When they had finished their meal, she said to the king from behind the door: 'You have eaten your dinner, but there is one thing that remains.'

'Send it in,' replied the king, thinking that she would offer them green tea after the meal.

Knowing that there were eight men, the vizier's wife had boiled eight eggs and had painted each a different colour. She put them in a tray and asked a servant to place them before the king. When the servant had done this, she spoke again from the next room: 'There are eight eggs, each of a different colour, and each man should choose the egg he wishes.'

'All right,' said the king, and he took a red egg himself, and gave a green one to his vizier, a black one to his military commander, a blue one to his chief magistrate, and so on. When all the eggs had been distributed, each man broke his egg and ate it.

Then the vizier's wife asked each of her guests the colour of his egg. When they had told her, she asked each one in turn the same question: 'What did your egg taste like.'

'They all taste alike,' they replied.

Then the vizier's wife addressed the king: 'Women may look different, but they are all alike. You had evil ideas in your heart. That is why your vizier, my husband, prepared your dinner, but left and did not want to call you. He thought that your intentions toward me were not good.'

The king felt ashamed and asked her forgiveness. 'Henceforth,' he said, 'I shall not have evil designs on another man's wife or sister.'

'Have I shown you enough honour?' she asked. 'Or should I do you more honour?'

The mortified king left the house without answering her question.

Next morning, as her husband, the vizier, was returning home, he said to himself: 'If my wife has invited the king to dinner, I shall throw her out of the house. I didn't want to invite him, so why should she wish to do so?' On his way home he asked three men, 'Did the king come to my house?'

'Yes,' they replied.

He therefore became very angry and broke a stick from a tree. When his wife saw him approaching the house with a stick in his hand, she withdrew to her room.

'Don't hide,' he shouted. 'I shall give you what you deserve.'

'What wrong have I done?' asked his innocent wife.

'I didn't want to invite the king,' replied the vizier. 'Why did you invite him?'

His wife did not give him a straight answer. 'I did invite him,' she said, 'and if you want to turn me out of the house, I am not one of those women who leave when you tell them to. You will have to remove me by force and take me to a place where wild animals live. God will prove my innocence by saving me.'

'I'll take you to a jungle where you won't survive for very long,' said the vizier angrily. And with these words, he dragged his wife from the house and took her to a place where only date palms grew. He left her alone there and returned home.

She found some palm leaves and made herself a hut. Since there was no water, she performed her ablutions with a smooth stone[2] and made a special prayer. She prayed that God might slay her at once if she were at fault, but that if she were innocent, He should spare her life until such time as she might speak with her husband once again.

God granted her prayers. All the beasts would pass by her hut, but they did her no harm. At meal times food and water appeared out of nowhere. And so nine months passed, and she gave birth to a son. When the child had learnt how to talk, she used to teach him different things as befitted his age and growing intelligence.

Every day the young boy would journey to where the king and the vizier, his father, lived, and he would play there and return in the evening.

One day the king thought: 'My daughter has been separated from me for such a long time. Let me see how she is and what she is doing.' So he disguised himself as an old man and went in the direction of his daughter's house. When he arrived at the crossroads, the young boy saw him. The boy said to himself: 'He looks like a thief. Perhaps he is going to steal from somebody. Instead of going home, I shall follow him. When he has committed the theft, I shall see where he hides the goods, and when he returns to his house, I shall find out where he lives. Then, when an innocent person is accused of theft, I shall go to the king and say, "This man is innocent." I shall point to the real thief and inform the king where the goods are hidden.' With these thoughts in mind, he followed the king.

The king walked for miles and miles until at last he reached his daughter's house. He approached the door and peered inside. His daughter saw him. 'There is a man at the door,' she said to her maid. 'Go and fetch him.' Meanwhile, the boy had also arrived at the house, but he remained in hiding.

The king was invited to enter. Four chairs and a table were placed in the middle of the room, and he was asked to sit down. Then the princess ordered the servant to close the door. As soon as the door was closed the boy stood behind it, so that, by looking through the keyhole and listening, he could see and hear everything without being seen.

'Bring it,' said the princess to her servant.

The servant opened a cupboard. Inside there were oranges. She took one, and placed it on a tray with a knife, and brought it to the princess. The princess cut the orange in two and gave it to the king. The king took half and ate it, leaving the other half on the tray.

'You fool,' said the princess, picking up her shoe. 'I didn't cut the orange so that you could eat it. There is a long story behind this. Now I have the right to kill you and you cannot escape; if you dare say anything or try to escape, no good will come of it. In future you had better listen to what I say.'

With her shoe she hit the king on one cheek and then on the other. When she had given him a thorough beating, she pushed him towards the door. 'Get out of my house. Why did you enter my house when you were unable to answer my question?'

The boy had been listening to all this from behind the door. 'The old man failed to understand the meaning of your question,' he said to the princess after the king had left, 'and if you threw him out of the house, you had a good right to do so.' In fact the boy felt sorry for the old man and intended to take revenge on his behalf.

Next evening the king was sitting near the princess's house when he saw the boy and followed him.

'Somebody's at the door. Please go and fetch him,' said the princess to her servant, for she had seen the boy peeping into the house. The boy was invited to enter. Four chairs and a table were placed in the middle of the room.

'Sit down,' she said.

He sat down on one of the chairs, and she sat on the chair facing him. Then she asked the servant to close the door. This time the king in disguise was standing behind the door. The princess then turned to her servant. 'Bring it,' she ordered.

The servant opened the cupboard, put an orange on a tray with a knife, and gave it to the princess. The princess cut the orange in two and placed the knife on the table in front of the boy. The boy picked up the knife, and cut the two pieces into four, and placed the knife on the tray. 'Take it,' he said to the princess. The princess picked up the knife and cut the four pieces into eight. 'Take it,' she said to the boy. The boy picked up the eight pieces, and put them together again, then cut them into sixteen pieces, and put them on the tray. 'Take it,' he said. The princess put the sixteen pieces together and, with one stroke of the knife, cut them into thirty-two pieces, and placed them on the tray on front of the boy. The boy picked up the thirty-two pieces, put them together, and cut them into sixty-four pieces, and put them on the tray. 'Take it,' he said.

At this point the princess took the sixty-four pieces and threw them away. 'You cut the orange with me in the correct fashion,' she said, 'but you must explain the meaning of the question. If you don't, I shall punish you.' Then she asked, 'When I cut the orange in two, what did it mean?'

'Your meaning was: "You have come to my house. If anybody cuts you in two and asks you where you went, will you tell them?" When I cut the two pieces into four, that was my answer: "If I were cut into four pieces, I would not tell them."'

'When I cut the four pieces into eight then?' she asked.

'You tested me by putting pressure on me. "What if you were cut into eight pieces?" In answer to that, I cut the eight pieces into sixteen, meaning that even if I were cut into sixteen pieces, I would not tell.'

'When I cut the sixteen pieces into thirty-two then?' she asked.

'It meant: "If you were cut into thirty-two pieces, then would you tell?" So I cut the thirty-two pieces into sixty-four. By doing this, I meant that even if I were sliced into tiny pieces, I still would not reveal that I had come here, nor that I had met you.'

The princess was finally satisfied. 'You have given me the answer to the question concerning the orange. I shall now ask you another question. Since you are only ten years old, how did you acquire such intelligence?'

'I acquired it from my mother,' he replied. 'Every morning, when I wake up, my mother teaches me that when this happens it means this, and when that happens it means that, and so on.'

As the boy was leaving the house, the king caught hold of him. 'Why did you go to that woman's house?'

The boy refused to answer. So the king took him to the palace, and ordered that he be tied to the mouth of a cannon and blown to pieces. The boy was tied to the mouth of a cannon, but still refused to talk. When the princess heard about this, she sent her servant with a pitcher full of water. The servant brought the pitcher and broke it in front of the boy. As it broke the water began to flow out. The boy knew that this was a signal from the woman that he was permitted to talk. Then the boy recounted his story to the king.

The king was astonished that such a young boy should be endowed with so much intelligence. 'Where did you acquire such intelligence?' he asked.

'I acquired it from my mother who lives in the jungle,' he replied.

'I shall have your mother brought here,' said the king, and he instructed his guards to go and fetch the boy's mother and bring her back with them.

'Is this your son?' asked the king.

'Yes,' she replied.

'I want to make him my servant.'

The mother agreed: 'If it pleases you, you are welcome to do so.'

Then the king said: 'I shall make him my vizier.'

'No,' said the mother, 'you can make him anything, but not vizier.'

'Why?' asked the king.

'His father is your vizier,' replied the woman, 'and he will lose his job if you make the boy your vizier.'

'Are you the vizier's wife?'

'Yes,' she answered.

'How can this be? The vizier lives here and you live in the jungle?'

The boy's mother explained: 'I am the same woman who invited you to the vizier's house for dinner, and gave you eggs of different colours at the end of the meal; and because I had invited you to dinner that evening, the vizier became angry and threw me out of the house and abandoned me in the jungle.'

The king was amazed: 'Is my vizier such an unworthy man and so lacking in intelligence?' And he gave orders that the vizier was to be tied to the mouth of the cannon and blown to pieces. The boy was thus appointed vizier, and was told by the king that he was free to marry the princess, his only daughter, and that his mother was welcome to live in the palace. 'But first,' said the king, 'since you are now my vizier, you must answer this question. One day my daughter came to me and said:"There is a tray. On it there is a melon and a knife. The knife cannot cut the melon, and if it does, the melon cannot fill the tray." What does this mean?'

The boy answered: 'The tray means this earth, and the melon means man, and the knife represents Izrail, the angel of death. The knife cannot cut the melon: death cannot come to a man until he has completed his time on earth. When death comes, he is buried in the ground. Many men die, but the earth cannot be filled.'

Congratulations,' said the king. 'You won and I lost.'

II

Virtues and Vices

7

The Greedy King

Once there was a king who was known for his kindness and generosity. He had no love of worldly things, and gave money and gifts to all his servants. Every morning he rose at dawn, and after offering his prayers, he would walk to the river that flowed near his palace and throw flour to the fish. When many years had passed, the king found that, as a result of his generosity and the dishonesty of his chief minister, he had lost all his wealth. He was left penniless and became a wandering fakir.

The fakir travelled from place to place begging and looking for work until he passed into another country beyond his kingdom. He made his way to the palace of the king of that country and, after much difficulty, was given an audience. The king was sitting on his throne holding a sword studded with priceless diamonds. The fakir bowed down before the king and greeted him.

'Your Majesty,' he said, 'I am a poor fakir and I have come a long way in search of work. I will give you God's blessings if you will help me.'

The king returned the fakir's greeting and then paused for some time to consider his words. 'I shall give you work,' he said finally, 'but in return there is one condition which you must fulfil.'

As the fakir was exhausted and starving, he readily agreed, and then asked, 'What is your condition?'

The king did not explain, but sought to reassure him. 'For six months you will live and eat well, and you will be well paid. But after six months, I shall expect you to fulfil the condition that we have agreed upon.' With these words, the king dismissed the fakir from his presence and ordered his vizier to give him food, clothing, and anything else that he might desire.

Time passed, and the fakir continued to live at court in the lap of luxury. After six months had elapsed, the king summoned the fakir. 'Tomorrow is the day I have been paying you for,' he said. 'I shall then expect you to do your duty. Prepare yourself for a journey and bring with you an ox and a donkey.'

'Your Majesty, I am at your service,' replied the fakir. So saying, he went off to make preparations for the journey.

Next morning, at first light, the king set out with the fakir, the ox, and the donkey. After travelling for many days, they came to a mountain which was as steep and smooth as a mirror and as high as Mount Qaf. They halted at the foot of the mountain. Then the king slaughtered the ox and made a large leather bag from its skin. Having done this, he turned to the fakir, and said: 'Enter this bag and I shall sew you in.'

'Why?' questioned the fakir in amazement.

The king grew angry. 'Have I not paid you handsomely for the last six months? And did I not warn you that one day you would be called upon to fulfil the one condition I set and to which you willingly agreed?' The fakir bowed his head and could find no answer.

'Make haste,' said the king, 'it is getting late.'

So the fakir obediently entered the bag, and the king sewed him in with strong thread. At that moment, a giant bird swooped down from the mountain and, lifting the bag in its talons, soared with it to the very summit. Here it deposited the bag and pecked hungrily at the leather with its beak until it burst open and the fakir was able to struggle out. The huge bird then flew off and perched on a nearby rock.

When the fakir looked around and saw where he was, he trembled with fear and shouted to the king, who seemed no bigger than a speck at the foot of the mountain, 'Why have you done this to me?'

'Be patient,' bellowed the king, 'I shall bring you down safely once you have finished your work. Now don't waste time. Look and see if you can find any diamonds.'

The fakir looked around and was astonished to discover that the ground was thickly covered with diamonds of all shapes and sizes. Their glitter was blinding. 'Your Majesty, there are priceless diamonds here,' he cried out excitedly.

'Throw down as many diamonds as you can,' ordered the king.

'First show me the way down,' replied the fakir.

'Throw down the diamonds, and then I'll show you the way down.'

So the fakir did as he was told. He threw down the biggest and the best diamonds that he could find, and the king collected them carefully, one by one, and filled the saddlebags on the donkey's back. When he had loaded the donkey with as much as it could carry, he shouted, 'Stop, don't throw any more diamonds down. I have no more place for them.'

'All right,' agreed the fakir, 'now show me the way down.'

'Are there any bones lying at the top of the mountain?' inquired the king.

The fakir looked and saw to his horror that there were human bones among the diamonds. 'Yes, there are bones here,' he groaned aloud.

'They belong to men like you,' cried the greedy king in a cruel voice, and he went on his way, leading his donkey laden with diamonds.

The fakir was left wringing his hands in anger and despair. He looked for a way down, but on all sides there were steep slopes that no man could scale. On the further side of the mountain flowed a deep river. The fakir thought to himself: 'If I throw myself into the river, the fish will eat me, or else I shall drown. But that is surely better than dying of thirst and hunger.' So he leapt, and fell into the river far below, and lost consciousness.

It so happened that this river was the very same river that flowed through the kingdom where the fakir had once been king. Now one of the fish recognized the fakir as the king who used to come and feed them each morning. So the fish called out to its companions, and they all helped to carry the king to safety, laying his head gently on the bank of the river. When the fakir recovered his senses, he sat up and saw a straight path leading to the king's palace. He rose to his feet and followed it until he reached the palace. He went inside at once and sat down in his usual place. When the king arrived, some time later, he was taken aback to find the fakir sitting in his usual place, as if nothing had happened, and wondered what miracle had brought him there. The fakir stood up and greeted the king.

The king returned the greeting, and asked: 'How on earth did you come down the mountain?'

'It was very easy,' answered the fakir. 'You frightened me for no reason. There is a straight path leading down from the other side of the mountain.'

The king's eyes glittered at the thought of laying his hands on more diamonds. 'Tomorrow,' he said, 'we shall travel again to the Mountain of Diamonds and you will show me the way down, so that whenever I need diamonds, I shall go and fetch them myself.'

'I am at your service,' agreed the fakir.

Next morning, at first light, the king set off once again with the fakir, an ox, and a donkey. When they reached the foot of the mountain, they rested for a while. Then the king slaughtered the ox and made a large bag with its skin. He entered the bag and the fakir sewed it up with strong thread. No sooner had he done this than the same gigantic bird flew down from the mountain, and lifted the bag in its talons, and flew with it to the top of the mountain, and deposited it there. The bird pecked at the bag until it burst open and the king came out. Then it flew off and perched on a nearby rock.

The king was overjoyed and marvelled at the sparkling diamonds that lay all around him. Never had he set eyes on such an abundance of treasure. He was so delighted that it was some time before he noticed that the fakir was walking away. 'Wait,' screamed the king, 'you haven't shown me the way down the mountain.'

'You love diamonds,' replied the fakir, 'so now you can stay there and play with diamonds for the rest of your life.' So saying, he left the king and returned to the palace.

The king remained on the mountain. His subjects awaited his return for many days, but when he failed to come, they made the fakir their king instead. They say that even the river cannot wash away good deeds.

8

The Sin of Pride

Once upon a time there was a man called Gulzamani. He had land, much wealth, and five wives. In short, he had everything he could have wished for, save that he had no children. This was a great disappointment to him, and he was troubled that he had no heir to inherit his wealth.

One day he was sitting on his bed in the courtyard of his house, brooding over this problem, when he heard the voice of a fakir begging: 'I've eaten nothing all day and I'm starving. Give me some food in the name of Allah.' Gulzamani invited him into his guest-house and served him a meal with his own hands. When the fakir had finished eating, and had washed his hands and mouth, he sat down on the bed beside Gulzamani.

'Why are you so discontented?' asked the fakir. 'God has blessed you with good fortune.'

'I have five wives,' replied Gulzamani, 'but none of them has borne me a child, and when I die there will be no one to whom I can leave my wealth.'

The fakir put his hand into his pockets and took out five berries. He gave them to Gulzamani, saying, 'Give one to each of your wives.' Having uttered these words of advice, he disappeared.

Gulzamani immediately went into the house and gave four of his wives one berry each. Then he went in search of his fifth wife Zubaydah, and discovered that she was having a bath. He explained how he had met the fakir and what the fakir had advised him to do.

'Leave my berry to one side,' she said, 'and when I've finished my bath, I shall eat it.'

Following his wife's suggestion, Gulzamani carefully placed the berry to one side. However, when Zubaydah had finished having her bath, she found that more than half the berry had been nibbled away by a mouse. All she could do was to eat what remained of it.

Some time passed, and each wife gave birth to a beautiful son, except Zubaydah. Since she had eaten less than half the berry, she gave birth to a stillborn child. All the wives were content with their lot, except Zubaydah who wept at her misfortune. In his pride and self-satisfaction, Gulzamani ceased to take any interest in her, and gradually the other wives started hating her. So one day Gulzamani told her to leave his house.

Zubaydah was miserable. Since she had no idea where to go, she just wandered aimlessly until she reached a forest. With great difficulty, she built a hut for herself and began living there. She ate wild fruits and drank water from the river, and spent every day in prayer.

One day, the same fakir who had given the berries to Gulzamani happened to be passing through that forest, and saw her. 'Why are you living all alone in this dangerous forest?' he asked. Zubaydah began to cry and told the fakir the whole story.

When the fakir heard what had happened, he gave a deep sigh and said, 'I gave those berries to Gulzamani. He has shown himself to be unduly proud and will be punished for it.' Then he gave some ointment to Zubaydah and said to her: 'Travel two furlongs and you will reach a cave. Rub this ointment on your eyes and enter the cave. Whatever you find there will be destined for you.' Having uttered these words of advice, he disappeared.

Following the fakir's instructions, Zubaydah walked until she reached a cave. Then she rubbed the ointment on her eyes and went inside. When she opened her eyes, she was amazed to see gold, jewels, and other riches on every side of her. She was very pleased by this and began living in the cave. Little by little, by means of her new-found wealth, she made a clearing in the forest and built a beautiful city, in the middle of which she erected a magnificent palace. Poor people from all the neighbouring kingdoms flocked to the city, and each family received a free house. In this way the city was populated and became important in its own right.

Time passed, and Gulzamani's sons grew up to be useless and lazy young men. They spent all day in idle pursuits such as gambling, and they never did a stroke of work. They soon squandered the fortune that they had inherited, and Gulzamani was left penniless.

Weary of living with his family, Gulzamani left his four wives and his four sons, and travelled until he came to the same forest where his fifth wife lived. In the middle of the forest, he found, to his amazement, a rich and thriving city. He walked to the main door of the palace and asked the guard, 'Who lives there?'

'Zubaydah,' answered the guard.

'My youngest wife had that same name,' thought Gulzamani. 'God alone knows where she is and what has become of her now.' Whilst these questions were running through his mind, Zubaydah's carriage passed. He looked up and saw her. He could not believe his eyes. He was so overcome by emotion that he began to weep and beat his head, and then he fell into a faint. Zubaydah, who had also seen him, ordered her servants to carry him into the palace.

When Gulzamani came to his senses, he felt ashamed of how he had treated Zubaydah. He fell at her feet and begged for her pardon. She was quick to forgive him, and from that day onwards he lived in her palace in great comfort.

Meanwhile, Gulzamani's four wiv es and four sons were reduced to poverty and became beggars. They begged from place to place until they came to the city in the forest. Zubaydah heard the voices of people begging for food, so she personally went to offer them something to eat. Recognizing the four wives and their sons, she immediately invited them into the palace. When they realized who she was, they fell at her feet and asked her to forgive them. Zubaydah forgave them with all her heart, and after that they lived happily together.

9

The Two Viziers

Once there was a king who had two viziers. One was a Hindu and the other was a Muslim. The king preferred his Muslim vizier, and in every situation he would consult him first; it was only after they had come to a decision that he would approach his Hindu vizier. Consequently, the Hindu vizier had no choice but to agree with the king's decision.

Many days passed, and the king continued to favour his Muslim vizier. So the Hindu vizier thought to himself: 'I don't have any work to do because the king always turns to his Muslim vizier for advice. Therefore I shall play a trick on him that will disgrace him in the king's eyes.'

One day the Muslim vizier was late in attending court. The Hindu vizier thought to himself: 'This is the chance I've been waiting for.' So he rose to his feet and paid his salaams to the king, and said, 'Your Majesty, I have a statement which I wish to make.'

'Tell me, what is it?' said the king.

The Hindu vizier continued: 'You decide many cases in court. Most of your judgements are correct, but some may be incorrect.

If a judgement is incorrect, it could have serious consequences. I myself cannot be held responsible for the consequences, because it is the Muslim vizier who advises you what decision to take, and very often he passes judgement without your knowledge, favouring those from whom he receives bribes.'

After some time the Muslim vizier arrived and presented himself before the king. After exchanging salaams, the king asked him, 'Is it true that you judge cases without my knowledge?'

'Yes,' replied the vizier, 'there are some simple cases which are not important enough to bring to your attention. For example, if a man comes and tells me that his cow has been stolen, I summon all the parties concerned, and after listening to their defence, I give my judgement.'

The Hindu vizier interrupted: 'Your Majesty, the Muslim vizier has in his possession a bird which is worth more than your whole kingdom. He received this bird as a bribe from a man whose case he judged.'

The king turned to the Muslim vizier, and said, 'Go and bring me this bird which is in your possession.'

'Your Majesty,' protested the vizier, 'I have no such bird in my possession.'

'Bring it at once,' ordered the king.

The Muslim vizier knew that it was useless to argue. 'Very well,' he said, 'I shall go and fetch it.'

The Muslim vizier lived with his young daughter and it was she who looked after him. When he entered the house, his daughter could tell from the expression on his face that something was troubling him. 'Father, why are you so worried?' she asked.

'The Hindu vizier has played a trick on me,' he answered. 'He has told the king that a man gave me a bird as a bribe, and that this bird is worth more than his whole kingdom; and the king has ordered me to bring the bird to him.'

The daughter thought for a while, and then said: 'Go to the city and rent the best house you can find. Once you have done this, go and buy two large jars, and take them to the rented house. Fill one jar first with water and then with gum; and fill the other jar with the feathers of many different birds. When you have done this, come and tell me, and I will go and sit there. Then on Sunday,' she continued, 'you must think of some pretext to bring the Hindu vizier near the house. As you pass the house, you must say to him, 'Look, what a beautiful house! I've never seen such a beautiful house in my life.' But when he looks up at the house, you must lower your eyes. You must repeat these words to him three times, and each time you must walk on ahead and then return to the same spot. After that you must excuse yourself, saying that you have an important appointment, and leave him in front of the house.'

The Muslim vizier went to the city and rented a beautiful house. He then went to the bazaar and bought two enormous earthenware jars. He had them transported to the house, and he filled the first with water and gum and the second with the feathers of many different birds. Then, after informing his daughter, he went to the house of the Hindu vizier, and said, 'Let us go for a walk together.' The Hindu vizier agreed, and they walked in the direction of the rented house.

When they approached the house, the Muslim vizier exclaimed: 'Look, what a beautiful house! I've never seen such a beautiful house in my life.' The Hindu vizier looked up and there he saw a beautiful girl sitting at the window. She made a sign to him to come in.

Then the two viziers walked on together, and after some time, they returned to the same spot. Once again the Muslim vizier exclaimed: 'Look, what a beautiful house! I've never seen such a beautiful house.' Once again, the Hindu vizier looked up and saw the beautiful girl at the window. She again made a sign to him to come in.

After this happened a third time, the Muslim vizier excused himself. 'My friend, I must leave you,' he said, 'because I have an important appointment.' They bade each other farewell, and each went his separate way. The Hindu vizier went straight to the beautiful house, and the Muslim vizier, who had pretended to go in the other direction, secretly followed him.

When the Hindu vizier reached the house, the girl was still sitting at the window. She made a sign inviting him to come in, and then went downstairs to open the door. 'I'm in a hurry; I must leave soon,' he muttered, once he was inside the house.

'Oh no!' said the girl. 'You mustn't leave yet.'

In the meantime, the Muslim vizier arrived at the house and knocked at the door. 'Open the door,' he cried in a loud voice.

The Hindu vizier became frightened. 'Who could it be?' he asked.

'My father,' replied the girl.

'What should I do?' he asked in dismay.

The girl pushed him towards the jar containing water and gum. 'Quick,' she said, 'hide in this.'

When he had climbed inside the jar, she told him to bend down so that she could cover it with the lid. As she placed the lid over the jar all the gum inside stuck to his body, and before she had time to open the door, the Hindu put his head up and lifted the lid. 'I've had enough of this jar,' he complained. 'God knows what it contains. It's very sticky and I must get out.'

'All right, then you'd better hide in the other jar,' said the girl.

Following her advice, the Hindu vizier climbed out of the first jar and concealed himself in the second. This jar contained the feathers of many different birds and, as his body was covered in gum, these stuck to him, so that he looked like a strange and exotic bird. The girl told him to bend his head so that she could replace the lid, and having done so, she opened the door for her father.

'Who were you talking to?' asked the father angrily as soon as he had entered.

'Nobody, father,' replied the daughter.

The Muslim vizier insisted: 'I definitely heard voices. Who was it?'

'Look for yourself,' she replied.

The Muslim vizier lifted the lid of the first jar, but that was empty. Then he lifted the lid of the second jar and saw the Hindu vizier, who was covered in feathers and looked like a bird. He was very pleased. 'I was looking for this bird,' he said, 'and here I have found it hidden in my own house.'

The Hindu vizier realized that a trick had been played on him, and he begged, 'Please let me go, in the name of Allah! And don't take me to the king. I promise never to try and harm you again.'

But the Muslim vizier turned a deaf ear to his pleas. He took him home with him and sent a message to the king, saying: 'The bird that you wished to see is in my possession. Fix a date, and invite all the people to come and see it.'

When the king received the message, he made an appointment for the following day, and invited everyone to his court to see the rare bird said to be worth more than his whole kingdom. Meanwhile, the Hindu vizier continued to plead for mercy, but the Muslim vizier would not listen.

Next day, people from all over the world arrived at the court to see the rare bird. At the appointed time the Muslim vizier led the bird into the court-room. There was a complete hush as he presented the bird to the king, and said: 'This is your bird.'

At that moment the Hindu vizier, with feathers of many colours clinging to his body, fell at the king's feet, and cried, 'For the love of Allah, forgive me. Accord me any punishment you wish, but do not dishonour me in front of the people.' And because he was covered in feathers, the people never recognized the Hindu vizier.

The king spoke to the bird: 'I am glad that the truth came to light before I had my Muslim vizier executed. As you yourself once said, an incorrect judgement may have serious consequences. You accused him of having committed a very grave offence and you have received your punishment.' Thus the king forgave the Hindu vizier.

10

The Lion of the Jungle

There was once a poor man who left his village to go to the city in search of work. On his way he had to pass through a thick jungle. As he was walking through the jungle, he saw a lion writhing in pain. He approached the lion with some apprehension and sat down beside him.

'Brother, tell me, what is the matter?' he asked.

'I hurt my foot two days ago, and I am in great pain,' replied the lion.

The man carefully examined the lion's paw and discovered that there was a large thorn stuck in it. 'A thorn has got stuck in your foot,' he said, 'and I shall try to remove it for you.' So saying, he took hold of the lion's paw in one hand and pulled the thorn out with the other. As he did so, the lion gave out a loud groan, and the whole jungle trembled at the sound. Even the man began to shiver with fear, but the lion sought to reassure him.

'Brother,' he said, 'you have been very good to me, so you have no need to be afraid. Tell me,' he continued, 'what brings you to the jungle, and what service can I do for you in return?'

The man was still somewhat nervous. 'I am a poor man,' he said. 'I don't have enough money to buy food for my family. I have three daughters; they have reached a marriageable age and I'm worried about them.[1] I haven't been able to find any work in the village where I live, so I was on my way to the city in search of work.'

When the lion heard this, he said to the man, 'Follow me.'

The lion limped in front and the man followed him. They passed a field where some labourers were digging. When the labourers saw the lion, they dropped their spades and fled.

'Go and get a spade,' said the lion to the man. 'We shall be needing one soon.'

The man picked up a spade, and they continued on their way until they came to the foot of a mountain.

'Dig here,' said the lion.

So the man began digging. When many hours had passed, and the hole was very deep, he came upon a treasure of gold coins.

'Take as many coins as you need,' said the lion, 'and tie them in your turban.'

The poor man was delighted. He filled his turban with gold coins and tied it in a knot. Then, after thanking the lion for his kindness and bidding him farewell, he set off home.

The man never forgot his debt of gratitude to the lion. After that day, he used to visit the lion in the jungle from time to time, and he would take with him any choice foods that his wife had cooked; and they used to sit together and chat for hours.In this way the lion and the man became close friends.

Many months passed and the man arranged the marriage of his eldest daughter. He made a special journey to the jungle to invite his friend to the wedding. The lion was very touched, but declined the invitation. 'The people of your village will be afraid of me,' he said, 'otherwise I would gladly have come to your daughter's wedding.'

'You have to come,' the man insisted. 'Without you, the marriage won't take place.'

The lion tried to explain, but the man would not listen or take no for an answer. So the lion finally gave in and agreed to attend the wedding.

On the day of the wedding, the lion went to the village. When the wedding party saw the lion approaching, all of them fled to the safety of their houses. The man shouted to them: 'Why are you so afraid? The lion is my friend and wouldn't hurt a flea. Come out of your houses.' The people came out cautiously, one by one. The man, who was now the owner of the biggest house in the village, invited the lion to sit with the other guests and make himself at home, while he went off to supervise preparations for the wedding.

When the other guests saw the lion sitting meekly in a corner, they decided to poke fun at him. Some began throwing stones at him, others their shoes. Each of the guests joined in the game and did his best to tease the noble beast. The lion was burning with rage, but managed to control himself. He thought that eventually they were bound to stop teasing him and, for the sake of his friend, he kept quiet and patiently endured the insults.

Meanwhile, after completing the wedding preparations, the host returned to his guests. When he entered the guestquarters, he found the lion sitting in a corner surrounded by sticks, stones, and shoes. He felt ashamed that his friend had been forced to suffer such insults, so he knelt down before the lion and apologized.

'If it hadn't been for you,' said the lion, 'I would have given them a good taste of their own medicine. But I didn't want to ruin the wedding, so I tolerated the abuse. However,' continued the lion, 'from today our friendship is over. Everything is good in its proper place. My place is in the jungle, and your place is in the village.' With these words, the lion left the village and returned to the jungle where he belonged.

III

Miracles and Magic

11

The Great Saint

Once, long ago, there was a great saint.[1] From an early age he had dedicated his life to the worship of God. In God's service, his black hair and beard had become as white as snow and his body had become knotted with age. He had visited many shrines and had made the pilgrimage to Mecca on several occasions. Such was his spiritual authority that he could perform miracles and heal the sick. Since he knew that his life was nearing its completion, he set off to pay his last respects to all the famous shrines in the district. He carried his begging bowl and was accompanied by his disciple.

After many days, the saint and his disciple reached the outskirts of a big city. Here they pitched their tent so that they could rest for a few days. Once the tent had been erected, the saint told his disciple to go to the bazaar to buy some provisions.

The disciple was a very beautiful young boy. He had large dark eyes and curly hair, and his face was as round as the moon; and when he walked through the streets, the crowds would stop to gaze at him. As the boy was walking round the bazaar, a dervish saw him and was so struck by his beauty that his heart was filled with passion. He accosted him and declared his love for him: 'I have fallen in love with you. From this day onwards you should abandon everybody and follow me.'

'I am a servant of the great saint and I do not care for anyone else,' answered the boy.

The dervish became angry, and in his rage he uttered a curse: 'I wish to God you would die tomorrow.'

The boy was very upset when he heard these words, and he quickly returned to his master. The great saint immediately knew that something was worrying his disciple. 'What is the matter? What is the cause of your worry?' he asked.

'In the bazaar I met a dervish,' replied the disciple. 'He fell in love with me and told me to abandon everybody and follow him. When I refused, he cursed me and prayed to God that I should die tomorrow.'

The great saint said nothing. He took the begging bowl that hung from his shoulder by a chain, placed it upside down on the ground, and prayed to God. Then he turned to his disciple and said: 'The night will continue forever and tomorrow will never come unless the dervish takes back his curse.'

They say it was the longest night that people had ever witnessed. The mullahs came and went, and wondered when dawn would break so that they could give the call to prayer. The children cried with hunger, because their mothers were waiting for daybreak before giving them food. Everyone wondered why the day never dawned. The people of the city went to the dervish. 'Why,' they asked, 'does the day never break?'

The dervish suddenly realized that it was the power of the disciple's spiritual master that had caused the night to continue. So he went to the great saint and asked, 'Why does the night never end?'

The saint explained: 'If the night ends, my young disciple will die, so I have prayed that the day will never come.'

The dervish fell at the saint's feet and begged for his forgiveness. 'I take back my curse,' he said. 'I pray to God that your disciple may live.'

When the saint heard this, he lifted his begging bowl and turned it the right way up. No sooner had he done so than the first rays of light appeared in the sky, and the mullahs gave the call to prayer, and the children ceased crying. The whole city recognized the spiritual authority of the great saint.

12

The Saint of Baghdad

A famous saint used to sit in a mosque in Baghdad, and his disciples used to sit round him while he repeated the name of God. One day, as he was sitting in his usual place, some drops of water fell on his head, and he asked, 'What is the meaning of this?' Looking up, he saw the *jinn* Dhobi Deo[1] flying in the sky. So he picked up his shoe. 'Go at once and fetch that *deo*,' he commanded.

The shoe went swiftly to Dhobi, and gave him a kick, and said: 'The saint has asked for you. Come with me.' Dhobi did as he was told; he returned with the shoe and sat down beside the saint.

'What work do you do?' asked the saint.

'I'm one of the disciples of a tribal elder whose name is Jabar Jhan,' answered the *deo*. 'Whenever he feels thirsty, it's my duty to go to Mecca and fetch water from the sacred well of Zamzam. His disciples all take turns to bring him this water, and today it was my turn. It was just my ill luck that I spilt some of it on you and so became your prisoner.'

The saint seemed well satisfied. 'Because you have told the truth, you may go on your way,' he said.

The *deo* thanked him and returned to his master. Jabar Jhan was in a rage: 'I shall no longer accept you as one of my disciples. I sent you for water, and where did you go? From now on you had better watch your step.'

Dhobi answered: 'In Baghdad there is a saint with a hundred thousand followers. He is famous for his miracles. As I was returning with your water and passing over the place where he sat, I was so filled with fear that my hand loosened its grip over the mouth of my water-bag, and some water fell on his head. So strong was his spiritual power that he was able to send his shoe after me. The shoe kicked me and brought me into his presence. He asked me what work I did, and I told him that I was your disciple, and that it had been my turn to bring you Zamzam water.'

Jabar Jhan was very angry that the saint had insulted one of his disciples. So he summoned all his disciples, and said, 'We are going to visit the saint of Baghdad.'

He took his disciples and his army, and they travelled to Baghdad. When they reached the mosque, they all entered and sat down in front of the saint, and said: 'You have insulted our Dhobi.'

The saint listened to their complaint. Then, within seconds, he ascended Mount Qaf, the highest mountain in the world. There he picked up two pigeon's eggs. On his return, he held them up in his closed fists and asked Jabar Jhan, 'What do I have in my hands?'

Jabar Jhan looked round the world. 'Great saint,' he replied, 'you have two very white pigeon's eggs which come from the summit of Mount Qaf.'

The saint then turned to Jabar Jhan, and said, 'Now show me your miraculous powers.'

Whereupon, within seconds, Jabar Jhan dived into the deepest river and caught a small fish. He returned with it and asked the saint, 'What do I have in my hand?'

'Jabar Jhan, in your hand there is a fish which comes from the deepest river in the world,' replied the saint.

The saint thought to himself: 'This infidel sees into every corner of this world, but God has not given him admittance to the garden of paradise. This time I shall trick him.' So the saint flew up to paradise and plucked a flower from the garden. Then he returned with it and asked Jabar Jhan, 'Tell me what do I have in my hand, which I have hidden from you with great care?'

Jabar Jhan looked round the world, examining every nook and cranny, but saw nothing. So he turned to the saint, and said: 'Your hands are empty, because I cannot see anything in the world which you could have brought.'

The saint opened his hand to reveal the beautiful flower that he had brought back from paradise. As soon as Jabar Jhan saw the flower, he recognized the saint's great spiritual power, and all his disciples and his army of unbelievers embraced Islam.

13

The Fakir and the Princess

here was once a fakir who used to go begging from house to house. One day he went to the king's palace and began begging for alms in his usual manner. Hearing the fakir's voice, the king's daughter came to the door and offered him charity with her own hands. The princess was very beautiful, and no sooner had the fakir set eyes on her than he fell in love with her. So when he left the palace, he visited the shrine of Loe Zwan, and prayed: 'I am very poor. I have fallen in love with the king's daughter and would like to marry her. I cannot give you anything in return, but if you are willing to grant my prayer, I am willing to lay down my life for you.'

Loe Zwan heard this prayer and decided to put the fakir to the test. That night the saint appeared to the fakir in a dream, and said: 'You must go to the king and ask him for his daughter's hand in marriage.'

So the fakir set off for the king's palace. There he introduced himself and greeted the king. 'Peace be with you,' he said.

'And peace be with you too,' answered the king. 'What is it that brings you here?'

'You have a daughter and I have come to ask for her hand in marriage,' the fakir replied.

The king looked the fakir up and down disapprovingly. 'What should I do with him?' he said, turning to his vizier.

'I suggest that you order a deep well to be dug,' said the vizier. 'Tell the fakir that he can marry your daughter when he has filled the well with diamonds. Since he could never do such a thing, you will be rid of him once and for all.'

The king instructed his guards to dig a deep well, and when they had done so, he said to the fakir: 'If you can fill this well with diamonds, I will give you my daughter's hand in marriage.'

When the fakir heard this, he visited the shrine once again, and said: 'Master, I asked the king to give me his daughter's hand in marriage, but he told me that I would first have to fill a well full of diamonds. What can I do? I am utterly penniless. Please can you help me?'

The voice of the holy man answered: 'Tomorrow morning, go to the king and tell him to look in the well. When he looks, he will find it full of diamonds.'

So the next morning the fakir once again presented himself at court and addressed the king: 'Now will you allow me to marry your daughter? I have fulfilled your condition: the well is full of diamonds.'

When the king and the vizier went to examine the well, they were amazed to discover that it really was full of diamonds. Then the king turned to the vizier for advice. 'What am I to do now? I cannot give my daughter to this man.'

'Have seven wells dug,' replied the vizier, 'and tell him that one well is not sufficient, and that he must fill all of them with diamonds.'

The king had seven wells dug, and said to the fakir: 'If you can fill all these wells with precious jewels, you can marry my daughter.'

For the third time, the fakir went to the shrine of Loe Zwan. 'O holy master,' he prayed, 'please fill the seven wells with precious jewels, otherwise the king will not give me his daughter.'

Loe Zwan appeared to the fakir in a dream, and said: 'I shall go to the king myself and speak to him.'

That same night Loe Zwan lifted the king's bed into the sky, then woke him up, and said: 'Why do you refuse to marry your daughter to the fakir?'

When the king looked around him and discovered that his bed was suspended in the sky far above the ground, he was terrified. At once he asked for God's forgiveness, touching each ear with the right hand to ward off evil, and began pleading with Loe Zwan to bring him back to earth: 'If you bring me back to earth again, I not only promise to give the fakir my daughter but also my kingdom.'

So Loe Zwan told the king to close his eyes. The king did as he was told, and when he opened them again, he found himself lying on his bed in the palace. As soon as the fakir came, the king ordered the mullah to perform the marriage ceremony. Then he arranged for his daughter to be transported with the fakir in a fine palanquin.

The first thing that the fakir did after kissing his new bride was to take her to the shrine of Loe Zwan. He made her wait in the palanquin and entered the shrine alone. He then took out a sharp knife and cut off his head, thereby fulfilling his vow.

The princess's brother, who knew nothing of his sister's marriage, was returning from a hunting expedition. As he was passing the shrine, he decided to go in and pray. Just as he was about to enter, he saw his sister in the palanquin. He was overcome with wrath. 'You have put us all to shame. You have come here to meet your lover,' he said.

The princess tried her best to explain. 'Today my father married me to a fakir, and after the marriage ceremony, my husband brought me to the shrine. He left me here while he went inside. I have been waiting for him for some time, but he hasn't come out yet.'

Learning that his father had given his sister's hand in marriage to a common fakir, the prince grew even more furious. So he drew his sword, entered the shrine, and killed himself.

Meanwhile, the princess waited and waited, and wondered what had happened. 'First the fakir went in and never returned,' she thought, 'and now my brother has done the same.'

When the princess entered the shrine and saw the fakir and her brother lying dead on the floor, she was stricken with grief, and she too decided to kill herself. She had picked up her brother's sword, and was about to cut off her head, when she heard a voice: 'Princess, do not kill yourself. Take the severed heads of these two men and place them close to their bodies.'

The princess was so upset and confused that she put the fakir's head on the prince's body and the prince's head on the fakir's body. She covered them with her veil and prayed to God to restore them to life. Then she lifted the veil and the two men rose to their feet. 'This is my wife,' said the fakir's head. 'This is my sister,' said the body to which it was attached.

The prince and the fakir were about to start fighting when a loud voice said: 'Be quiet!' The voice then addressed the princess: 'Cut off both heads, and place each head on the correct body.'

The princess asked the two men to lie down. Then she cut off their heads, and placed the fakir's head on the fakir's body and the prince's head on the prince's body. She then covered the two bodies with her veil and prayed to God to restore them to life again. God restored them to life. The prince asked God's forgiveness and returned to his father's palace. But the fakir and the princess remained in the shrine.

14

Musa Khan Deo

*O*nce upon a time there was a king who had seven daughters. All of them were married save the youngest. The king was worried that he had no male heirs, but he kept his thoughts to himself.

One day, he was sitting in the courtyard of his palace, his head bent in thought, when he heard the voice of a fakir begging for alms: 'Give me something, in the name of Allah.' The king stood up and called for his vizier. When the vizier came, he told him to go and fetch a bag of gold. The vizier did as the king had commanded. The king took the bag of gold and handed it to the fakir. But the fakir rejected it, saying, 'I cannot accept your alms until you tell me the reason for your sorrow.'

The king explained the reason for his sorrow: 'God has only blessed me with daughters, and I have no sons who will be my heirs.'

The fakir answered as follows: 'There is a *jinn* called Musa Khan. In his garden there is a certain flower. If you smell the scent of that flower, you will have a son.' With these words, the fakir departed.

The king did not know what to do. He was an old man, and he could not go in search of the flower, leaving his kingdom unguarded. But he had no sons who would go in his stead. While he was thus bemoaning his misfortune, his youngest daughter entered the courtyard. She noticed that something was worrying her father. 'Father, what is the reason for your sorrow?' she asked, after greeting him.

'I have no sons who will be my heirs,' replied the king, 'and I met a fakir who told me that if I smell the scent of a certain flower that grows in the garden of Musa Khan Deo, then I shall have a son. But I cannot go in search of that flower, leaving my kingdom unguarded.'

'I shall go in your stead,' announced the young princess.

The king did not approve of this idea, but when his daughter insisted, he finally agreed. After changing into a man's waistcoat and felt cap, the princess chose the fastest horse and set out on the long journey. Beside her flew the starling that she kept as a pet. They say that starlings can understand and speak man's language.

After travelling for many days, the princess reached the kingdom of Musa Khan Deo. As soon as she arrived, she went straight to Musa Khan's guest-house. Many men were sitting there on *charpoy* beds, talking to one another. The princess entered and greeted each of them in turn. They invited her to join them, and a relative of Musa Khan was sent to Musa Khan's house to inform him that he had a new guest. Musa Khan had no sooner set eyes on the princess than he suspected that she was not a man but a woman. Without even greeting his new guest, he returned home and said to his mother: 'There is a youth in my guest-house, but his face looks like that of a woman.'

'My son,' said the mother, 'there are certain actions whereby one can tell the difference between a man and a woman. Listen and I shall tell you some of them. First, you must persuade the youth to go for a walk with you. Walk towards the canal in the fields. When you reach it, jump first; then wait and ask him to jump. When he jumps, you must observe which foot he puts forward. If it is the right foot, then the youth is a man; if it is the left foot, then the youth is a woman. If, for some reason, you do not discover the answer, then the second thing you should do is to ask him to come and bathe with you, and in this way you are bound to discover the truth. But if this too fails, the third way to find out is to invite the youth to your room and place weapons and jewellery before him. You must then watch him carefully: if the youth is a woman, her hand will instinctively reach out for the jewellery; if the youth is a man, his hand will be drawn towards the weapons.'

The starling, who had been flying round the house to see if she could detect anything unusual, overheard this conversation between mother and son. She flew back to the princess and whispered into her ear what she had just heard.

Musa Khan returned to the guest-house and invited the youth to take a walk with him. They walked until they reached the canal in the fields. Musa Khan jumped with his right leg forward and waited for the youth. The princes remembered what the starling had told her, and knew that this was a test, so she too jumped with her right leg forward.

This did not satisfy the *deo*. So he took the youth to a stream, and he suggested that they should bathe together. But the princess refused and returned to the guest-house.

In the guest-house the *deo* made a pile of gold and precious jewels, and a pile of weapons, such as pistols, knives, and swords. He then turned to the youth, and said: 'You may choose whatever you like from these two piles.' The princess again remembered what the starling had told her, and she picked up a sword. Musa Khan still suspected that the youth was a woman, and he was irritated that his suspicions had not been confirmed by her actions.

In the evening Musa Khan invited the youth to have dinner with him in the guest-house. After dinner green tea was served. When the tea had been poured out, Musa Khan took the youth's cup and secretly slipped some opium into it. The starling noticed him doing this and reported it to the princess. When Musa Khan gave her the tea, she accepted it graciously and waited for the right moment to act. While he was busily engaged in a conversation with his friends, she swiftly exchanged her cup with his. Thus Musa Khan drank the tea containing the opium. It had an immediate effect on him and he soon dropped asleep.

When everybody was fast asleep, the princess crept out of bed and cut off Musa Khan's moustache and beard withher sword. And she wrote a note on a piece of paper and pinned it to his shirt. Then she quietly slipped out of the guest-house and entered the *deo*'s house. She tiptoed into the garden, without waking any of the family, plucked the flower for which she had been searching, and then returned to the place near the guest-house where she had tethered her horse. She mounted her horse and rode away as fast as she could, with the starling flying beside her. As soon as she arrived home, her father took the flower and smelt its perfume.

When Musa Khan awoke the next morning and read what the princess had written, he groaned with rage, for it read: 'I was a woman, but I did the work of a man.' He was even more furious when, having gone down to the river to wash his face, he saw his own reflection. His moustache and beard had vanished. Never in his life had he received such an insult. He swore by the honour of his tribe to take revenge and not to rest until he had drunk the princess's blood. With this intention,he mounted his horse and set off in pursuit of her,

After travelling for a long time he reached her kingdom. He made inquiries to find out whether the king's daughter was indeed the same girl as the girl who had come to his guest-house. After talking to many people, he finally met an old woman who informed him that the king had seven daughters, all of whom were married save the youngest. She also informed him that a fakir had told the king that he would have a son if he smelt a certain flower from the garden of Musa Khan Deo. 'The king's youngest daughter went in search of the flower,' said the old woman, 'and she returned with it and gave it to her father.'

Hearing this news, Musa Khan stormed into the royal palace and addressed the king: 'I have come to ask for your daughter's hand in marriage. If you refuse to give her to me, I shall destroy your kingdom. Not a man, woman, or child will be left alive.'

The king did not know what to do, but the vizier advised him not to contradict the *deo*: 'Give your daughter to Musa Khan or we shall all be killed.' So the king agreed and fixed a date for the marriage.

When the princess heard the news, she became very worried, because she knew that Musa Khan would never spare her. She ordered her servants to make a statue in her likeness out of clay, and she instructed them to leave a small opening at the top. When the statue was ready, she filled it with red sherbet from the opening at the top, and then had it sealed.

After the wedding celebrations were over, the princess heard the *deo* approaching her room. She told her servants to place the statue in the bed and to cover its head with a gold-embroidered veil. She then sent her servants away and hid under the bed. The *deo* entered the room with a dagger in his hand. He approached the statue in the dark and stabbed it in the stomach. When the blood poured out, he drank it. It tasted deliciously sweet. 'What a pity I have killed her,' he thought, 'because her blood is so sweet that she must indeed have been a beautiful woman.' But he consoled himself by saying that there was nothing else he could have done: it was a question of honour, and he had been obliged to take his revenge.

At that very moment the princess emerged from underneath the bed, and said to the *deo*: 'I beg you to forgive me. You have kept your oath and taken your revenge; now you can be forgiving.' When Musa Khan saw her he was very pleased, and they both lived happily ever after, and the king had many sons.

15

Khurram Deo

There was once a king who had two daughters, and every day these daughters used to go down to the river to bathe. One day they were bathing in the river as usual when one of them lost her nose-ring. At that moment a *deo* happened to be passing. When he saw the two pretty girls, he said to them, 'One of you must marry me.' Now this *deo* was very strong and handsome. So the girl who had lost her nose-ring replied: 'I am willing to marry you on condition that you find my nose-ring, which I must have dropped in the river.'

Hearing this, the *deo* dived into the river and, within minutes, reappeared with the princess's nose-ring. The princess therefore had no choice but to accompany the *deo*. He took her to a cave deep in the forest. The mouth of this cave was blocked by a large boulder. The *deo* lifted the boulder and took her inside.

In this way the princess and the *deo* began living as man and wife. The *deo* used to leave the cave each morning and return home at night. But when he left the cave in the morning, he always used to push the boulder back over the mouth of the cave to prevent the princess from escaping.

Many months passed and God blessed the princess with a son. They named him Khurram. When Khurram was two years old, he said to his mother: 'I will lift the stone to let light into the cave; I have never seen light.' The little child used all his strength, but he could only move the boulder very slightly. So he said to his mother: 'I cannot lift the stone because my body is still too weak, but tomorrow I shall lift it.'

Khurram's mother was very happy because she longed to see the sunlight again. 'When the *deo*, your father, leaves tomorrow morning,' she said, 'we shall leave the cave and pay a visit to your grandfather.'

Khurram agreed: 'Yes, mother, I would like to meet grandfather.'

Next morning, when the *deo* had left the cave, Khurram pushed aside the boulder that blocked the entrance, and he and his mother escaped and travelled to the palace where the princess's father lived. There they settled down to a new life.

Khurram used to play with the local children. But he was so strong that if, while playing, he caught a child's arm, the arm would come out of its socket. People became angry and used to complain to the king. Growing weary of the complaints brought to him every day, the king warned Khurram, 'You must stop mistreating others, otherwise don't blame me if you come to grief.'

Khurram was so offended by his grandfather's words that he ran away from home. He travelled from one kingdom to another, and wherever he went he became renowned for his strength.

Many years passed, and Khurram continued on his way until he reached a certain kingdom. While he was sitting in the bazaar, a man approached him. 'Who are you?' he asked. Khurram recounted his story. After listening with attention, the man said: 'There is a famous wrestler in our town. He wears chains round his neck and claims to be stronger than Khurram Deo.'

'Take me to him,' said Khurram, rising to his feet. The man agreed and took Khurram to the wrestler.

'Come, let us wrestle together at once,' said the wrestler. With the greatest of ease, Khurram lifted his opponent into the air and dropped him on the ground. The man was astonished by Khurram's strength; he fell at his feet and declared: 'I recognize you as my master.'

Khurram thus travelled on with his disciple, challenging other famous wrestlers to compete with him in strength. Each time he won, and each time his opponent would fall at his feet and become his pupil. In this way the number of his disciples increased every day, and they followed him wherever he went.

One day, they entered a country where nothing grew but rice, and that country was inhabited by a *deo*. In order to feed themselves, Khurram and his disciples would go out hunting each morning, leaving one of their companions behind to prepare the rice. But each evening, before they returned from hunting, the *deo* of that country used to come and devour all the cooked rice, so that the companion had to prepare more rice in a hurry. As a result, the rice was never cooked properly. On their return, Khurram and his disciples used to complain about the food, but the companion never told them about the *deo*.

This happened several times. So one day Khurram decided to stay behind himself and prepare the rice. When the food was ready, the *deo* of that country suddenly appeared before him. 'Give me the rice,' he said, 'or else I shall strangle you with my bare hands.' But Khurram was not afraid. He lifted a blazing stick from the fire and hit the *deo* with it. The *deo* fled in fright and Khurram pursued him. The *deo* then took refuge in a deep well, where there were two beautiful fairies whom he had imprisoned. The sides of this well were very slippery, and it was easier to climb in than to climb out again. Khurram followed the *deo* into the well and killed him.

Khurram's disciples had heard the noise and had followed their master to the well. So he shouted to them: 'Get me out of this well.'

'Don't worry,' replied the disciples. 'We will lend you a hand as soon as we have helped the fairies out.'

Khurram agreed. The disciples then helped the fairies to escape, but they left their master in the well.

16

The Man-eater

There was once a shepherd with a bald head who used to graze all the sheep and goats in his village, and wherever he took his flock, he used to sow a seed of the jujube tree. One day, while his flock was grazing, he quickly sowed one of these seeds and said to the seed: 'O jujube seed, when I come back here tomorrow, by the grace of God, your seedling will have grown above the ground.' When he returned next day, the seedling had grown above the ground. 'O seedling,' he said, after watering it with care, 'when I come here tomorrow, by the grace of God, you will be a full-grown tree.' When he came on the following day, the seedling had grown into a tree. 'O tree,' he said, after watering it with care, 'when I come back here tomorrow, by the grace of God, you will be laden with fruit.' Next day he returned to find the tree laden with berries. 'Tomorrow, by the grace of God, your berries will be ripe,' he said, after watering it. Next day, when the shepherd returned once again, the berries were ripe and had turned bright red. He was very pleased and climbed into the tree to eat the ripe fruit.

After some time, the shepherd looked down and saw an old woman looking up at him. She was sitting under the tree and she carried a big sack. Little did the shepherd realize that she was a man-eater.

'My son,' cried the old woman, 'Throw down some berries to a poor old lady.' He immediately responded by throwing down two berries. 'My bald son,' cried the old woman, 'the ground here is very muddy. Tie some berries in one corner of your *chadur* [turban-cloth] and tie the other end to your foot. Then lower your foot so that I can untie the *chadur* and take out the berries.'

The shepherd did as the old woman had instructed: he tied the berries in one corner of his turban-cloth and, after attaching the other end to his foot, he lowered it. No sooner was the turban-cloth within the old woman's reach than she held it tight and pulled with all her might, so that the shepherd fell from the tree and landed on the ground with a heavy thump. She seized him, swiftly pushed him into her sack, and, after tying up the mouth of the sack with several knots, set off home.

On the way she stopped at a village. Having first concealed the sack in a nearby field, she went to the blacksmith to have her teeth sharpened. A farmer was ploughing the field where the sack was hidden, and every time he goaded on his bullocks, shouting 'Ho! Ho!' the same sound 'Ho! Ho!' came from the sack. When the farmer shouted 'Gowat! Gowat!' to steer the bullocks round at the edge of the field, the same sound 'Gowat! Gowat!' came from the sack.

The farmer said to himself: 'Whatever is making this noise is in this sack.' So he went to the sack and untied it, and was astonished to discover a young man inside. He helped him out, then filled the sack with stones, thorns, and earth, and tied up the mouth with several knots. The shepherd thanked the farmer and went on his way.

When the old woman returned from the blacksmith, after having had her teeth sharpened, she picked up the sack and went home.

'My son,' she warned, when she felt the thorns poking into her, 'don't pinch me, or I shall deal with you later.'

As soon as she reached home, she opened the sack, and found to her horror that it was full of stones and thorns and earth. She was furious that she had been tricked.

Several days later the old woman disguised herself carefully and sat under the same jujube tree. Looking up, she saw the shepherd perched in the tree, eating berries. So she said to him: 'My son, please be kind and throw me down some berries.'

'Old woman, go away,' replied the shepherd. 'The other day I showed kindness by giving some berries to an old woman, and she repaid me by tying me up in a sack. If it hadn't been for a kind farmer who helped me to escape, I don't know what would have become of me.'

'So that's how the rascal escaped,' thought the old woman. 'That farmer is the culprit and one day I shall punish him.' She then turned to the shepherd with an innocent face. 'My son,' she said, 'Don't talk to me like that. I'm a poor woman, all alone in the world, and I'm also cursed with failing eyesight. Bring me down some berries and I shall say some prayers for you.'

The shepherd filled his turban-cloth with berries and then climbed down the tree. He had barely set foot on the ground when the man-eater jumped on him and caught him and tied him tightly in her sack. This time she went straight home. She gave the sack to her daughter, and said: 'I have to go on some urgent business, but I shall be back soon. In the meantime, take the man out of the sack, chop him up into little pieces, and prepare the pieces for us to eat.' Having said this, she went once again to visit the blacksmith.

When the old woman's daughter took the shepherd out of the sack, she noticed that his bald head was as round as a ball. So she said to him: 'Shepherd, why is your head so round?'

'My mother made it round by placing it in a stone mortar,' he replied.

'My head is crooked,' remarked the girl. 'Could you please make it round like yours?'

'Come here,' he said, picking up a stone mortar. 'If you put your head in this stone mortar, I can make it round.'

The girl p ut her head in the mortar, and the shepherd, gripping a stone pestle in his hand, hit her so hard that her head split into smithereens. He quickly changed into her clothes and picked up an empty water-pitcher and went to the river. Then he sat on the upturned water-pitcher and crossed the river as fast as he could.

Meanwhile, the man-eater had returned home to find her daughter dead. She immediately ran to the river, but by the time she arrived, the shepherd had safely reached the other side.

'My son, you were my guest,' said the old woman reproachfully. 'Why did you run away?'

'No, old woman,' replied the shepherd, 'I will not come to you. If you would like to join me, tie your mill-stone round your neck and jump into the river. In this way you will certainly reach the other side.'

The old woman went home and returned with the mill-stone. She tied it round her neck and jumped into the river. She drowned immediately.

17

The Prince and the Fairy

There was once a king who had seven sons, and of the seven sons, the youngest was the most handsome. When the princes came of age, the king called his vizier and said to him, 'My sons have come of age; we must think about getting them married.' To which the vizier replied: 'But first we must find a king who has seven daughters, so that each of them can marry one of the princes. In this way there will be unity in the family and no quarrelling.' The king immediately approved of the idea, and said to the vizier: 'Go and search for such a king, and ask him whether he will offer his daughters in marriage to my sons.'

The vizier travelled from one kingdom to another until he reached the kingdom of a king who had seven daughters. Having obtained an audience with him, he delivered his message. The king was very pleased with the proposal, and he said to the vizier: 'Tell your king that I agree to marry my seven daughters to his seven sons.'

The vizier returned to his country and gave the king the good news. The king was delighted, and he ordered that preparations be made without delay, because he wanted the marriages to be celebrated with great pomp and ceremony.

On the appointed day, there was rejoicing throughout the kingdom. The princes, accompanied by a large wedding procession, set off to the palace where the princesses lived. They travelled until evening; then they broke their journey. The king had made arrangements in advance for everyone's food and shelter. Some servants put up tents, while others lit a big fire and cooked a feast for the wedding party. After the feast, there was singing and dancing late into the night; and when everyone was exhausted, they retired to their tents.

The tent of the youngest prince was at the furthest corner of the encampment. As soon as he entered it, he lay down on his bed and fell fast asleep. Late that night a fairy, who happened to be passing, peeped into the tent, and no sooner had she set eyes on the prince than she fell in love with him. She woke him and declared: 'I have fallen in love with you. I shall kill you and take you away with me.'

'No, you mustn't do that,' replied the prince. 'This is a day of rejoicing; my mother and father and brothers are very happy today, and my death would cause them great sorrow. The day after tomorrow is the day of my wedding. If you want, you can kill me then.' The fairy agreed.

Next morning, the wedding procession set off once again. They travelled all day, and that evening they arrived at the princesses' palace. They were made welcome by the king and a huge dinner was served in their honour. The wedding ceremony took place on the following morning, attended by all the guests. In the evening each prince and princess was shown to a separate room in the palace.

As soon as the youngest prince entered his room, the fairy appeared before him once again, and made him smell her handkerchief. No sooner had he done so than he collapsed and died. When the princess and her maidservant entered the room and found the prince lying dead on the floor, they were filled with grief.

'We ought to inform the prince's parents,' said the maidservant.

'No,' replied the princess, 'we should wait until morning.'

The two women spent the night weeping over the prince's dead body. In the morning the prince's mother and father learnt the sad news. The wedding celebrations came to an abrupt end and the whole kingdom mourned the prince's death. The prince's mother called the princess aside, and said to her: 'We shall be returning at once to our country. I leave it to you to decide whether you would rather remain here in your father's house, or whether you wish to accompany us.'

'I shall accompany you,' replied the princess, 'and spend the rest of my life praying at my husband's grave.'

That same day the wedding procession set out on the homeward journey with the prince's body. After travelling all day, they reached the same spot where they had camped previously. Once again they broke their journey for the night. Once again the tents were pitched and the food was prepared. But this time there was no singing and no dancing. People sat and prayed near the body of the prince until late into the night. Then they retired to their tents to rest before the next day's journey. Only the princess and her maidservant remained to keep vigil over the prince's body. While they were sitting and weeping, the fairy appeared once again, and carried off the prince and the bed on which he was lying.

In the morning, when the king and queen were told what had happened, they said to the princess: 'We can do nothing. It is the will of God. You must be patient and bear your grief in silence.' Then they asked her: 'What would you like to do now? Do you still wish to accompany us, or would you prefer to return home?'

'Now that I have lost everything, I shall return to my father's house,' she replied.

The wedding procession continued on its way, and the princess, with her maidservant and two guards, returned home.

The princess took up her abode in a secluded wing of the palace, and here she would spend the whole day in prayer. She never went out, except when she went to offer alms to the poor. Any beggar who came to her door would receive food, money, or clothing from her own hands.

Many years passed. One day, as the princess was completing here evening prayers, she heard the voices of two fakirs begging for alms. The princess took them some food. When they had eaten, she addressed the elder of the two: 'Respected father, have you seen or heard about any unusual event?'

'Yes, my lady,' he replied, 'I have seen one strange thing. On the Mountain of Qaf a human being, a son of Adam, is lying on a beautiful bed. Many years have passed, yet he still lies there just as he did on the first day.' The elder fakir then described what the man looked like.

The princess was certain that this man was the prince, her lost husband, and she asked the fakirs to take her to the spot where he lay. The fakirs at first refused: 'No, my lady, it is very far away. The journey is impossible for a man, let alone for a woman.' But the princess insisted, and the fakirs finally consented.

After making the necessary preparations, they set off on their journey. They travelled for many days and had to overcome countless obstacles; on some days, they had to do without food or water; but the princess's determination to find her husband kept her alive. The slopes of Mount Qaf were steep and slippery. When, at last, they reached the summit, the princess was amazed to discover her long-lost husband. He was reclining on the same bed as that on which he had been lying when the fairy had carried him away. But she had barely had time to approach the bed when the fairy suddenly appeared and lifted the bed into the air and flew away. The fakirs and the princess were powerless to do anything.

The fakirs asked leave of the princess to continue on their wanderings. She bade them farewell, and told them that she had decided to remain where she was. She made her home in a cave, eating wild fruits and drinking water from a nearby stream. She spent her days searching for the prince, but could see no trace of him. Time passed; and she scarcely had any clothes left to cover her back.

One day the King of the Fairies happened to be flying over the Mountain of Qaf when he noticed some creature running into a cave. He swooped down and stood at the mouth of the cave. The princess, dressed in rags, was crouching in a corner in the dark.

'Who are you and what are you doing here?' he shouted. 'Tell me the truth or your life is in danger.'

'I am a daughter of Adam,' replied the princess, 'but I have spent a long time here and I am naked.'

At this the fairy king threw his turban-cloth towards her. She picked it up and covered herself, and then came outside.

'Pray forgive me,' said the fairy king when he beheld her. 'From today you shall be my sister, for I have no sister.' With these words, he gathered her up in his arms and carried her to his palace.

A few days after the princess's arrival in the kingdom of the fairies, a big festival took place. In accordance with the fairy custom, fairies from all over the world came to attend it, and there was singing and rejoicing throughout the land. The fairy who had stolen the princess's husband was also there, and she was wearing a beautiful red flower in her hair. When she entered the palace, the princess saw her and guessed at once that she had transformed the prince into a flower. She tried to catch hold of the flower, but it disintegrated in her hands and the petals fell on the floor. The fairy quickly collected the petals and rushed out of t he palace. But the fairy king, who had been watching, beckoned to his guards: 'My sister likes flowers. Go and bring her the finest flowers in the kingdom.'

The princess turned to the fairy king. 'No, brother,' she said, 'I do not like flowers. The fairy, whom you have just seen, has killed my husband and has made him into a flower, and I have been searching for him for many years.'

When the fairy king heard this, he was very angry, and ordered his guards to summon all the male and female fairies. When they had gathered before him, he addressed them sternly: 'Which of you has transformed a son of Adam into a flower?'

A fairy clasping red petals in her hands stepped forward,

'Make that flower into a human being immediately,' commanded the fairy king, 'or you will be severely punished.'

Without hesitation, the fairy transformed the flower into the young prince. When the princess beheld her husband, she was filled with joy. After thanking the fairy king for all his help, the prince and the princess set off on their homeward journey. First they visited the princess's father and paid him their salaams. Then they travelled to the prince's palace. The prince's parents and brothers rejoiced when they saw him, and there were celebrations in the land for many days.

IV

Courtship and Infidelity

Kandahar Lady of Rank (Rattray, pl. 29)

Mosque of Ahmad Shah (Rattray, pl. 27)

9. Hawkers of Kohistan (Rattray, pl. 3)

10. Kabul Costumes (Atkinson, pl. 25)

1. Muhammad Nain Sharif (Rattray, pl. 15)

12. Dost Muhammad Khan, two of his sons and his cousin (Eden, pl. 1)

18

The Parrot and the Starling

They say that both the parrot and the starling make their nests in holes, usually in a tree or a mud wall. There were two trees standing side by side, and in the trunk of each there was a hole. A parrot lived in one hole, and a starling and her daughter lived in the other.

They say that the parrot belongs to the royal tribe and the starling belongs to the menial tribe, and it is well known that these tribes do not normally inter-marry.

One day, there was a fearful storm with rain, wind, and hail. The wind raged through the trees with such ferocity that rain and hailstones were blown into the parrot's nest. Soon the nest was flooded with water, and the parrot came out of his hole and perched on a branch. The storm, however, showed no signs of abating, and he thought that if one single hailstone were to fall on his head, he would surely die. He therefore decided that it would be wiser to enter the starling's nest.

'Leave my house immediately,' screamed the starling as soon as he had entered. 'You have broken my daughter's purdah. No male is permitted to set eyes on her, except the one she is to marry.'

'There is a dreadful hailstorm outside,' replied the parrot. 'If I go out, I shall die.'

'Leave my house immediately,' repeated the starling. 'I don't care if you die. You have broken my daughter's purdah.'

'I'm not leaving,' said the parrot stubbornly.

The starling thought for a moment; then said: 'If you refuse to leave, you can stay, but only on one condition, that you marry my daughter.'

'God forbid!' cried the parrot. 'How could such a thing be possible? I belong to the royal tribe and you belong to the menial tribe. Till this day no member of the royal tribe has ever been known to marry into the menial tribe. So why do you even suggest such an thing?'

The starling did not wish to startan argument. 'If you don't want to marry my daughter, then, as I said, you must leave immediately.'

The parrot thought to himself: 'If I go out, I sh all die; therefore, in order to save my life, I shall agree to the marriage, but on one condition.' So he turned to the starling, and said: 'In the royal tribe it is the custom that the wife should remain indoors. I shall marry your daughter on condition that she respects this custom. The moment she leaves the house she shall cease to be my wife.'

The starling agreed happily. 'If youcan look after her in the house, and give her plenty of food and drink, she will have no need to go out.'

It was thus that a marriage took place, there and then, between the starling's daughter and the parrot. Next day, when the storm had subsided, the parrot went out in search of food. In the evening he brought back more than enough food to satisfy the needs of his wife and her mother. Every morning thereafter he would go out foraging for food, and he would always bring back the tastiest fruit from the orchard. The starling and her daughter had previously lived on insects; never before had they tasted or even seen fruit. So time passed, and with good food and much pampering the starling's daughter became rebellious.

One day, when the parrot had gone out as usual in search of food, the starling's daughter said to her mother: 'I'm so bored here in this dark hole. Let's go out and take some fresh air and eat a few insects; my husband will not return before dusk.'

The mother disagreed. 'We lead an easy life,' she said, 'and the parrot brings us good food. Suppose we go out and he happens to see us, we're bound to be in trouble.'

But the starling's daughter refused to listen. 'If you don't come with me, I shall go alone.' With these words, she flew out of the nest.

The mother then grew anxious. She thought to herself: 'I don't know how long my daughter will be absent, so I had better go after her and bring her back before the parrot returns.'

The starling's daughter had not flown far before she came upon some lovely fresh cow-dung. At once she sat on it and began to poke around for food with her beak. Soon her head and feet became filthy. A few moments later her mother, who had followed her, sat down beside her. 'Hurry!' she said. 'We don't want to be found here by the parrot.' But no sooner had she uttered these words than the parrot flew past.

'My marriage to your daughter is now annulled,' squawked the parrot, unable to contain his wrath.

'But that's impossible,' protested the starling. 'The marriage can't be broken so easily.'

'I married on one condition,' retorted the parrot, 'that my wife should remain indoors. Now look at her beak and feet,' he said, pointing at his wife. 'I cannot possibly live with her in such a disgusting state.'

The starling was not one to give in so easily. 'Let us go to the mullah,' she said, 'and he will consider the matter and pronounce his judgement.'

The parrot agreed, and so the three birds went to the mullah's house.

'We have come to you with a problem which you must solve,' they said when they were all seated.

'Who is the accuser and who is the accused?' asked the mullah.

The parrot stood up. 'I am the accuser,' he said in a loud voice, and he pointed to the starling's daughter: 'I accuse her of breaking the condition on which I agreed to marry her.'

The mullah straightened his robes, stroked his beard, and then addressed the parrot. 'Please make your statement,' he said solemnly.

The parrot recounted how his nest had been flooded in a hailstorm, and how he had sought refuge in the starling's nest, where he had been tricked into marrying the starling's daughter because he had broken her purdah and feared that, if he were to brave such a storm, he would certainly die. 'But,' continued the parrot, 'I made it a condition of the marriage that my wife should remain indoors. I warned the starling that if her daughter ever broke her word, I would consider the marriage null and void. But today, as I was returning home earlier than usual, I caught my wife red-handed. She was sitting on a cow-pat, poking in it with her beak. If you don't believe me, just look at her beak and feet.'

After listening attentively to the parrot's statement, the mullah turned to the starling. 'What do you have to say in defence of your daughter?' he asked solemnly.

'He is incapable of looking after his wife,' said the starling. 'He is making excuses so that he can again lead a bachelor's life.' Then she turned to the mullah, and said: 'Now I shall tell you a story.'

The Glittering Necklace

'Once upon a time there was a king whose son refused to have an arranged marriage, declaring that he would marry the girl of his choice. Some years passed, but the prince did not marry because he still had not found a girl to his liking. The king was growing old, and he thought to himself, "If I leave the choice to my son, he will never marry." So, without consulting his son, he had him betrothed to a princess in the neighbouring kingdom. When the prince heard the news, he was very upset, and he went to his father to complain: "I was waiting to choose a girl whom I liked. You should not have engaged me to marry a girl whom I've never even met without obtaining my consent. If I like her, our house will be sweeter than paradise, but if I dislike her, it will be worse than hell."

'The prince therefore decided to find out for himself what sort of a girl had been promised to him in marriage. He filled his purse with money and travelled to the neighbouring kingdom. When he reached the town where the girl lived, a thought suddenly occurred to him: Supposing he were to see his future wife, how would he recognize her? Then he had an idea: "I shall stay in one of the local inns. There I shall probably meet the young men of the town and overhear all their gossip. If I hear in the inn that the girl I am to marry is good, I shall agree to the marriage; if not, I shall inform my father that I wish to break off the engagement." So he went to an inn and took rooms there.

'In the inn the prince spent much of his time eating and drinking, and when the other guests went out to work, he would remain behind, lying in bed all day doing nothing. After three days, the innkeeper said to himself: "This man eats, drinks, and does no work. He must be a thief." So, as soon as the innkeeper had a moment to spare, he approached the new guest and inquired what work he did.

'"I do no work," replied the prince. "I am looking for work."

'When the innkeeper heard this, he said: "A friend of mine is very rich and he is looking for a servant. When he returns home in the evening, I shall introduce you to him. He has a flock of a thousand sheep. Your job will be to look after them from dawn to dusk, regardless of the weather, and he will pay you whatever you ask."

'In the evening the innkeeper's friend returned home and the innkeeper introduced the young prince to him. The friend then asked the prince, "How much money do you want for your services?"

'"Whatever you think is just," answered the prince.

'The friend asked the same question three times and each time he received the same answer. Then he said: 'Come home with me. I shall introduce you to my mother, and from today you may consider yourself my brother. We shall live together, and work together, and half my wealth shall be yours. Moreover, I shall go and look for two sisters who are equally beautiful and similar to each other in every way, and you can marry one, and I shall marry the other. For the first three days, I shall accompany you," he added, "so that you know where to graze the sheep, but on the fourth day you will have to go alone."

'For the next three days the rich man accompanied the prince when he took the sheep to graze. On the way to the grazing ground they had to pass a place that had a foul smell. On the third day the prince turned to the rich man. "Brother," he said, "this place smells foul; it makes me feel sick."

'"This is the king's rest-house, and people come here with their horses and use it as a stable," explained the rich man. "That's why it smells so bad. Today is only the third day – after a few days you will grow accustomed to the smell."'

The starling interrupted her story and turned to the mullah, and said, 'Now listen carefully to what I have to say.'

Then she resumed her story: 'For three days the rich man accompanied the prince, showing him how to reach the grazing ground and how to look after the flock. On the fourth day he left the prince to perform his duties by himself, and he set off in search of two beautiful sisters whom he and the prince might marry.

'They say that in those days there was a severe drought in that district. The king had ordered a deep well to be dug, so that all men and women, whatever their colour or tribe, might come by turn and draw one jar of water each. Travellers were permitted to take one jar of water without queuing like the others, and a woman had been appointed as keeper of the well to ensure that each one received a fair share.'

Again the starling turned to the mullah, and said: 'Now listen carefully to what I have to say. One day a merchant arrived in the kingdom with a camel caravan laden with goods. His tents were pitched and arrangements were made for food, but there was no water to be found. The merchant told his servants to continue their work while he made inquiries. When he asked the local people where he could find water, they informed him that there was a drought and that, by the king's command, a deep well had been dug from which each citizen was entitled to draw water by turn. But travellers, so they said, could go and draw water without having to queue for it.

'Now it so happened that the princess to whom the prince was betrothed had gone for an outing with her friends on that same day, taking her water-jar with her. There was a long queue of people waiting near the well. The princess placed her jar in the queue and stood a little apart from the others, watching the scene. It was at that very moment that the merchant arrived with his water-jar. When he saw the princess standing there, he was struck by her beauty. He stepped forward and handed his jar to the old woman who guarded the well. Knowing that he was a stranger to those parts, she filled it for him without delay.

'"Who is that beautiful girl?" he asked, when she gave the jar back to him.

'"You shouldn't ask such questions," replied the old woman. "That is the princess. She is already engaged to be married. She has come here to take a walk with some of her friends."

'The merchant said nothing to his servants when he returned, but he was very agitated, and his mind was lost in thought. He arranged for the sale of his goods at half price and was pleased to be rid of them. He then dismissed his servants and became a guest of the old woman who had been appointed keeper of the well.

'"Respected mother, what does the king pay you for your duties at the well?" he asked.

'"One *maund* of wheat every six months," answered the old woman.

'"For every errand you do for me, I shall offer you eighty *maunds* of wheat," said the merchant.

'"First tell me what I have to do for you?" replied the old woman, with a cunning smile.

'"You will have to go to the queen and give her a message. You will tell her that if her daughter is willing to spend one night with me, I will give her a necklace which is so rare and precious that it is worth a thousand rupees." [In those days, you must remember, this was a vast sum of money.] "Whatever the queen may say," he added, "you must say nothing more, but return to me with her reply."

'The old woman did not like the sound of what she heard, but she was tempted by the offer of wheat. She told the merchant that she would go at once to the palace and persuade the king to dismiss her from his service. The crafty old woman then went to the king, and said, "Your Majesty, I cannot continue in your service because the girls tease me and take water from me by force." In this way she managed to have her name struck off the king's pay-roll. After that she obtained an audience with the queen. When she was brought before the queen, she did not beat about the bush, but came straight to the point: "Respected queen, there is a merchant here who has sent me to you to plead on his behalf. He says that if your daughter is willing to spend one night with him, he will give her a necklace that is worth a thousand rupees."

'At this the queen rose to her feet in anger. "Kick this woman out," she screamed to her maidservants, "for she has insulted me."

'The maidservants came running into the room and roughly pushed the old woman out of the palace, warning her never to show her face there again. But the old woman often returned to the palace, and several times she was able to gain admittance by bribing a guard or an old acquaintance. Each time she repeated the merchant's request to the queen, and each time the queen reacted in exactly the same manner as she had done on the first occasion: she cursed the old woman and had her thrown out of the palace.

'One day, the princess happened to pass her mother's room when the old woman was there. She later asked her mother, "What was the old woman saying to you?"

'The mother explained: "She has come here many times, and she talks nonsense. She speaks of a merchant who has seen you, and who is willing to give you a necklace worth a thousand rupees if you spend one night with him. We have scolded her and warned her not to show her face here again, but she keeps returning with the same request."

'The princess thought for a while, then said: "Mother, I will win the necklace from the merchant. Next time the old woman comes, you must arrange a rendezvous."

'The mother was shocked, but could not argue, because once her daughter had made up her mind, nobody could contradict her. So finally she agreed and sent for the old woman. When the old woman appeared, the queen said to her: "Go and tell the merchant to have the necklace ready. My daughter will meet him next Friday, in a week's time, at the king's rest-house." The queen then ordered her servants to clean the rest-house. For seven days the servants worked day and night, cleaning, painting, and perfuming the place. The queen herself inspected the work and, following her daughter's instructions, had a beautiful bed placed just inside the door.

'That Friday evening the young prince was returning with his flock when he noticed a smell of exotic perfume that seemed to come from the royal rest-house. He was puzzled, and thought that there was something strange about this place, since in the past it had smelt foul, yet now it smelt of the finest perfume in the land. So he decided to go and take a closer look.

'In the twilight the prince now saw from afar the princess approaching with her friends. She had a knife in one hand and a gun in the other. She entered the rest-house, and put the knife on one side of her bed and the gun on the other. Then she asked her companions to leave her. Soon after their departure, the merchant arrived, carrying a glittering necklace in one hand.

'"Beware!" warned the princess. "I shall shoot you if you dare to come any nearer, and if you escape my bullets, I shall finish you off with this knife." So saying, she flashed the knife in his direction. The knife glinted in the moonlight, and the merchant thought to himself: "If I go any closer, she will certainly kill me, so I shall have to be content to remain outside and to gaze at her all night, and lose the necklace. But next time, I shall make it a condition that, for the next necklace, I should spend the night in the room with her; and the time after that, I shall make it a condition that I spend the night in bed with her; and in this way I shall surely win her."

'So the night passed, with the merchant standing at the gate and the princess reclining on the bed just inside the open door. She was in full view of the merchant and on her guard lest he should take one step closer.

'The prince, who had come to discover why the rest-house was smelling so sweet, was crouching in the darkness near the gate and had witnessed this whole scene. Moreover, he had overheard the conversation between the princess and the merchant. When the merchant had begged to be allowed into the rest-house, the princess had replied that she was betrothed to the son of a certain king, and that if she were to marry the very next day, and if her husband were to hear that she had allowed a man to enter her room, then what would she say? The prince heard all this, and was eager to step forward and make himself known, but he restrained himself and waited patiently.

'At the first light of dawn the merchant departed, leaving the necklace behind with the princess. Soon afterwards, the princess returned to the palace. Once the road was clear, the prince ran as fast as he could to the rich man's house, and said, "I am no longer willing to work for anybody; I must return home at once." So saying, he saddled his horse and rode at a gallop to his father's kingdom. When he reached the palace, he asked his father to make arrangements for his marriage, explaining that he had seen and liked the princess to whom he was betrothed.

'Respected mullah,' said the starling, 'my daughter is as brave and impulsive as this princess. The parrot is just making excuses because he prefers to lead a bachelor's life.'

'The starling is right,' said the mullah, turning to the parrot. 'You have lost the case and must keep her daughter.'

The parrot looked rather worried, but with great dignity he addressed the mullah: 'The starling and her daughter are dirty, and what's more, they are liars. Now it's my turn to tell you a story.'

The Man-eaters

'Once upon a time there was a king who had three sons. When the king died, his sons buried him. That evening the sons were sitting at home, and the elder brother said to his younger brothers, "Tomorrow I shall sit on the throne and rule the kingdom in my father's place." He turned to the second brother, and said, "You will assist me in the affairs of state." He then turned to his youngest brother, and said, "You will be in charge of the royal household."

'Next day, the elder brother sat on the throne and held court; the second brother was sent to settle some local dispute; and the third brother stayed at home to supervise the preparation of the food and other household tasks.

'As time passed, the elder brother grew bored with his royal duties. So he called his two younger brothers, and told them that they would all go out hunting. "I shall hunt," he said; "you, my second brother, will collect the game, and you, the youngest, will cook it for me." They set out hunting early in the morning. The eldest brother hunted; the second brother collected the game; and the third brother began to pluck the dead birds. The elder brothers had already shot and collected twenty wild duck, but, as the plucking and cooking was evidently going to take some time, they went out again in search of more game.

'While the youngest brother was gathering sticks for a fire, he realized that he had lost his matches. They had obviously fallen out of his pocket. He became very worried, and searched everywhere, but to no avail, not realizing that, in his search, he had wandered deeper and deeper into the forest. Suddenly he found himself in a clearing and saw a house. Three beautiful sisters lived in this house, and they were man-eaters. When the young prince knocked on the door, the elder sister came out.

'"Excuse me," he said, "I need some matches to light a fire, so that I can cook the game my brothers have hunted."

'"We have a good fire here," replied the eldest sister. "Call your brothers and you can cook the game in our house."

'So the young prince went running to his brothers, and told them that he had met three beautiful girls who had invited him to prepare the meal in their house in the forest. The three brothers could not resist such an invitation. They went to the house of the three sisters and cooked their game, having decided among themselves to spend the night there.

'"Listen," said the elder brother to the second brother, "when we've finished the meal, I shall turn to you and say, 'We had better be going now – it's getting late.' The girls will then ask us to spend the night in their house, and we will agree."

'The elder brother's plan was successful, and it was thus that the princes spent the night in the house of the three sisters.'

The parrot interrupted his story, and said to the mullah, 'Respected mullah, listen very carefully to what I have to say.'

Then he continued the story: 'When it was growing late, the elder sister said to the brothers: "What more could one wish for? We are three sisters and you are three brothers. I should marry the eldest brother; my next sister should marry the second brother, and the youngest sister should marry the youngest brother." After making this proposal, she showed the princes round the house. The first room contained beautiful beds; the second room contained bedding; the third room was full of the finest crockery and cutlery; the fourth room was full of silver; the fifth room was full of gold. Then, turning to the brothers, she said, "We shall live here, or if you prefer it, we can go and live in your house." The brothers said that they would be very pleased to live in that house. So the three brothers married the three sisters, and each couple had a separate room.

'Next morning the brothers went to bathe in the river.[1] After bathing, when they were sitting on the bank of the river, the eldest brother said: "I have such a wonderful wife. Everyone should have a wife like mine." The second brother said: "My wife is so kind. Anyone who sees her is bound to admit that she is better than yours." The third brother said nothing, so his brothers asked him, "What is your wife like?"

'"My wife cried all night," he answered.

'"Did you ask her why she was crying?"

141

'"I did," he continued, "but she only replied: 'You look after your sorrow and I shall look after mine.' I insisted, but she refused to tell me."

'The two elder brothers were puzzled by this, and they said to their younger brother, "Tonight, whatever happens, you must find out why your wife was crying."

'That night, when the youngest brother entered his room, he noticed that his wife had carefully prepared the bed for him. But, instead of getting into bed, he lay on the floor.

'"Why do you lie on the floor when I've just made your bed?" she asked.

'"I shall sleep here until you tell me why you were crying," he answered.

'"If I cry, that's my own affair," said the girl.

'"If you don't tell me why you were crying, our marriage and friendship are finished," said the girl's husband.

'But the girl still refused to speak, and the youngest brother slept on the floor.

'Next morning, when the three brothers went down to the river to bathe, the two elder brothers asked the younger one, "Did your wife tell you why she was crying?"

'"I tried all night to persuade her," he replied apologetically, "but she wouldn't tell me."

'The elder brothers were very angry. "If you don't find out by this time tomorrow night," they said, "we shall kill you and throw you into the river."

'On the third night they went to their rooms and prepared for bed.'

The parrot interrupted the story once again, and said to the mullah, 'Respected mullah, please listen carefully to what I have to say.'

Then he continued the story: 'That night the youngest prince left his room and sat outside the door. When his wife asked him what he was doing, he replied, "Everything is finished between us until you tell me what makes you cry." His wife hesitated for a moment, and then she told him that if he came into the room, she would tell him. When he had entered the room, his wife explained the reason for her sorrow: "We three sisters are man-eaters. None of the wealth you have seen in our house belongs to us by right: we have stolen it all from men like you whom we have entertained. This is how we make our living. You and your brothers have only a few more days to live; then we will cut you into pieces and eat you. That is why I am crying, because I like you and I don't want to kill you."

"'If you love me so much, can't you think of some way of escape?" asked the young prince.

"'I myself am powerless to do anything," answered the girl, "but I'll tell you a trick which could save your life. Tomorrow morning, tell your eldest brother to tell my eldest sister that a certain king owes him three thousand rupees, and that all of you must go and visit him to retrieve the money. My sister will say that it's not worth bothering about such a small amount of money, and she will offer to give him twenty thousand rupees instead. But you must insist, and say that you will return in four days' time. For four days you must disappear somewhere. Upon your return, your eldest brother must say, within earshot of my sisters, that he doubts whether the king will ever repay the loan, and that you should therefore go and stay in his palace until he produces the money. Again my sister will urge you not to go, saying that for every thousand rupees she would give forty thousand instead. Your eldest brother should then reply that it is not a question of money, but a question of honour. When you leave for the second time, you must flee for your lives and never return. I will show you the route to take. After travelling for eight days, you will reach a river that you will have to cross. If you can cross the river, you will be safe. If you fail to do what I say, my sisters will eat you alive."

'Next morning, when the brothers were bathing in the river, the youngest recounted what he had heard the previous night. So the brothers did as the youngest sister had suggested and the plan worked well. But as the brothers prepared to leave the house for the second time, the eldest sister began to suspect that they might never come back. After the brothers had leftthe house, she told her younger sisters to come with her and pursue them.

'The brothers took the route which the youngest sister had told them to follow. After travelling for eight days, they reached the river. First the eldest brother's horse waded across the river. Then the second brother's horse waded across the river. But only the two front legs of the third brother's horse were in the river when the three sisters arrived, and the eldest sister tried at once to catch the horse by the tail.

'"Catch the horse by some other part, or else he will cut off the tail and escape," cried the youngest sister, seeing that the prince was in danger. She said this to warn the prince and to advise him what to do.

'Hearing these words, the prince quickly drew his sword and cut off the tail of his horse. Thus he managed to reach the far bank of the river while the eldest sister still stood clutching the horse's tail.[2]

'"You were lucky to escape," shouted the eldest sister, "but tell me who told you our secret?"

'"Your younger sister," they answered.

'Hearing this, the two elder sisters pounced on the younger sister, sliced her into little pieces, and devoured her.'

The parrot turned to the mullah, and said: 'The starling is from the same tribe as these women.'

The mullah thought for a moment, then solemnly addressed the starling: 'The parrot has won the case.'

'Respected mullah,' said the starling, 'please listen and I shall tell you another story.'

The Widow and the Missing Corpse

'In the olden days there was a wealthy king. One night six thieves broke into his palace. The guards opened fire. One thief was shot dead, and the other five escaped. In the morning the guards went to the king and told him what had happened. The king ordered them to hang the thief's corpse onthe palace gate, and he made it known that if anyone came to claim the corpse, he too would be executed and his corpse would be strung up beside that of the thief. Everybody, including the five thieves, saw the corpse hanging from the gate, but no one dared to say that he knew the dead man.

'The five thieves conferred with one another, and one of them said: "It's not right to leave our friend without giving him a decent burial. Tonight I suggest that we go to the palace and kill the sentry. Then we can take our friend's body and bury it."

'When it grew dark, the five thieves crept to the gate where the corpse was hanging. The sentry was leaning on his gun and seemed to be fast asleep. They cleared their throats to check if he was indeed asleep. Thus reassured, they decided that there was no need to kill him. They untied the corpse and took it away with them. A few minutes later the sentry awoke and discovered that the corpse had vanished. He thought to himself: "There is only one place where one could take a corpse, and that is the graveyard." He therefore decided to go there at once.

'When the sentry was inspecting the graveyard, he met a woman who appeared to be weeping over her husband's grave. "What are you doing here at this time of night?" he asked.

'"My husband died recently, and I have come to pray at his grave," she replied.

'The sentry felt sorry for her, and promised to marry her. Then the woman asked, "What brings you here?" The sentry related his story: "I was guarding the corpse of a thief that had been strung up on the palace gate when I fell asleep and it was stolen. I came here to look for it, because if I don't find it, and if the king demands an explanation, I don't know what excuse I can make."

"'If you don't find the missing corpse, the king will have you executed," said the woman, "but don't worry, you can take the body of my dead husband and hang him on the gate instead." So together they dug up the husband's corpse and dragged it to the palace gate. But once they had strung up the corpse, the sentry grew worried, because it suddenly occurred to him that the thief had no beard, whereas the woman's dead husband had a beard. The woman noticed his look of anxiety. "Why are you so lost in thought?" she asked. "Haven't we solved your problem?"

"'No,' replied the sentry, and he explained: "The thief didn't have a beard and your husband has a beard. Tomorrow morning, when the king sees him, he'll know what we have done, and he'll ask me what happened to the thief's corpse."

"'Don't worry." said the woman. "Lift me up on your shoulders and I shall pull out his beard."

'The sentry lifted the woman up on his shoulders and she removed her husband's beard. This was not difficult, since it is an easy matter to remove hair from a dead man. But when the sentry saw her doing this, he thought: "If she is prepared to do this to her dead husband, what will she do to me?" So he gave her a push. "Get out of my sight," he cried. "If you can do this to your dead husband, what, I wonder, will you do to me?"

'Respected mullah,' said the starling, 'the parrot is from the same tribe as that woman.'

The mullah turned to the parrot. 'Respected parrot,' he said, 'I'm afraid you have lost the case. What do you have to say in your defence?'

The parrot then began his second story:

The Two Unfaithful Wives

'In the olden days there was a prince who had a friend called Gulkandan. Gulkandan was a poor man, and every day he would go to work in the fields. The prince often used to go and sit with him, and after work they would have dinner together in the village guest-house.

'The prince was engaged to marry a princess. On the wedding day the prince and his other friends were travelling in a procession to fetch the girl from her father's palace, and they passed Gulkandan's house. The prince stopped and asked Gulkandan to accompany them. Gulkandan accepted the invitation, but explained that he would first have to change his clothes. The prince waited at the door while he went in to change.

'"What are you doing?" asked Gulkandan's wife, when she saw her husband changing.

'"I am going to take part in the prince's wedding procession," he replied. "I may be away for two days."

'She seemed displeased that her husband would be away for such a long time. She tried to stop him, but he insisted, saying that the prince was his best friend and he had to go. "I don't want you to leave," she said, "but if you insist, I shall let you go on one condition: you must hang your picture on the wall and prepare the bed, and I shall sit on the bed and contemplate it."

'The prince overheard this discussion, and thought to himself: "It will be some time before Gulkandan is ready." So he continued on his way with the rest of the party. Meanwhile, Gulkandan prepared the bed, placed the bed against the wall, hung up his picture, and then left the house.

'Now Gulkandan's wife had a lover who was a black man. She had sent word to him that her husband would be taking part in the prince's wedding procession, and she urged him to come to her immediately.

'When Gulkandan left the house, he discovered that the prince had already gone, so he hurried after him. On the way he met a black man who was walking in the other direction. This black man was evidently very happy and was smiling to himself. So Gulkandan asked him, "What makes you so happy?" Failing to recognize him, the black man replied: "Gulkandan is taking part in the prince's wedding procession, and his wife has invited me to come to her house so that we can enjoy ourselves."

'When Gulkandan heard this, he said nothing, but waited until the black man was out of sight, then returned home. When he arrived home, the black man was already in bed with his wife. Seeing the two of them in bed together, Gulkandan took out his sword, and with one single blow, he cut them both in two. Then he covered them with a sheet and went to join the prince.

'When Gulkandan reached the fort belonging to the prince's father-in-law, the gates were already closed. This was because strict orders had been issued not to permit anyone to enter until the guests had departed in order to avoid any risk of theft. He went up to the gates, and asked the sentry to open them for him.

'"The king has commanded that these gates shall not be opened until after the departure of the wedding procession," said the sentry.

'"But the prince is my friend," complained Gulkandan, "and he is expecting me."

'"That's too bad," retorted the sentry. "These are my orders and I have to follow them."

'So Gulkandan was forced to remain outside the gates.

'Now the princess whom the prince was about to marry also had a black man for a lover. In the middle of the night Gulkandan heard the tinkling sound of anklets. When he went to investigate, he saw the princess climbing down a ladder on one side of the fort. As soon as she reached the ground she ran into the jungle. Gulkandan followed her. She ran to a small hut in the jungle and knocked at the door. A black man appeared.

She went inside, and Gulkandan stood near the door listening to their conversation.

'"Very soon I shall be a married woman," said the princess. "In the past I used to come to your house, but now you must come to mine."

'The black man complained that he didn't know the way; then he thought of a solution: "Your father must have prepared a large dowry for you, and the prince must have brought hundreds of boxes for transporting the dowry. Take me with you, and I shall hide in one of the boxes, and whenever the prince is absent, I shall come out."

'The princess agreed that this was an excellent idea. Then she and the black man left the hut and walked stealthily, hand in hand, to the wall of the fort. Gulkandan followed them. Once the two lovers had climbed the ladder, they pulled it up and lowered it on the other side. In this way they entered the fort, confident that no one had seen them.

'Next day the prince returned to his father's palace with his new wife. In the evening the prince and Gulkandan were sitting and talking to each other in the village guest-house, as they always used to do, when the prince said: "It's getting late. You should go home to your wife. She must be waiting for you. I too must go, as my wife must be waiting for me." With these words, the prince rose to his feet and set off to the palace, and Gulkandan quietly followed him.

'When the prince entered his wife's chamber, all her maidservants and friends, who had been sitting there, rose to their feet and left. The princess was seated on a bed, which was covered with soft cushions and garlands of flowers. When the prince approached her bed, she cried in a cunning voice, "Oh, something has bitten me!" The prince picked up the flowers and threw them on the floor, and asked her to sit down again. She sat down, and then again screamed, "Oh, something has bitten me!"

The prince removed the sheet and asked her to sit on the cushions.

'Meanwhile, Gulkandan had reached the door of the chamber, and was listening to this conversation. The door was locked from the inside, but Gulkandan bolted it from the outside. The princess screamed once again. Hearing this, Gulkandan chuckled aloud. The prince and his wife heard the laughter, and the prince wondered who on earth it could be. Then he said to himself: "It must be my friend Gulkandan. He has come to tease me on my wedding night." So he swore at him and went to the door. But when he tried to open the door, he was unable to do so, because it was bolted from the outside.

'"Gulkandan, open the door," he shouted angrily.

'"If I open the door, you will hit me," replied Gulkandan.

'"I promise not to hit you," said the prince, "but please open the door."

'"First unbuckle your sword and put it in the corner," said Gulkandan, "and then I will open the door."

'After the prince had placed his sword in one corner of the room, Gulkandan opened the door. "Take the princess's keys from her," he said, as soon as he had entered. "Open that big box over there. Her lover is inside."

'The princess cunningly tried to distract the prince. "Your friend has come here to dishonour you," she said. "I shall bring the key tomorrow from my mother's house, and you will see that he is blaming me for nothing."

'"She is lying," said Gulkandan. "She has the keys. You must take them from her."

'"I don't have the keys with me," she insisted.

'Gulkandan then told the prince, "Take the stone which is lying there and smash the box open."

'The prince took the stone, smashed the lock of the box, and opened the lid. He could hardly believe his eyes, for there, inside the box, sat a black man, shivering with fright. Gulkandan was standing near the door, and when the black man tried to make a quick escape, he wielded his sword and struck him a mortal blow. Then he turned round and slew the princess. At this the prince grew angry. "The black man deserved to die, but why the princess?"

'"Please don't be angry," replied Gulkandan. "Come with me and I shall show you something."

'He took the prince to his house, and lifted the sheet that covered the dead bodies of his wife and her lover. After witnessing this spectacle, they both asked God to protect them from women and vowed never to marry again.'

Having finished his story, the parrot turned to the mullah, and said: 'The starling is from the same tribe as these two unfaithful women.'

Addressing the starling, the mullah now gave his final verdict: 'The parrot is right. He has won the case and you have lost it.'

19

The Prince and the Fakir

There was once a king who had only one son, and this son was very dear to him. When the prince came of age, the king wanted to arrange his marriage in the normal way. However, the prince refused to marry, because his teachers had taught him that women are fickle and cunning. The king insisted that he must marry, so he finally agreed to do so, but on one condition.

'I shall take a girl who is two years old,' he told his father, 'and I shall look after her myself. When she is old enough to marry, I shall marry her. If you do not agree to my condition, then I shall never marry at all.'

The king had no choice; so he accepted this arrangement. He chose a two-year old girl and gave her to his son. The prince took her to a house that he had built in the forest, and there he looked after her and educated her. He did not allow her to meet anyone.

Many years passed; and when the girl reached the age of sixteen, he married her. He had great faith in his wife's love, believing that she loved him with total devotion because he had brought her up himself. He would go out hunting early in the morning and return in the evening. While he was away, the young girl did all the housework and then went to the stream to fetch water. Her husband had instructed her to return home at once if she ever happened to encounter anyone at the stream.

One day, when she went to fetch water from the stream, she saw a young man. This man had gone out hunting with his companions and, feeling thirsty, he had come down to the stream to have a drink. When he saw the prince's wife, he fell in love with her. Never in his life had he seen anyone so pure and innocent. When the girl saw the young man near the stream, she hurried home.

The young man rejoined his companions, and said: 'Who is that girl? If I don't meet her, I shall go mad.' His companions advised him to go to the city and find an old woman who would act as a go-between.

So the young man went to the city and searched for a cunning old woman. Having found one, he told her his story and gave her a bag of gold, and promised her more if she could arrange for him to meet the young girl in the forest. The old woman reassured him: 'Leave everything to me. You must meet me every three days in the forest.'

Then the old woman went to the forest, and for many days she watched the prince's movements. She noted that every morning he used to pass the stream on his way to go hunting. So one day she sat down near the stream, and when he was due to pass, she began weeping loudly. The prince drew up his horse and dismounted.

'Respected mother, what is the matter?' he asked.

'I've been abandoned here, and I'm dying of hunger, and I've nobody in the world to care for me,' replied the old woman. The prince took pity on her and brought her to his house.

'Who is she?' asked his wife.

'She is a helpless old woman,' he replied, 'and from now on she will stay with us.'

By means of this ruse, the old woman began living with the prince and his wife, and was soon able to win their confidence and respect. One day, when the prince was out hunting, the old woman said to the girl: 'Daughter, there is a handsome young man who lives nearby, and he would like to meet you.'

The girl was shocked by these words. 'For me there is nobody more handsome than my husband,' she said. 'You had better beware! If you speak to me like that again, I'll tell him.' The old woman kept quiet, but she was not deterred.

Whenever the prince left the house, the old woman used to talk to the young girl about the outside world and its attractions. So time passed, and the princess became interested in people and things. The old woman thought that the time was now ripe, and again she said: 'There is a very handsome young man who lives near here.'

'Who is he?' asked the princess.

'He is the son of a rich merchant, and he is in love with you. Would you like to meet him?'

The girl thought for a moment, and said: 'I don't see any harm in it.'

The old woman was pleased with this reply. She left the house and came back bringing the young man with her. When the young girl saw the young man, she at once fell in love with him.

As time passed, the prince noticed a change in his wife. She always seemed to be lost in thought and she did not show him the same attentions. He decided to find out the reason for this. Next day he pretended to set out on a hunting expedition, but instead, he walked a short distance and climbed a tree, so that he could see clearly what went on inside his house. He waited there the whole morning, but nothing happened. In the early afternoon, as he was about to climb down the tree, he saw the

154

old woman leave the house and return soon afterwards with a young man. His wife greeted the young man in the courtyard, and they both entered the bedroom. The old woman climbed on to the roof to keep a lookout in case the prince should return. The prince observed all this from the tree.

He was about to come down and catch his wife and her lover red-handed when a strange thing happened. A fakir had come and had sat down under the tree. This fakir drew a female doll out of his pocket. He repeated a magic spell three times and blew on the doll. When he did this, the doll was transformed into a beautiful young girl. The fakir addressed words of love to her and spoke with her for a long time. Then he lay down his head on the girl's lap and fell fast asleep. The girl sat there quietly for some time. Then she lifted the fakir's head from her lap and placed it gently on a stone. Having done this, she put her hand in her pocket and drew out a male doll. After repeating the same magic spell that the fakir had used on her, she blew on the doll, and the doll was transformed into a handsome young man with whom she exchanged words of love.

A long time passed, and the fakir began to stir in his sleep. The moment the girl saw this, she warned her lover, 'Get ready, so I can turn you back into a doll, because the fakir is about to wake up.' She recited another magic spell and blew the words on the young man, and again he took the form of a male doll. She barely had time to put the doll back in her pocket, lift the fakir's head from the stone and place it on her lap before the fakir awoke.

The fakir thanked the girl for watching over him while he slept. Then he repeated his magic spell three times, and again the girl took the form of a female doll. He carefully hid the doll in the pocket of his robes.

The prince was amazed by what he had seen. He waited for the fakir to get up and walk away. Then he climbed down the tree and ran to catch up with him. 'Dear sir,' he said, 'you are a stranger in these parts. I would be honoured if you would be my guest tonight.' The fakir thanked him and accompanied him to the house.

When the old woman saw the prince approaching the house with another man, she climbed down from the roof and hurried to the princess's room to warn her. The girl quickly hid her lover underneath the bed, and then came out to greet the prince and the fakir as they were entering the courtyard. Without betraying his thoughts, the prince said to his wife: 'Go and cook five *seers*[1] of rice. We have guests for dinner.'

The princess was puzzled, because five *seers* of rice would be sufficient to feed four guests, and was much too much for one guest. Nevertheless, she did as she was told without arguing.

When the princess and the old woman had prepared the rice and meat, and had placed it on the floor where the prince and the fakir were seated, the prince said, as they were about to retire from the room, 'Today you will eat with us.'

'The men can eat first,' said the princess. 'Then the old woman and I can take our meal together.'

But the prince ordered the two women to join them, so they obediently sat down. Then he turned to the fakir. 'My dear sir,' he said. 'There is a doll in your pocket. Make it into a woman so that she too can eat with us.' The fakir looked troubled. 'There isn't a doll in my pocket,' he said. The prince put his hand in the fakir's robes and produced the doll. 'Here it is,' he said. 'Make it into a woman, or else I shall kill you.'

The fakir obeyed. He repeated the magic spell three times and blew on the doll, and it was transformed into a beautiful young girl. Then the prince told this young girl to take out the male doll that she had in her pocket and turn it into a man. With an air of innocence, the girl denied that she had a doll in her pocket, but before she had finished protesting, the prince had taken the doll out of her pocket. She knew that it was no use arguing, so she repeated the magic spell three times and blew on the doll, and it was transformed into a handsome young man.

Then the prince turned to his wife, and said: 'Go and fetch your lover so that he too can eat with us.'

'There isn't anybody here,' replied the princess, yellow with fright.

The prince rose to his feet and went to the bedroom, and told the young man who was hiding under the bed to come out and join them for a meal. Taking him by the arm, he brought him to the room where the guests were seated. 'Here he is!' he said to his wife.

As soon as they had all finished eating, the prince turned to the old woman, and said to her: 'I brought you to my house because you had no one in the world to care for you. I expected that, in return, you would guard my honour, instead of sullying it.' Then he turned to his wife's lover, and said to him: 'Was there no other woman in the world, that you had to enter my house and dishonour it?'

With these words, the prince took out a sword and, with a single stroke, he cut off the heads of the old woman, the lover, and his wife.[2] Then he turned to the fakir and handed him his sword. The fakir, with a single stroke, cut off the heads of the beautiful young girl and her young man. After this the prince and the fakir embraced and became brothers, vowing never to marry again.

20

The Dancing Dolls

hey say that there was once a peasant who had a very cunning wife. The peasant was not cunning, but at least he could tell the difference between wheat and barley, and he noticed that although he grew wheat, his wife always used to give him barley bread when he returned home in the evening.

'How is it,' he asked his wife one day, 'that although I grow wheat, I always eat barley?'

'Listen, and I shall explain,' she replied. 'Whenever your sister sneezes, the wheat stored in our sacks turns to barley.'

The peasant was very angry and went in search of his sister. On the way he met a man who saw his troubled look. 'Brother, what is the matter?' he asked.

The peasant recounted his story: 'I am a farmer, and although I grow wheat, my wife gives me barley bread to eat. Today I complained about this, and she told me that whenever my sister sneezes, the wheat stored in our sacks turns to barley. So I am on my way to find my sister.'

'Brother, return home,' said the man. 'Your sister is not to blame as you yourself will soon discover.' The man then gave the peasant two dolls and taught him to say two words, Jaranz and Kharanz. 'When you utter the word Jaranz, the two dolls will begin to dance. When you utter the word Kharanz, they will immediately stop dancing.' After saying these words, the stranger said farewell.

The peasant returned home with the two dolls and gave them to his wife, explaining that if she wished to make them dance, she should use the word Jaranz, and that if she wished them to stop dancing, she should use the word Kharanz.

Early the next morning the peasant went off to the fields with his bullocks. His wife had a lover who used to visit her while he was out working. She made some big *parathas* for him with butter and wheat flour. 'But,' she said, 'before we have tea, I will show you something amusing.' She picked up the two dolls that were lying in the corner and placed them in the middle of the room. Then slowly she pronounced the word, 'Jaranz.' No sooner had she said this than the dolls began to dance. After some time, she wished to make them stop dancing, but she had forgotten the word that her husband had taught her to make them stop. Her lover tried to stop them dancing, but when he touched them, he himself began to dance. Then the peasant's wife tried to stop him dancing, but when she touched him, she too began to dance.

The mullah who looked after the mosque lived next door, and that day his wife had woken up late. So he sent his daughter to fetch water from the peasant's house. When the mullah's daughter entered the house, she saw the peasant's wife and her lover dancing. 'Why are you dancing?' she asked, but when she touched them, she too began to dance.

Soon the mullah arrived, angrily calling for his daughter. When he beheld the strange scene, he said nothing, but went to the peasant who was ploughing his fields, and said to him: 'Come quickly – your wife is dancing with her lover.'

The husband returned home and saw his wife and her lover dancing. The *paratha*s, which his wife had made for her lover, were lying in the corner. He first ate them. Then he uttered the word 'Kharanz,' and they all stopped dancing. Then he turned to his wife, and said: 'So this is how my sister's sneeze turns the wheat to barley.' With these words, he killed his wife and her lover.

21

The Merchant and the Parrot

Once upon a time there was a rich merchant who used to buy goods in one town and sell them in another. One day he went to a big city and there he bought some merchandise, intending to sell it elsewhere. It should be explained that it was the custom in these city bazaars for men to stand about and gossip. In the bazaar the merchant learnt that a certain man in the city had a very beautiful daughter, whose hand would only be given in marriage in exchange for her weight in gold.

Hearing this, the merchant held his tongue and spoke to no one. Instead he waited and considered how he would win the girl's hand. Next morning he auctioned his goods for gold. Then he inquired from the people of the city where he could find an old woman to serve as a go-between. He was told that in a certain street he would find the person he needed. After much searching, he located her house and knocked on the door. An old woman opened it. He greeted her, and said: 'Respected mother, go to the man with the beautiful daughter, and tell him that there is a merchant who wishes to marry her.'

'My son,' said the old woman, 'her father is only willing to give her to the man who can offer him her weight in gold. If you are able to fulfil this condition, then I shall gladly take your message. If not, please don't waste my time for nothing.'

The merchant reassured her: 'I shall offer him even more wealth than her weight in gold.'

The old woman was satisfied: 'Then I shall go immediately.'

She covered her head and hurried to the father's house, and said to him: 'There is a merchant who wishes to marry your daughter.'

'Tell him to come to my house tomorrow and introduce himself,' replied the father.

Next day the merchant loaded all his gold on to a donkey's back and took it to the girl's house. On the way he stopped in the bazaar to buy a large pair of scales. When he reached the house, he greeted the father and said to him: 'Make your daughter wear a lot of clothes and heavy jewellery so that you can claim more than her weight in gold.'

The father made his daughter wear a lot of clothes and heavy jewellery, and told her to sit on one of the scales. The merchant loaded his gold on to the other scale in the presence of the mullah and several witnesses. 'Stop,' shouted the witnesses, when the weight of the gold was exactly equal to the weight of the girl. But the merchant continued to add gold until the scale would hold no more. He then turned to the girl's father, and said, 'All this is yours.' The mullah then stepped forward and performed the marriage ceremony.

'Now you can take her away,' said the father.

'No, not yet,' replied the merchant; 'she must stay with you until I have purchased a house for her.'

The merchant spent several days searching for a suitable house. Having eventually found one, he had it furnished and decorated, and then went to the girl's father and told him to put his daughter in a palanquin. When this had been done, he took his bride home.

After his marriage the merchant gave up his trade and stayed at home with his wife. As time passed, he began to deteriorate physically, so much so that his weight and stature diminished to half their former size. 'How can I be rid of this man?' thought the wife. One evening she asked him: 'What work did you do before you married me?'

'I was a merchant,' replied her husband. 'I used to buy goods in one town and sell them in another.'

The wife thought to herself: 'If my husband were to become a merchant again, he would always be away from home.' So she said to him: 'You are still young; you should continue to earn money. Later, when you are old, you will no longer be able to do so.'

'Don't worry,' replied the merchant. 'I've earned enough money to enable us to live comfortably for the rest of our lives.'

'But what if we have children?' said the wife. 'We must think of them.'

'Yes,' he agreed, 'but my trade involves much travelling, and I cannot live away from you.'

The wife was silenced. She could not think of an appropriate reply. But she was not deterred, and whenever the opportunity arose, she would reproach her husband for wasting his life and doing no work. Finally the merchant grew tired of her reproaches, and in order to please her, he decided to take up his trade again.

Next morning he went to the bazaar, and said to one of the shopkeepers: 'Please give me 60 *maund*s of molasses in about twenty sacks, so that I can sell them in the neighbouring city.'

'Your order will be ready by this afternoon,' replied the shopkeeper.

The merchant then went to make other arrangements for his journey. On the way he met a hunter, who had caught a starling and had put her in a cage. It is said that in those days some birds could understand and speak human language. Since merchants have a habit of asking the price of all the goods that they see in the bazaar, whether they intend to buy them or not, the ·merchant addressed the hunter: 'Where did you find this starling?'

The hunter answered: 'It's my trade to catch birds of all kinds and to sell them in the bazaar.'

When the starling heard this, she asked her captor, 'Is it true that you have captured me to sell me?'

'Yes,' replied the hunter.

'In that case, I shall set my own price,' said the starling.

'And what price would that be?' inquired the merchant; 'for I should very much like to buy you.'

'A hundred rupees,' answered the starling, 'because each piece of advice I give is worth a hundred rupees.' The merchant promptly gave the hunter one hundred rupees and took the starling.

In the afternoon he went back to the bazaar to pick up the merchandise that he had ordered. On the way he met another hunter, who was carrying a parrot in a cage. So again, out of curiosity, he asked him a number of questions.

'What do you intend to do with that parrot?' he asked.

'I'm going to sell it,' replied the hunter.

'Is it true that you are going to sell me?' the parrot asked his captor.

'Yes,' replied the hunter.

'In that case, I shall set my own price,' said the parrot.

'And what price would that be?' inquired the merchant.

'A thousand rupees,' answered the parrot, 'because I am able to predict the price of goods as far in advance as a year from now.' The merchant promptly gave the hunter one thousand rupees and took the parrot.

As the merchant proceeded on his way, the parrot asked him, 'O merchant, you bought me in great haste, but tell me are you a rich man?'

'Yes,' answered the merchant, 'I am very wealthy.'

'Good,' said the parrot. 'If your house is nearby, take me there and leave me. You must then go to the bazaar, and for a period of eight days you must buy all the flowers in the city at one rupee each. On the eighth day each flower will be worth five times more than you bought it for, and if you follow my advice, you will certainly make a profit.'

The merchant took the parrot and the starling home and left them there. Following the parrot's advice, he went to the bazaar and hired some servants. He sent them to all the flower growers in the city and the surrounding areas, and told them to take a lease on all the flower gardens for the next eight days, paying one rupee for each flower. The servants did as they were instructed.

Now it so happened that at that time the marriage of a princess was to be celebrated in the neighbouring kingdom, and there was a shortage of flowers. So the king sent a message to the king of the country where the merchant lived, asking him to send all the flowers that he could find for the wedding celebration. The king ordered his guards to carry out the purchase, but wherever they went, they were told that no flowers were for sale, because a certain merchant had bought every flower in the kingdom. The guards returned and told the king, 'There are no flowers available; a certain merchant has bought every flower in this country.'

'Then go and fetch this merchant,' ordered the king.

When the merchant was brought before him, the king said, 'Is it true that you have bought every single flower in this country?'

'Yes, Your Majesty,' answered the merchant.

'Then state your price.'

'Five rupees per flower,' said the merchant.

The king agreed because he had no choice, and bought all the flowers in the kingdom. As a result, the merchant made so much money that every room in his house was filled with riches. When his wife realized what had happened, she was disappointed. She thought to herself: 'I had hoped that my husband would travel to another city, but now he has made so much money that we shall never be able to spend it all!' However, she was not deterred, and next day she said to her husband: 'You followed my advice and we are richer than we were before. Now you must travel to another city and do more business.'

'I wish you would let me live in peace,' complained the merchant. 'We have so much wealth that even our children won't be able to spend it all in their lifetime.' But since his wife kept nagging him, he once again gave in to her wishes.

Next morning the merchant bought 800 sacks of molasses from one of the shopkeepers, and arranged to have them transported to another city. Then he returned home.

'Tomorrow, I shall be transporting some goods to another city,' he announced to his wife in the presence of the starling and the parrot. 'While I'm away, you mustn't do anything without first consulting the starling and the parrot.'

At daybreak the merchant set out on his journey. No sooner had he left the house than his wife perfumed herself and put on her best clothes and jewellery. Then she summoned her maidservant, and instructed her to go to the house of a certain man to inform him that she would like to have a word with him.

The starling and the parrot overheard her say this, and the starling said to the parrot: 'Before the merchant left the house, he told his wife not to do anything without asking our advice; but she has just ordered her servant to invite a strange man here, and she hasn't consulted us.'

'Yes, I heard that too,' said the parrot. 'We must think of a way of stopping her.'

'I know a way of stopping her,' whispered the starling, 'but she'll kill me if I try, and if she is prepared to kill me,she won't hesitate to kill you.'

'That, I am afraid, is a risk we'll have to take,' said the parrot.

The starling chided the merchant's wife: 'It wasn't right of you to ask your servant to invite a strange man to our house. Why do you want to dishonour our master, your husband? Have you already forgotten that the merchant told you not to do anything without first consulting us?'

'Yes, I do remember,' she answered, 'but the servant has already left the house and it's impossible to call her back now; but I promise that in future I shall never do anything without first consulting you.'

The servant had been reluctant to invite a strange man to the house during her master's absence, so she had gone to the gate of the house to wait there, hoping that her mistress would change her mind and call her back.

'She couldn't have gone far,' insisted the starling. 'Why don't you call her?'

'My servant must be far away by now,' thought the merchant's wife, 'but to pacify the starling, I shall call out her name.' So she called out to her servant in a loud voice. The servant heard her and came running back to the house. When the merchant's wife saw her, she was furious: 'I thought I had sent you with a message. What are you doing here?' Then she turned to the starling and pleaded: 'You are a female and I am a female, and we understand each other's ways; so please don't interfere with my life.'

'I sympathize with you,' said the starling, 'but the merchant bought me for a hundred rupees, and as long as I'm alive, I shan't allow you to dishonour him.'

The merchant's wife lost her temper, and in her rage she opened the door of the cage, seized the starling, and broke her neck, and then threw the dead body on to the roof of the house. Having done this, she warned the parrot, 'If you dare to open your mouth, you too will be lying dead beside your friend.'

Once her anger had subsided, the merchant's wife grew worried, and wondered what she would tell her husband when he returned. But she was quick to make up lies: 'I'll tell him that a cat entered the house while I was saying my prayers and terrified the starling. By the time I had finished my prayers, the cat had fled and the bird had died of fright. After three days you still hadn't returned home, so I threw the dead body on the roof.'

Next morning, after serving the parrot an excellent meal of fruit, the merchant's wife asked him very sweetly, 'Respected parrot, do you mind if I invite a friend of mine to our house?'

'Yes, I do mind,' replied the parrot. 'I will never allow you to do such a thing. You have already committed a grave sin by killing the starling.'

The merchant's wife begged and pleaded, but the parrot was adamant: 'As long as I'm alive, I'll never give you my permission.'

Finally the merchant's wife lost her patience. She took the parrot out of his cage by the scruff of his neck. 'Now how do you feel about it? Should I invite my friend or not?' she asked in a threatening tone of voice.

'My answer is the same,' replied the brave parrot.

She then pulled out one of his feathers and repeated the question. The parrot gave the same answer. She pulled out another feather, and another, and each time she would ask, 'Now parrot, what is your answer?' and he would reply, 'My answer is no.' In this way she plucked out all the parrot's feathers, and he was left naked. Then she threatened him for the last time: 'If you don't allow me to call my friend, I'll kill you.'

'You're welcome to kill me,' he replied.

The merchant's wife could no longer restrain herself. 'I'll throw him over the wall,' she thought. 'If he survives the fall, a cat or a dog will no doubt eat him up, because he has no feathers and cannot fly.' So she threw the bird over the wall. The parrot landed on his beak and was badly hurt, but he got up quickly and began to walk as fast as his legs could carry him. He walked and walked until he reached a graveyard. He found a hole in a mound of earth marking an old grave, and there he made a home for himself. In the daytime he used to stay indoors, and at night he went out in search of food.

In the meantime, the merchant's wife did as she pleased. After several months, when the merchant returned home from his travels, he was shocked to discover that the bird-cages were empty. So he picked up the first cage, and said to his wife: 'When I left home there was a starling in this cage which I entrusted to your care. Where is she now?'

She began to weep, and between her sobs she recounted her version of what had happened: 'One day, while I was saying my prayers, a cat entered the house and started to prowl round the starling's cage. By the time I had finished praying and had rushed to the rescue, the cat had already fled. But the starling had fluttered about so much in her cage that she died. I kept the corpse for three days, but you didn't return home. So I threw it on to the roof. Some animal may have eaten it by now, but the feathers may still be there.'

'Can you give me your word of honour that the starling died in this manner?'

'Yes, I promise,' replied the merchant's wife.

Then the merchant picked up the second cage, and said: 'In this cage there was a parrot which I entrusted to your care. Where is he now?'

'He was a demon, not a parrot,' replied the wife. 'He pestered me every day, saying that the cat which had killed the starling would soon kill him. He insisted that I leave his cage door open, so that if the cat should chance to come again while I was away, he would be able to fly to safety. I told him that if I left his cage door open, he would probably fly away. But he assured me that he wouldn't. So I left the cage door open. After that, he used to perch outside his cage. One day, as he was perching on the courtyard wall, some parrots came and perched with him. He talked to them in their own language and then flew away with them and has never returned since.'

'Can you give me your word of honour that the parrot left our house in this manner?'

'Yes,' lied the merchant's wife, 'I swear on the Holy Quran that he left in this manner.'

'The starling left my house dead,' said the merchant, 'but the parrot left it alive. So now you too must leave my house.'

The merchant's wife left the house and went to live with her parents. She began to say her prayers five times a day,[1] and every day she used to visit a shrine near her parents' house.[2] Here she would weep aloud, and pray that her husband would forgive her and take her back.

Now it so happened that this shrine was in the graveyard where the parrot had made his home. The parrot's feathers had grown, and he was able to go out during the day without danger. He at once recognized the merchant's wife and noticed that she came to pray at the shrine every day.

One day the parrot flew to the shrine and hid there. The merchant's wife came as usual to pray for help. 'O master of the tomb,' she prayed, 'please ask God to make my husband take me back, and I promise I shall give alms to the poor.'

When the parrot heard this, he spoke in a solemn voice: 'Young woman, I am tired of listening to your prayers. So I shall ask God to grant them. But in view of the gravity of your sins, I cannot ask God to fulfil your request unless you agree to do penance.'

'O master,' answered the merchant's wife, 'I am willing to do penance for my sins.'

'You had a starling,' said the parrot. 'What did you do with her?' Then he added: 'Before you begin, I warn you not to tell lies as I know the truth.'

'I broke her neck,' she confessed.

'After you broke her neck, what did you do?' asked the parrot.

'I threw the dead body on to the roof,' she said.

'When your husband returned home and asked you about the starling, what was your reply?' continued the parrot.

'I told him that a cat had killed her,' she answered.

'Was he satisfied, and did he forgive you?'

'Yes, he did,' she replied.

'You had a parrot too. What became of him?'

The merchant's wife confessed how she had pulled out all the parrot's feathers, one by one, until he was completely naked, because he would not allow her to invite her lover to the house, and had then thrown him over the wall.

'When your husband asked you about the parrot, what did you say?' inquired the voice from the shrine.

The merchant's wife confessed that again she had lied to her husband, telling him that the parrot had flown away with some other parrots, after insisting that his cage door be left open for fear that the cat might return. 'My husband told me that, since the parrot had left the house alive, I too must leave the house.'

'Your husband forgave you the death of the starling, and I too shall do the same,' said the voice. 'But your husband made you leave the house because of the parrot, therefore I too must take revenge on his behalf. You plucked out all the parrot's feathers and made him naked. Now, since I cannot come out of the grave, you must pull out all the hairs on your head, one by one. Having done this, you must climb the graveyard wall and throw yourself over on the other side.'

The merchant's wife obediently pulled out every hair on her head; then she climbed the graveyard wall and threw herself over on the other side. By the time she had picked herself up and returned to the shrine, the parrot had come out of his hiding place and was perching on the branch of a tree.

'You foolish woman,' he said to her, 'the master of the tomb doesn't talk to anyone. It was I who told you to pull out all your hair. It was I who made you fall from the wall. Now I have satisfied my honour, because I have taken my revenge. But I also promised to grant your request that your husband would take you back; so come with me.'

'How can I go with you?' she said. 'I'm completely bald.'

'It doesn't matter,' said the parrot. 'Cover your head with a veil and follow me.'

So they travelled together to the merchant's house. When they reached the gate of the house, the parrot asked the merchant's wife to wait there while he made some investigations. He quietly entered the house and found the merchant sitting on his bed. The merchant was brooding over the past, wondering whether it had been a mistake to send his wife away. The parrot hopped about in front of him, but the merchant was so lost in thought that he did not notice. So the bird gave him a peck on the leg. The merchant was delighted to see the parrot. 'O unfaithful bird,' he said, taking him in his arms and kissing him, 'why did you sneak away?'

'I will explain,' replied the parrot. 'One day I was perching on the courtyard wall when some other parrots came and perched beside me. They asked me to accompany them to an orchard. We all went and feasted on the fruit. While I was busily eating, I failed to observe that a hunter had crept up and had cast a net over my tree. When we had all eaten to the full, my companions began leaving the orchard. I tried to join them, but fell into the hunter's net. The hunter caught me and cut my pinions. I remained with him until my feathers had grown again, and as soon as I could fly, I escaped and returned home. On the way I stopped at your father-in-law's house and saw your wife. I asked her why she was living there, and she told me you had turned her out of the house because of me. So I brought her back with me. She is standing at the gate.'

When the merchant heard this, he was very pleased, and asked his wife to come back and live with him. Thus the merchant, his wife, and the parrot began living together once again. But the parrot would always turn his head away whenever the merchant's wife passed him. The merchant noticed this and wondered what the reason could be. One day, when his wife had gone to her father's house, he asked the parrot, 'Why are you angry with my wife? You must tell me the reason.'

'Don't ask me, I beg you,' said the parrot. 'If I tell you, you will surely kill your wife, and your home will be destroyed, and you will curse me for it.' But since the merchant insisted on knowing the truth, the parrot finally gave in. 'All right,' he said, 'I'll tell you, but let the ruin be on your own head.'

And he recounted how he and the starling had t ried to prevent the merchant's wife from inviting a strange man to the house, how she had broken the starling's neck, how she had tortured him by pulling his feathers out one by one, and how he had taken revenge on her at the shrine by pretending to be a holy man speaking from the grave.

'I invented the story which I told you previously about being caught by a hunter,' said the parrot, 'because I had given my word to your wife that you would take her back. But what I have just told you is the whole truth.'

After this, the merchant refused to speak to his wife. He began to hate the very sight of her, and whenever she passed in front of him, he would turn his head away. The parrot noticed this, and said to the merchant: 'I warned you not to ask me to tell you the truth. Now look, your home has been destroyed. You cannot continue like this. You should dig a hole in the ground, kill your wife, and bury her there.[3] I shall arrange for you to marry a young girl who is not only beautiful but also faithful, honest, and sincere.'

The merchant followed the clever parrot's advice. He dug a hole in the ground, killed his wife, and buried her there. Then he said to the parrot, 'How soon can you arrange my marriage, now that you have destroyed my home?'

'Collect all your wealth,' answered the parrot, 'and I shall take you to see Princess Padama. She looked after me when I was a mere fledgling. She brought me up and always used to listen to my advice. The servants became jealous of our friendship, and they persuaded the king to get rid of me. The king ordered his vizier to make sure I was eaten by a cat when his daughter wasn't looking. Luckily I learnt about this plot and told Padama about it. Then I begged her to allow me to leave, and she gave me her permission. I flew away and have never returned since. But today I shall take you to Padama myself, because she once promised me that she would marry the man whom I chose for her. When we reach her kingdom, you will stay in the city, and I shall visit her and tell her about you, and then I shall bring her to your house.' It was thus that the merchant and the parrot set off together to Princess Padama's kingdom.

Every morning, since the day of the parrot's departure, Padama had ordered that one *maund* of *churi* should be prepared for her. This is the favourite food of parrots. It is made of dried fruit, with breadcrumbs or flour, fried in ghee. She used to scatter it on her roof in the hope that her beloved parrot would come back. Other parrots used to come to eat the *churi*, but not her parrot.

When they reached Princess Padama's kingdom, the parrot found a house for the merchant, and then went on his own to visit the princess. She was delighted to see him. 'O unfaithful bird,' she said, taking him in her arms and kissing him, 'where have you been? I've been waiting for you for such a long time.'

'What do you know of the troubles I've had to endure!' said the parrot with a sigh. 'Even to this day my feathers have not fully regrown. When I left you I fell into one trap after another, and I'm grateful to God to be still alive.'

They continued to talk in this manner for many hours, and then the parrot remarked: 'I'm staying with a merchant. He is a very good man, and I would like you to be his wife.'

'If you like him, I shall marry him,' said the princess, 'because I once promised to marry the man whom you chose for me.'

The parrot seemed to hesitate for a moment: 'Husbands and wives fight among themselves, and tomorrow, if something goes wrong, then I shall no doubt be blamed. You should therefore make the decision yourself.'

'No,' said the princess, 'I leave the decision to you.'

Then they spoke of other things; and once again the parrot remarked: 'It would be wonderful if you could marry him, and we could all live together.'

'If you like him so much,' said the princess, 'I shall marry him, come what may.'

'Good,' said the parrot, 'then I shall take you to see him tomorrow.'

Having said this, the bird flew back to his master and gave him some further advice: 'Buy fruit and beautiful flowers, and decorate your house well, because the princess will be coming here tomorrow.' Since the merchant was very rich, it was easy for him to buy the very best of everything.

Next day, all the necessary preparations had been made, and the merchant awaited the princess's arrival. When the parrot brought the princess to the house, he asked her to wait at the gate while he went on ahead to inform the merchant of her arrival. When he met the merchant, he spoke in a loud voice so that the princess could hear what he said: 'Have you done anything about your marriage?'

'No,' answered the merchant, 'I was waiting for you to choose a girl for me.'

'I've already chosen a girl,' said the parrot. 'She's waiting at your gate, but I don't know whether you will like her or not.'

'If you like her, then I'm sure I shall like her,' said the merchant, 'so please bring her in.'

The parrot left the room and soon returned with the princess. They say that the first thing a woman does when she enters a house is to look around and examine the interior. The parrot and the merchant had decorated the house with such good taste that the princess liked it immediately. The merchant then said to the princess: 'We are hungry. In the cupboard you will find food of all kinds. Cook something and bring it to us.'

The princess opened the cupboard and took out some vermicelli, knowing that it could be cooked quickly, and placed it in boiling water. Nowadays there are many kinds of vermicelli, and some can even be cooked without water.

'This is the girl I've chosen for you. Would you like to marry her?' said the parrot to the merchant when they had finished eating.

'Yes,' answered the merchant.

The parrot went to fetch the mullah to perform the marriage ceremony, and from that day onwards the merchant and his wife and the parrot lived happily ever after.

22

Gul and Sanobar

There was a king who had a son called Sanobar. When Sanobar came of age, his father arranged his marriage to a beautiful girl called Gul. Now Sanobar had a very close friend who was a rich merchant, with whom he used to spend most of his time. He would spend the whole day with him, only returning home in the evening.

One evening, when he returned home and touched his wife's hands and feet, he noticed that they were cold. He thought to himself: 'Gul must have taken a bath.' So he asked her, 'Why are your hands and feet cold?'

'I have just washed for prayers,' replied Gul. 'That is why my hands and feet are cold.'[1]

Sanobar did not raise the subject again, but his suspicions had not been dispelled. Time passed, and one day, Sanobar went to his stables, intending to go for a ride on his favourite horse. But he found that this horse, and all his best horses, looked worn out. So he asked the grooms, 'Why are my best horses in such a wretched condition?'

'If we tell you the truth, our heads will be cut off,' they replied.

Sanobar insisted that he wanted an answer, and the grooms finally told him the truth: 'These horses are ridden every night to the jungle, and by the time they return at daybreak, they are so worn out that they refuse to touch their food, and as a result their condition is poor.'

Sanobar was very upset when he heard this. He went home without saying a word to anyone. In the evening he lay in bed, pretending to be asleep. When Gul was satisfied that her husband was asleep, she combed her hair, perfumed her body, and put black antimony on her eyelids. Then she wound a man's turban round her head and left the house. Sanobar leapt out of bed and followed her.

Now Gul had a lover who was a black man. He lived in the jungle, and at night she used to go and visit him.

Sanobar said to himself: 'If I follow Gul on horseback, she is bound to see me.' Therefore he decided to go on foot. In the dark he bumped into trees, and several times he tripped and fell, but each time he quickly rose to his feet and ran to keep up with the speed of Gul's horse.

After travelling for some time, Gul came to a fort in the middle of the jungle. She dismounted and greeted her lover. Eventually, after much difficulty and breathless with running, Sanobar reached the same place and sat down under a tree.

The lover asked Gul, 'Why are you so late tonight?'

Gul explained: 'I had a strange feeling that my husband suspected something, so I waited until he was fast asleep before coming.'

When the black man heard this, he said to himself: 'But supposing her husband has followed her.' So he called his servants, and said to them: 'Go and check if there is anyone outside the fort.' The servants went outside and saw Sanobar sitting under a tree. So they seized him and brought him to their master.

'Tie him hand and foot and throw him into one of the dungeons,' ordered the black man. The servants did as they were told, and Sanobar was thrown into one of the dungeons.

Now Sanobar had a dog who was very loyal and devoted to him. When it was morning, the dog became aware that his master was absent. She searched for him everywhere in the city, but he was nowhere to be found. Then by chance she came to the stables and saw the hoof-marks of her master's horse. She followed them until she reached the fort in the jungle. The fort was encircled by high walls, but there was a narrow water-channel leading into the fort, and the dog entered through this opening and managed to make her way to the dungeon where her master had been tied up. Wasting no time, she gnawed through the strong ropes until Sanobar was free.

Once the dog had freed him, Sanobar rose to his feet and immediately went in search of Gul. He found her lying fast asleep beside the black man. A sword lay on the floor. He picked it up, and was just about to cut off the black man's head when Gul awoke and shouted, 'Don't kill him.' Sanobar turned to his wife in anger, and as he did so, the black man escaped. Gul tried to follow him, but Sanobar caught hold of her by the arm. 'I will not kill you,' he said, 'but we can no longer return home. If people ever find out what has happened, we shall be dishonoured for life.'[2]

Sanobar took his wife and the dog, and they travelled for many days until they came to a wide river. In the middle of the river there was an uninhabited island. Sanobar paid a fisherman to row them across to the island, and there they made their new home.

In the meantime, Sanobar's father wondered what had become of his son. He searched for Gul and Sanobar everywhere, but they were nowhere to be found. So he sent for Sanobar's

friend the merchant, and said to him: 'If you know whether my
son is dead or alive, please tell me.'

'I don't know where he is,' replied the merchant, 'but I shall
go and search for him, and if he is alive, I shall bring him back
to you.' So the merchant collected his sword and some
provisions, and set off in search of his friend.

He travelled for many days. On the first day, he passed
through the jungle where the black man lived. But there was no
sign of Sanobar. So he continued on his way until he reached a
desert. Weak from hunger and thirst, he sat down in the shade
of a tall tree. It was in this tree that a gigantic bird feared even by
elephants had made her nest.[3]

They say that every year, when this bird laid her eggs, a cobra
used to come and devour her young. When the merchant fell
asleep under the tree, the mother bird was absent, and the time
had come for the cobra's annual visit. The snake crawled to the
foot of the tree, and said to himself: 'First I shall eat the baby
birds that have hatched, and then I shall eat the merchant.'

When the young birds saw the snake sliding up the tree, they
began to cry for help. They say that in the olden days all the
birds and beasts could speak human language. 'Help! Help!'
cried the little birds. 'We are going to be eaten alive.' The
merchant was roused from his sleep by their cries. He rose to his
feet, and asked the cobra, 'Why do you want to eat them alive?'

'At this time, every year, I eat them,' replied the cobra. 'I was
going to eat them first and you afterwards. But if you tell me not
to eat them, I shall eat you first and eat them afterwards.'
Having said this, the cobra began to slither down the tree
towards the merchant.

'This is the best moment for me to kill him,' thought the
merchant. So he drew out his sword and cut the cobra in two,
and the two halves fell wriggling to the ground.

The mother bird had gone in search of food, but she returned
after a short while, sensing that her young were in danger. Seeing

the dead cobra and the merchant standing over it with his sword, she said to her young: 'I shall pick up this man and drop him from such a height that he will never again enter the earth's atmosphere.'

'What are you saying?' exclaimed the fledglings. 'We have no better friend in the world than this man. If he hadn't killed the snake, we would all have been gobbled up. You must therefore help him, whatever his task may be.'

So the bird flew off to the blessed city of Mecca and dipped her wings in the sacred well of Zamzam. Then she returned and shook her feathers over the merchant to make him feel cool. 'Now you may sleep in peace,' she said, 'while I go and bring you something to eat.'

While the merchant was asleep, the bird gathered the best fruit in the land. Although the merchant had travelled widely, many of these fruits were unknown to him. When he had satisfied his hunger, the bird asked him what had brought him to these foreign parts.

'I have a friend called Sanobar,' replied the merchant. 'He and his wife have disappeared; his father, the king, has sent me in search of him.'

'I shall take you to your friend,' promised the bird, and she lifted him up in her huge claws and carried him to the island where Gul and Sanobar lived. 'Your friend Sanobar comes to bathe here,' said the bird. 'When he goes bathing, he always leaves his sword behind. As soon as he sees you, he will ask why you have come to the island. When you tell him that his father has sent you in search of him, he will say, "I shall return with you to my father's kingdom, but first I must go home." Then he will go home to fetch his sword. At that moment, I shall swoop down and lift you up into the air.' So saying, the bird flew down and left the merchant at the place where Sanobar used to bathe.

That day, when Sanobar came to have his usual morning bathe, he was surprised to see his friend waiting there for him.

The merchant greeted Sanobar, and said: 'Why did you leave your father's kingdom and never return?'

Sanobar sadly recounted in detail what had happened since the day that he had followed Gul into the jungle. 'So now you understand why, in our shame and dishonour, we have made this island our new home. My dog and I eat first, and the leftovers are given to my wife.'

When the merchant had heard Sanobar's story, he said: 'I shall now return and tell your father that you are still alive, and I shall explain why you haven't come home.'

'No, wait,' said Sanobar, 'I shall return with you to my father's kingdom, but first I must go home.' Sanobar then went home to fetch his sword in order to kill the merchant.

In the meantime, the bird flew down and lifted the merchant into the sky, and transported him to the king. The merchant informed the king: 'Sanobar has built a house on an island in the middle of a river where he lives with his wife and his dog.'

The king went there himself, and ordered his attendants to make him a raft out of reeds. He sat on it and was taken across to the island. He was very pleased to see his son Sanobar and took him back to his kingdom. The dog accompanied his master, but Gul remained on the island and no one knows what became of her.

23

The Three Friends

O nce there were three friends: a king, a vizier, and a peasant. One day the peasant gave a dinner in honour of his friends. At the appointed time he came to fetch them at the palace, and the three of them set off together to the peasant's house. On the way they chanced to find a very precious pink diamond. When they reached the village guest-house, they sat down on a *charpoy* bed and discussed what they should do with the diamond.

'There are three of us and there is only one diamond,' said the king. 'If we divide it, its value will be destroyed. So let us decide which of us should keep it.' It was agreed that each man should tell a strange, but true, story, and that the teller of the strangest tale should receive the diamond.

How the Prince Became a Dog

The king began his story first: 'When I came of age, my father married me to a very beautiful girl. We lived together happily and I had no complaints. Then, one evening, I was lying on my bed with my arms over my eyes considering my good fortune, when my wife entered the room. She looked at me and, thinking that I was fast asleep, hurried out. My curiosity was aroused, and I followed her to see what she was doing.

'She first prepared a large quantity of *pilau* rice, while I patiently awaited her next move. She then carefully placed the rice on a tray and left the house. I had just enough time to pick up my sword and follow her. She went to the jungle and continued to walk until she reached a small house. A black man was sitting on the verandah waiting for her. He was her lover. She placed the tray in front of him, and had barely seated herself beside him when he said to her, "Go and get water from the river."

'The river was at some distance from the house. My wife obediently rose to her feet, picked up the pitcher, balanced it on her head, and went to fetch water. I thought to myself: "I must kill the black man. This is my only chance." So I drew my sword and cut off the black man's head. He died instantly. I withdrew to my hiding-place and waited. My wife returned with water, and was shocked to discover that her lover was dead. She looked around to see who could have murdered him, but there was no one in sight. So she picked up the tray of rice and returned home. I also hurried back and arrived before her. I quickly lay down on the bed and pretended to be sound asleep. When my wife arrived, she placed the tray on one side and woke me up. "I've made this *pilau* for you; you must eat it," she said. I ate the rice and pretended to be very pleased.

'Some days passed, and one night I woke up feeling thirsty. So I said to my wife, "Go and get some water." She refused,[1] saying she was afraid. So I said to her in anger, "You are afraid in your own home, but you were not afraid in the jungle when the black man told you to go and fetch water from the river."

'"So it was you who followed me to the jungle and murdered my lover. Get out of here, you dog," she cursed.

'Now I should explain that my wife had magical powers. Therefore, when she uttered this curse, I immediately took the shape of a dog. Then she went to the courtyard and picked up some stones and began hurling them at me, so that I was forced to leave the house and join other dogs that roamed about in the streets.

'One day, I happened to pass the house of a friend. In shame I sat down on his doorstep and peered inside. The whole family was seated by the fireside eating rice. After some time an old woman who worked at my friend's house saw me. She at once recognized the smell of my breath and began smothering me with kisses.

'"How disgusting!" shouted the children. "Imagine kissing a dog! You must be completely mad."

'But the old woman, who was also a sorceress, did not heed their insults. "You are all blind," she said. "This is not a dog, but our prince." She drew some lines on the ground and performed an incantation, and thus I recovered my human form. She took me inside the house and bandaged the wounds that I had received in my quarrels with other dogs. I thanked her warmly.

'"Mother," I said, "I must now take my leave, or else my kingdom will be in ruins."

'The old woman tried to persuade me to stay for a few days, warning me that I might soon be in trouble again, but I insisted that I had to leave. So she cut two sticks from a tree, pronounced a magic charm over them, and gave them to me, saying, "If you want to do something, you can do it with the first stick; if you want to undo what you have done, use the second stick. But be careful," she added, "because I cannot compete with your wife:

she is too powerful a sorceress." Then I bade her farewell and went home.

'It was late in the evening when I arrived home. After removing my shoes, I quietly entered the bedroom. My wife was lying asleep in bed. I hit her with the first stick, and said, "Get up, donkey." She was instantly transformed into a donkey. I led the donkey to the house of the sweepers and, after the usual exchange of salaams, I explained the purpose of my visit: "Take this donkey and use her to carry your heavy loads. But I warn you that when you load her with sacks or other goods, don't put a saddle-cloth on her back. If you do, I shall take her back."

'That is the end of my story,' said the king. 'Now it's your turn,' he said, addressing the vizier.

How the Vizier Became a Woman

The vizier began his story: 'One day, feeling dejected, I went for a stroll in the forest. While I was walking, I suddenly became very thirsty, so I started to search for water. After some time, I discovered, much to my surprise, a deep dark well. I thought to myself: "I shall first throw a stone into the well, and if I hear the sound of it hitting water, I shall climb down and take a drink." I threw a stone into the well and heard a splash. At the same time, I heard a strange voice: "If you are a man, then become a woman; if you are a woman, then become a man." No sooner had I heard this voice than I took the form of a woman.

'I was puzzled by this extraordinary turn of events, and was still wondering what to do, when a king, who had gone out hunting and happened to pass that way, saw me. He fell in love with me and took me back to his kingdom. It was thus that I became his wife. Twelve years passed and twelve sons were born to us; and all this time I had been considering how to escape from my predicament.

'One day, I said to the king, "I must returnto the well in the forest where you found me, otherwise I shall die." The king agreed to take me there himself.

'Once we had reached the well, I pretended to be very thirsty, and said to my husband, "Please see if there is any water in the well." The king picked up a stone and dropped it down the well. When the stone hit the water, the strange voice spoke once again: "If you are a man, then become a woman; if you are a woman, then become a man."

'As soon as we heard these words, I became a man and the king became a woman. I took the woman home, and we lived together for twelve years, and twelve more sons were born to us. Then, one day, we decided to tell each other our stories, and when we had finished recounting our stories, we agreed that we should each go our own way. And so I returned to my own country.

'That is the end of my story. Now it's your turn,' said the vizier, addressing the peasant.

Why the Peasant Never Married

The peasant began his story: 'I had a very close friendship with a fairy. I used to go to her house to visit her, and she used to come and visit me, although she never actually entered my house. Many days passed, and I said to the fairy, "What sort of friendship do we have if you are not willing to be more intimate with me?"

'"I am willing to be a guest in your house on one condition," replied the fairy, "and that is that you must promise me never to take a wife."

'I immediately agreed to this condition and the fairy became a frequent visitor to my house. Days and nights passed, and one day, my father came and announced: "I have made arrangements for your wedding."

'When I next met the fairy, she said to me: "I hear that your father has arranged for you to marry. What will you do with me?"

'"Let him make the arrangements," said I.

'The fairy angrily reminded me of my promise: "Didn't you swear to me that you would never take a wife?"

'"It wasn't my idea," I replied. "Is it my fault if my father decides to arrange my marriage?"

'The fairy departed in a furious temper. "Very well," she said before leaving, "I shall take my revenge."

'That night, while I lay fast asleep, the fairy came and cut off my pecker. In the morning, I was bewildered to discover my loss, and went to the doctor to have the wound tended. Then, after sending a letter to my father asking him to postpone the wedding until I had attended to some urgent business, I went to the fairy and begged her to cure me.

'"I am willing to cure you on one condition," she said, "and that is that you will never take a wife."

'I asked her to forgive me and swore never to marry. She then ordered me to stand naked with my back to the wall. So I did as she told me. Then she threw my pecker at me from a distance, and it landed slightly squint. After that I was quite well again.'

Finishing his story, the peasant said to his friends, 'Look and see for yourselves whether or not I have told you the truth.' When they examined his pecker, they had to admit that it was indeed crooked, and they gave him the diamond.

V

Epic and Romance

24

The Shy Prince

Once there was a king who had a son who used to go hunting every day, departing at dawn and returning at dusk. Once he had gone out hunting as usual and had lost all sense of time. When he looked at the sky, he realized that it was much later than he had previously thought. In fact, it was already growing dark. So he turned his horse back and took a shortcut through some fields. This route passed through the neighbouring kingdom.

The ruler of this kingdom had a beautiful daughter, and it so happened that at that very moment she was sitting on the palace terrace. When the prince saw her, he reined in his horse and stopped. The princess thought: 'If somebody chances to see this man looking at me, they will say that there must be a secret liaison between us.' So she left the terrace and went inside.

The young prince had been so struck by the beauty of the princess that he no longer had the strength to ride his horse. But the horse took him back, without any need of guidance, to his father's *hujra,* which was where the young men of the household used to sleep. The servants helped him to dismount, and encouraged him to lie down and rest. He entered the guest-house and lay down on a broken *charpoy* that stood in a corner.

The prince had received some education. So he took a pen and ink, and drew a map of the district through which he had just passed, and he wrote down how he had seen the princess and how he had been struck by her beauty; then he put the piece of paper to one side and went to sleep.

The night passed, and the next day came, but still the prince lay there. On the second night, the king's wife asked the servants, 'Where is the prince?' They did not know, and answered, 'We saw him yesterday, but not today.'

On the third day, as the king was on his way to give public audience, his wife intercepted him: 'You are going to the court-room, yet the prince has been missing for the past three days and you haven't even inquired about him.' So the king mounted his throne and made an announcement: 'Everybody must go and look for the prince.'

All the king's subjects went out and searched for the prince, but they returned home in the evening and reported: 'The prince is nowhere to be found.' Meanwhile, the prince was still lying on the same *charpoy* where the servants had left him on his return from hunting. Nobody had thought of looking for him there.

On the following day, the king went to the court-room and made a second announcement: 'Whoever finds the prince, dead or alive, will receive one thousand rupees.' When the people heard this, all the strong young men set out to search for him in distant lands.

There was a lame man whose wife used to grumble at him all day long, and when she heard that the king had offered a reward of a thousand rupees for finding his son, she said to her husband: 'You never leave the house. Why don't you take your stick and go to the *hujra*? Perhaps you will find him there.' The lame man did not want to go, but as he wished to avoid being pestered by his wife, he decided to do what she suggested.

3. Durrani Chieftains in full armour (Rattray, tp)

14. Interior of the City of Kandahar (Rattray, pl. 23)

15. The Tomb of the Emperor Babur (Atkinson, pl. 24)

16.   The Main Street in the Bazaar at Kabul (Atkinson, pl. 19)

17. Entrance to the Bolan Pass (Atkinson, pl. 5)

The royal guest-house had a large number of rooms. He peeped into one and then into another, until finally he came to the room where the prince was lying, covered from head to foot by his turban-cloth.

'Who is there?' he called.

But there was no answer from the prince who was half unconscious. The lame man was astonished when he pulled aside the turban-cloth.

'I've found the prince. I've found the prince,' he shouted triumphantly.

When the servants heard the lame man's words, they came running. They lifted up the bed and carried the prince to the king, and said, 'Here is the prince, but he is dying.'

After sending the lame man a thousand rupees, the king summoned the best physicians in his kingdom and asked them to cure his son. The physicians conferred among themselves for hours, and then one of them spoke to the king: 'When we feel a patient's pulse, we can diagnose the nature of his disease, and so prescribe the necessary remedy. We have all felt the young prince's pulse, but, according to our diagnosis, he has no illness, therefore we cannot cure him.'

The king was very angry: 'He is lying there unconscious before your very eyes and you tell me he is not ill.'

Once again the physicians consulted among themselves, and decided to give the prince some medicine to make him strong. They carefully prepared three cups of this medicine, but when they gave the first cup to the prince, he was unable to swallow it and threw it up. Then the physicians went to the king, and said: 'The prince refuses to drink our medicine, so how do you expect us to cure him!' With these words, they left the palace.

The king ordered his servants to give the prince the second cup of medicine, but he threw that up too. The king again lost his temper: 'The prince is ill, but he refuses to drink the medicine. You will have to force him to drink it.'

When the king's wife overheard this, she called out: 'Bring him here. Don't force him to drink the third cup.' So they took the prince to his mother, and all the women of the house gathered round and tried to comfort her.

The king grew worried. Next day he summoned his vizier, and said to him: 'The prince is my only son, and if he dies, I shall have no heir. Advise me what I should do, otherwise I shall reclaim all the money I've ever given you.'

The vizier did not know what to advise the king. That evening he returned home and lay on his bed. His wife knew that something was troubling him, so she asked, 'Why are you so worried?'

The vizier answered: 'The young prince is ill, and the king has asked me either to find a remedy, or else to return all the money he has ever given me.'

'Don't worry,' said his wife reassuringly, 'I shall go and see the prince, and then search for a cure.'

'You are welcome to go,' said the vizier, 'but nothing will come of it.'

When the vizier's wife visited the prince, she knew at once that he had fallen in love. So she returned home and instructed her husband: 'Go to the bazaar and find a cunning old woman. Offer her one hundred rupees, and tell her that she will receive a further reward from the king if she can make the prince talk.'

Without a moment's delay, the vizier hurried to the bazaar and found a cunning old woman. He said to her: 'The king's son is not really ill, but he refuses to eat or to talk. Here are one hundred rupees; if you manage to cure him, you will receive a further reward from the king.' The old woman took the money, and said, 'Take me to him and I shall cure him.'

When the old woman reached the prince's room, a large number of women were crowding round the bed. She ordered them to leave, and when they had left, she stood in the doorway and addressed the prince in a loud voice: 'O foolish boy! You have only to mention the name of the girl whom you love and your father will arrange for her to marry you.'

'Come in,' shouted the prince, on hearing this.

When the old woman entered the room, the prince handed her the map that he had drawn, and asked her to give it to his father. She took it to the king. When the king had examined the map and what was written on it, he ordered his vizier and his magistrate to go in search of the girl.

The vizier and the magistrate said to one another, 'It is simple enough to find the place, but how will we meet the girl?' In the end they decided that it would be best to take their wives with them. When they reached the palace where the princess lived, they told their wives to go inside while they waited outside.

The two wives entered the palace, and met the princess and her mother. They asked the mother, 'What relation is this girl to you?'

'She is my daughter,' was her reply.

So they explained: 'We have come from the neighbouring kingdom on behalf of the prince to ask for her hand in marriage.'

The mother said: 'My daughter has had more than a hundred proposals, but her father, the king, hasn't made up his mind yet. You will have to go and ask him.'

So the two wives went outside and told their husbands to convey the marriage proposal to the king. The vizier and the magistrate presented themselves before the king, and announced: 'We are the vizier and the magistrate of the king of the neighbouring kingdom, and we have come on behalf of the prince to ask for your daughter's hand in marriage.'

As the king was weary of receiving proposals for his daughter and desired to remain on good terms with his neighbours, he granted his consent.

The vizier then said: 'Whatever is your custom and whatever you require as a bride-price, write it down and we shall take the message to our king.' The king wrote down the bride-price and the other items that he required for the wedding, and handed the message to the vizier. Then the vizier and the magistrate and their wives returned home.

People began preparing for the wedding and the prince's health began to improve. On the day of the wedding the prince and the people of the kingdom set out to fetch the bride. When the time came to read the marriage contract, two witnesses from the prince's family went to the princess and asked her if she was willing to enter into marriage with the prince.

'I cannot say yes until you bring the prince to my door,' she replied.

So the two witnesses brought the prince to the door of the princess's room. 'Young man,' said the princess, 'do you wish to marry me?'

'Yes,' answered the prince.

The princess issued a warning: 'You saw me for the first time from afar and look what happened to you. If you see me from close quarters, you will not survive. You have invited the guests and you have given them a wedding banquet, but this marriage is only acceptable to me in one condition. I shall give you eight days, and during this trial period I shall observe your conduct. If you are able to behave normally, and not like a madman, then I shall be your wife; if not, then I shall leave you. In the daytime I shall come to your house, and at night I shall return to my father's house; or, if you prefer, I shall spend the night in your house, and return to my father's house in the daytime.'

The prince accepted this arrangement, and the princess took an oath before several witnesses: 'I am willing to marry the prince, provided that he fulfils the conditions agreed upon.' Then she sat in the bridal palanquin and the people carried her to the prince's house. The princess slept in the prince's bedroom and he slept in the guest-house.

In the morning, after the barber had shaved him, the prince put on new clothes and went to visit the princess. But no sooner had he entered the bedroom and set eyes on the princess than he fainted and collapsed on the floor. The princess knelt down beside him and rubbed his hands and feet until he regained consciousness and stood up. That evening she returned to her father's house.

Next morning the princess came back, but as soon as the prince saw her, he fainted again and collapsed on the floor. Then, as before, she knelt down beside him and rubbed his hands and feet until he regained consciousness and stood up. In the evening she again returned to her father's house.

On the following morning the princess came back for the third time, but when the prince saw her, he fainted once again. After she had rubbed his hands and feet, he stood up and immediately left the room.

Instead of going to the royal guest-house, he went out into the fields. There he saw a *talib,* a student of Quranic law, seated on his prayer-mat reading the Quran. He sat down near him and listened to the recitation. Towards evening the student of religion rolled up his prayer-mat and set off home. The prince sat on the ground for a long time on his own. Then he made his way to the guest-house and spent the night there.

Next morning, instead of going to meet the princess, the prince returned to the place in the fields where the student of religion sat reading the Quran. When the student saw him, he said, 'May I ask you a question?'

'Read on,' replied the prince, 'there is no need to ask questions. Sorrow has turned my heart to ashes.'

The student of religion persisted: 'Before marriage young men always sit in the guest-house with their friends, but after the marriage ceremony they rarely leave their homes, and when they do leave, after three or four days, people tease them and say they have become like women because they are forever indoors. But I hear that you have just got married, and that this is only the fourth day of your marriage. Yet you are sitting here with me, and yesterday too you sat here with me throughout the day. Tell me please, what is the matter?'

The prince confided: 'My wife is so beautiful that whenever I set eyes on her, I become delirious and faint. She has sworn to observe my conduct for eight days, and if, during that period, I behave like a madman, she will cease to be my wife and leave me. I have already lost my mind and fainted three times, so today I have decided not to go home.'

The student of religion thought for a while, then said: 'I am only a novice, but I shall do what I can.' He went to the mosque, and returned with a piece of paper on which he had written a *taweez,* a prayer with magical power. He wrapped the piece of paper in a handkerchief and tied it to the prince's arm. Nearby a farmer was ploughing his field with bullocks. 'See if the charm works by testing it on the farmer,' suggested the student of religion.

The secret of this particular charm was that, when the prince wore it, he could see other people, but they could not see him. The prince approached the farmer and threw a stone at him. The farmer began cursing loudly and looked round to see who had hit him, but he could see nobody. 'Where are you?' he shouted. The prince picked up another stone and threw it at him. Once again the farmer began cursing loudly. He peered round him in all directions, but there was not a soul in sight. Then the prince picked up a huge stone and hurled it towards the farmer. The farmer picked up the stone, and thought: 'Nobody could throw such a big stone from a long way off; perhaps a *jinn* is throwing these stones from nearby.' So he abandoned his work and ran home as fast as his legs could carry him.

'What happened?' inquired the student of religion, when the prince returned.

'You saw what happened,' replied the prince. 'I kept hitting him with stones, and he kept looking round to see who it was, but he couldn't see me.'

'This charm is my special discovery,' said the student of religion, 'and I have now done all I can to help you. If you have any intelligence, and are the true son of your parents, you should be able to manage your affairs and keep your wife.' After their exchange of farewells, he asked, 'If you win your princess, will you reward me?'

'Yes, of course I shall,' replied the prince.

'Well then, if you are successful in your undertaking, you know that we students of religion are very fond of food, so I want you to send me a plate of *pilau* every morning and every evening.'

'Your wish will be granted,' promised the prince. 'Until the day you die, you will receive two plates of *pilau*, one in the morning and one in the evening.'

When the prince returned home it was evening, so he sent the princess back to her father's house in the palanquin. Then he attached the *taweez* to his arm and followed her. When she entered the palace, he too entered, but the charm prevented anyone from seeing him.

The princess had about sixty young companions. It was their duty to keep the princess company and to spend the night with her. When she arrived, these girls collected their bedding and placed their bedsteads round her bed in the usual way. Among them the princess was like a moon surrounded by stars.[2]

As soon as all the girls were fast asleep, the prince, who had been watching everything from the corner of the room, approached the princess's bed and nibbled her on the left cheek. The princess awoke with a start and shouted, 'Thief! Thief!' She looked around, but could see no one. So she lay down again and tried to sleep.

Then the prince approached her bed again and nibbled her on the right cheek. 'Thief! Thief!' shouted the princess once again. All her companions awoke and looked around for the intruder, but they could see no one. They searched until morning without success.

In the morning the prince returned to his village. On the way he met a bald man who was grazing his cows. The prince said to him: 'Come with me and take a walk round my garden. I shall call out to you, and when you come, I shall say, "I had a strange dream last night," and you must then ask me what the dream was about.' He took the bald man with him and gave instructions to his servants: 'When my wife's palanquin arrives, don't let her go indoors; bring her to the garden.'

When the princess arrived, the servants took her to the garden. The prince was sitting at one end of the garden, and the bald man was wandering around eating fruit. 'Come here,' shouted the prince, and the bald man came at his bidding. Then the prince said to him: 'I had a strange dream last night.'

'What was your dream about?' inquired the bald man.

The prince began relating his dream: 'Last night, when I was sleeping in the guest-house, I dreamt that I entered a palace. I was standing in a corner when sixty young girls appeared. These girls collected their bedding and placed their bedsteads in a circle round the bed of a beautiful princess. When it was dark, and everybody was fast asleep, I approached the princess's bed and nibbled her on the left cheek. She screamed, 'Thief! Thief!' and looked round the room, but could find no one.'

Meanwhile, the princess, who had been listening, thought to herself: 'But that is what really happened.'

The prince continued: 'I approached the princess's bed a second time and nibbled her on the right cheek. She sat up and shouted for help, and her companions began to hunt for me, but I was nowhere to be seen. In the morning, when I awoke, I was lying on my bed in the guest-house.'

'The beautiful princess sounds just like your wife,' remarked the bald man. 'You must visit her again tonight.'

That evening the princess was transported to her father's house in her palanquin. Once again the prince tied the *taweez* round his arm and followed her.

When the princess entered her bedchamber, she warned her companions: 'Be on your guard because the thief will come again tonight and we must catch him.' The prince, who was crouching against the wall, heard her say this.

When half the night had passed, and everyone had fallen asleep, the prince approached the princess's bed, lifted her blouse, and touched her on the left breast. The princess was furious and scolded her companions: 'I warned you to keep watch, but instead you went to sleep. We must search the palace. He couldn't have left, because the door is still locked, and there is a watchman outside.' They searched everywhere, but could find no one. Then she warned her companions: 'Don't fall asleep. The thief will come again.'

Despite the princess's warning, the girls fell asleep, and the prince approached the princess's bed, lifted her blouse, and touched her on the right breast. The princess screamed in anger, and she and her companions searched for the thief all night, but could find no one.

In the morning the prince returned home. On the way he met the bald man, and said to him: 'Come with me into the garden, and we shall repeat what we did yesterday.'

The bald man answered: 'Yesterday you gave me one rupee and I gave my cows to another man to graze, but he lost one of them, and I spent the whole night looking for it without success. So you must pay me forty rupees for that cow and one rupee for today, which I can give to the man who grazes my cows.'

The prince agreed and gave the bald man the money. They entered the garden. The prince sat down and the bald man wandered about eating fruit. When the princess arrived in her palanquin, the servants again directed her to the garden. At that moment the prince called out to the baldman: 'Come here, so I can tell you the dream I had last night.'

When the bald man approached, he began recounting his dream: 'I dreamt that I entered the same palace as I did last night, and everything was just as it was before. This time the princess told her sixty companions that the thief would come again and warned them to be on their guard. When half the night had passed, and they were fast asleep, I approached the princess's bed and touched her left breast. She woke up and angrily rebuked her companions for not obeying her orders, and told them to be on the alert for the rest of the night. They remained awake for some time, and then fell asleep again. I approached the princess's bed a second time and touched her right breast. The princess's screams woke up the whole household, and they searched for me all over the palace, but they couldn't find me. In the morning, when I awoke, I was lying on my bed in the guest-house.'

When the princess heard this, she said to herself: 'I'm sure that my companions have been concealing the prince. Perhaps he disguises himself as a girl and comes in the place of one of them. But tonight I shall catch him.'

That evening the princess returned home, and for the third time the prince put on his magic charm and followed her. When the princess entered her bedchamber, she scolded her companions: 'It is because of you that this man comes to tease me; he disguises himself as a girl and takes the place of one of you.' She searched them one by one, and discovered that they were all present. Annoyed at being insulted in this fashion, they left the room, and the princess was now obliged to sleep on her own.

When half the night had passed, the prince approached the bed and put a cloth over the princess's mouth to prevent her from screaming. Then he untied the cord of her *shalwar*, and having done this, he sat down near the wall.

In the morning the prince returned home. On the way he met the bald man, and invited him to come to the garden with him. When the princess arrived in her palanquin, she was directed once again to the garden. 'Come,' shouted the prince to the bald-headed man, 'let me tell you about the dream I had last night.' 'Beware!' cried the princess. 'Don't repeat the dream to that bald fool. Tell him to leave the garden at once.' The prince answered: 'I have no dealings with you. You have driven me mad, and there is only one day left of the eight days which you gave me, and then you will be free to go your own way.' As the princess was about to step out of her palanquin, the prince whispered to the bald man, 'You had better leave the garden, otherwise there will be trouble.'

The princess stepped out of her palanquin and embraced the prince, and said to him: 'Everything you have recounted is true, but you say that nobody could see you. How is this possible?'

The prince explained: 'I have a special *taweez*. When I tie it round my arm, I can see everybody, but nobody can see me.' He took out the magic charm and tied it round his arm. He then pinched the princess: 'Can you see me?'

'No,' she replied. 'Where are you?'

'Here,' he shouted.

She went to the place whence the voice had come, but could not see him. This was sufficient to convince her that it was the prince who had visited her on three consecutive nights. The prince took off the magic charm and appeared before her, and they lived happily ever after.

25

The King's Dream

here was once a king who had a strange dream. In this dream a woman entered the royal bedchamber and stood before him. He looked at her for a long time, transfixed by her beauty. It seemed that she was about to sit down beside him on the bed, but then she drew back. He tried to catch her, but she vanished and he fell on the floor. When the king awoke, he summoned his ministers and ordered them to hold a meeting.

When the vizier, the magistrate, the royal bodyguard, and others had assembled, the king told them what had occurred in his dream, and said: 'I want you to find this woman for me.'

'It was only a dream,' said the vizier, 'and you should be thankful you are not obliged to have a bath.[1] You shouldn't take your dream so seriously, because in their dreams some people even become kings. There is no truth in it.'

'No, I swear upon my word that she entered my room,' the king persisted. 'She was standing near my bed and looking at me, and I was looking at her. I tried to touch her, but she disappeared. As a result I fell from my bed. Yet when I awoke, there was no one in the room.'

The vizier and the others assured the king: 'There is no such woman. It was just a dream. But if you insist, we shall go in search of her.'

The king ordered that they should build a room near the palace, and he would describe the woman's features in such detail that they could draw her picture and hang it up. He would thus be able to contemplate the picture while they went in search of her.

The room was built, the picture was drawn and hung onthe wall, and a bed was placed in the room near the picture. Then the king's ministers set out on their quest.

The king had a son who was charged with the task of looking after the affairs of the kingdom while his father contemplated the picture. For ten years he governed his father's kingdom. Then he grew restless, and thought to himself: 'Either my father is too old to travel, or else he is too lazy to search for this woman herself. I am young and strong. I shall go in search of her.'

He summoned his advisers, and said to them: 'How can I see the picture? Tell me what time the king leaves the room so that I can go and look at it.' They arranged that one of them should spy for him and inform him when he could obtain a glimpse of the picture without any fear of encountering his father.

One day the spy came and told the prince that his father had just left the room. The prince hurried there, and when he saw the picture, he fell more deeply in love with the woman than his father. So he immediately filled his purse with money and set out to look for her.

For months and months hetravelled, until at last he reached the city of Lucknow. He was walking in the bazaar when a merchant of the city recognized him.

This merchant used to transport goods from Lucknow to the prince's kingdom, and had often been a guest of the king for several nights. At the time of his last visit, the prince had been a small child, so small that, when the merchant had asked to see him, the servant had brought him in his arms.

It was evening, and the merchant had just finished business, and was sitting on a mat in front of his closed shop, when he saw the prince pass. He at once recognized the little boy whom the servant had brought to him in his arms. 'This is the same boy,' he thought. 'Let me ask him what he is doing here so far from his father's kingdom.' So he stood up and called to the boy. After greeting him and embracing him, he asked after the prince's father.

'How do you know him?' the prince asked in surprise.

'I am a friend of your father,' the merchant explained. 'When I used to transport goods to his kingdom, I was often a guest in the palace. In those days you were just a small child, but today I recognized you and you must be my guest.'

The merchant then took the prince to his house, and here he was treated as one of the family, so much so, that the women of the house did not observe purdah when they conversed with him. The merchant gave him a meal and a bed for the night.

He imagined that the prince would leave the next morning, but the whole day passed and the prince never mentioned anything about leaving. Then he spent a second night there, and on the following day he still stayed and showed no intention of leaving.[2] The third night came, and the merchant thought to himself: 'I found this boy and brought him home. Since he has decided to stay here, it must mean that he has quarrelled with his father. Since he is an only son and his father's heir, his father must have dispatched all his guards in search of him. I shall therefore bind his hands and feet, and take him back to his father.'

On the morning of the third day, the merchant said to the prince: 'I have to go to your father's kingdom on business, so will you please accompany me?'

'You may have business there,' said the prince, 'but I have no business there.'

'O you rascal,' said the merchant, 'you don't want to go because you are angry with your father, but you must come with me.'

'I am not angry with my father,' explained the prince. 'What happened was that my father saw a woman in a dream and fell in love with her, and when I saw a picture of that woman, I too fell in love with her, and now I am searching for her.'

For a moment the merchant was bewildered by the prince's words. Then he said: 'Come with me and I will show you something.'

The merchant had a *deo* that belonged to him and had been with him ever since childhood. When the merchant was a child in his cradle, this *deo* had seen him and had said to his parents: 'I am in love with your child. If you don't want me to kidnap him, then make arrangements for my food and drink, and I shall live here and look at the child. I must be allowed to see him every morning and every evening.' The parents had agreed, and since that time the *deo* had stayed with them. He used to see the child every morning and every evening, then later once a week. But now that the *deo* had become old, the merchant was only expected to visit him once a month.

The merchant led the way to the *deo*'s room. He opened the door and embraced the *deo* and kissed him. 'I am so pleased,' said the *deo*. 'The month is not complete and you have come to see me.'

'I have a favour to ask you,' said the merchant.

The *deo* looked very happy. 'This is a great pleasure. What work can I do for you?'

The merchant asked the prince to relate the whole story, and the prince recounted everything up to the time of his meeting with the merchant in the bazaar.

'Can you describe the woman?' asked the *deo*.

Without a moment's hesitation, the prince described all the woman's features from head to toe.

The *deo* pondered for a while, then said: 'A long time has elapsed since I fell in love with the merchant, and at that time I remember having seen a woman like the one you describe. She was known as the Princess of the Tower. Her father was a king, and every young man, both from her kingdom and from other kingdoms, wished to marry her. Her father did not know what to do. If he gave her hand in marriage to one prince, then the other would be offended; and if he gave her to the other, then the next would be offended. He wondered where he could hide his daughter so that people would leave him in peace and cease to trouble him.

'His vizier advised him to lock up his daughter in a tower: "This tower should be built at some distance from the palace under the cover of darkness. The only window should be one large enough for passing food and drink inside. If any more suitors ask for your daughter's hand in marriage, you can deny that you have a daughter; and if they don't believe you, then they can search your palace and they will not find her, and will thus be convinced."

'This princess was so beautiful that her face shone with light. All those who saw her fell in love with her, and refused to be parted from her, and eventually went mad. Therefore lamps had been placed at the four corners of her bed. In this way it was possible to look at her without going insane.

'In that kingdom there was a special kind of grass, which the princess used to cut and rub on the soles of her feet, and until the liquid from the grass had dried on her feet, she was able to sit on her bed and fly through the air. When people looked up in the sky and saw the bed shining with light, they used to say: "Look! The king's daughter is going out for a ride." But when the king locked her up in the tower, she was no longer free to go out. So it is many years since I last saw her. I shall go and see whether she is alive in the tower, and if so, I shall find a way of bringing her to you.'

As the *deo* prepared to go, a famous proverb came to the prince's mind: 'Another man's trouble is as cold as ice.' This means that if I have a problem, another person will not go to great lengths to solve it. Mindful of this proverb, the prince said to the merchant: 'I want to accompany the *deo*. Otherwise, he will go and return and say she is not there.'

The merchant told the *deo* that the prince wished to accompany him. The *deo* did not approve of the idea. 'He will die, because I travel as fast as fire,' he warned.

'Whatever we do,' said the merchant, 'please remember that we are acting on his behalf. Therefore if he insists, you had better take him with you.'

With some reluctance, the *deo* agreed, and said: 'Going at my speed, the journey will take eight days. So cook enough food for the prince to last eight days. Wrap it up so that he can easily unwrap it and eat it on the way, and also so that it keeps fresh.'

The merchant ordered the food to be prepared for the journey. It was packed and given to the prince, who strapped himself to the *deo*'s stomach, and off they went.

After travelling for four days the *deo* felt hungry, so he stopped in a desert. He untied the prince and unbandaged his eyes, which had been blindfolded because of the speed of their flight.

'Are you well? Is everything all right?'

'Yes,' answered the prince.

Then the *deo* drew seven lines in a circle round the prince, and said: 'If a beautiful woman comes, or if somebody comes offering you wealth, or whoever comes, do not cross these seven circles. This is a form of defence, like a fort. If you cross the circles, then don't blame me if you die or come to harm.' It should be explained that these magic circles were a protection against *jinn*, demons, snakes and other hazards of the desert, including of course other *deo*s.

After drawing these lines on the ground, the *deo* went in search of food. He travelled a long way and reached the district where the princess's tower had been built. In the fields some children were grazing sheep, so he took the shape of a kindly old man with a long white beard, and said: 'The king had a daughter who had many suitors. The king grew tired of her suitors, so he built a tower outside the village, and in that tower he imprisoned his daughter. Do you know what has become of her?'

'She is still there,' answered the children.

'Is it possible to enter the tower?' asked the old man.

'No,' they replied. 'There is only a small hole through which food is passed.'

The *deo* left the children and approached the tower. It was built of solid stone. 'If I destroy this tower,' he thought, 'then the princess will be killed.' So he sat down near the tower and wondered what to do. By the time he had reached a decision, it was dark. He decided that he would push the tower with so much strength that it would fall far away, leaving the princess behind on her bed. Then he would be able to carry her off. It was night time and the princess lay fast asleep. So he pushed the tower over, lifted the bed, and flew with it to where he had left the prince. When they arrived, dawn was just breaking: one side of the sky was light, the other side was dark.

It was now five days since the *deo* had last eaten. He said to the prince: 'I must leave you again and search for food. I have lost so much energy pushing over the tower that if I were to travel immediately, we might bump into a mountain or a tree-top, and then you would both die.' He made seven circles round the prince and the princess, and made them swear never to cross them. Then he left in search of food.

In that area there was another *deo* who had dishonoured a woman in a nearby village. The villagers had caught him, and had bound him hand and foot in heavy chains so that a tiger or some other wild beast should come and devour him. This *deo* now turned himself into an old man, and shouted: 'Enemies have tied me up here, and last night I was saved from harm, but if I'm left here for another night, the wild beasts will surely devour me. So for the love of God, please help me.'

'I must go,' said the prince, who felt sorry for the old man, but the princess warned him not to cross the magic lines. 'Perhaps he is lying,' she said. 'If he hasn't committed any crime, then why have they bound him up in such heavy chains?'

The *deo* continued to plead for help, so the prince told the princess for the second time, 'I must go.' But once again she stopped him.

'Please, for the love of God, save me,' cried the *deo* for the third time.

This time the prince could no longer resist, and said, 'I must go and help him.'

As soon as the prince crossed the magic lines, the spell was broken; the charm read over them no longer had any effect. The old man now took his true form, that of a *deo*, and using all his strength, he broke free from his chains and was able to cross the lines.

'You wished to save me from death,' he said to the prince, 'so I shall not harm you, but what need do you have of her? I shall take her with me.' With one hand he picked up the princess, and with the other he drew seven new circles around the prince, and then left.

When the other *deo* returned, he was surprised to find the prince all alone and asked what had happened. The prince recounted how the old man had begged to be set free from his chains, and how, when he had crossed the lines to free him, the old man had assumed his true shape as a *deo* and had captured the princess.

The *deo* became very angry. 'You are worthy of death,' he said. 'I warned you not to cross the magic lines.' He was tempted to kill the prince, but thought to himself: 'What answer will I give to the merchant?' He was in two minds about what to do. After asking the prince which direction they had taken, he made him climb on his back, and after a brief journey they arrived in the kingdom of the *deo*s.

In that kingdom there was a sacred well called Zamzam. The water of this well was famous for its medicinal properties: when the blind drank from it, they regained their eyesight; when the sick drank from it, they were cured. *Deo*s drink a great deal of water, and they used to come to that well by turns to drink.

The *deo* hid near the well with the prince by his side, and whenever a *deo* came, he grabbed him and asked, 'Have you stolen my princess?' If he were satisfied with the answer, he would let him go.

One day a *deo* appeared, and he asked him the same question. 'What princess?' asked the *deo*.

The merchant's *deo* explained: 'We were travelling with a princess. A *deo* who had been chained up in the desert deceived us and stole her.'

This *deo* informed them that the *deo* whom they were looking for had been chained up because he had acquired a very bad reputation. 'Come,' he said, 'I shall take you to his house.'

They went to the house of the evil *deo* and broke open the door. He was sitting near the fire with the girl. 'I didn't know that this princess belonged to you,' he said, falling at the feet of the merchant's *deo*. 'Please forgive me and take her.' So the prince and the princess climbed on to the back of the merchant's *deo* and they left the kingdom of the *deo*s.

After journeying for several days, the *deo* once again grew tired. But before going in search of food, he picked up a huge boulder and hollowed out a space where the prince and princess could hide. Then he put the boulder back in its former position.

He thought that they would be safe there, because only a *deo* would have the strength to lift such a huge boulder.

Meanwhile, the father of the princess had heard that his daughter had been captured and his tower destroyed. He summoned the four *deo*s who worked for him as servants and told them what had happened. People had seen a strange light moving through the air: it was the light of the princess's face. They pointed in the direction to which the light had been heading. So the *deo*s led the way, and the king followed with his army, until they reached the boulder under which the prince and the princess were hidden. The four *deo*s sat down on that stone.

'Let us continue on our way,' said the king.

'That which we seek is under this stone,' replied the*deo*.

The king ordered the *deo*s to lift up the stone. But the *deo*s thought to themselves: 'Only a *deo* could have lifted a boulder like this, which means that whoever placed the prince and princess under it must belong to our tribe. We have done wrong to tell the king.' The king repeated his order three or four times, but the *deo*s turned their faces away as though they had not heard him.

At this very moment the merchant's*deo* returned. When the four *deo*s saw him, they immediately fell at his feet, because in the kingdom of the *deo*s they were his tenants, and they begged for his forgiveness, and told him to speak to the king, their master.

'Please remove your army,' said the *deo* to the king. 'Your daughter is under this stone, and the person for whose sake I brought her is also under this stone.'

In those days kings were very cunning. As soon as the king agreed to remove his army, the *deo* removed the boulder, and said to the prince, 'You will have to obtain the king's permission to marry his daughter.'

'You have had your say,' said the king to the *deo*. 'Now let me speak to him.' Then the king addressed the prince: 'If I hadn't caught up with you, then you would have escaped and I could have done nothing about it, but since I have now caught up with you, you must return with me to my kingdom and I shall marry you to my daughter with great pomp and ceremony. Afterwards, you may take her wherever you wish, but first you must come back to my kingdom and marry her.'

Without even discussing the matter with the merchant's *deo*, the prince agreed and at once departed with the king and the princess whom he hoped to marry.

On the way the vizier and the magistrate said to the king: 'What sort of death can we devise for him?' The king told them to lower their voices, otherwise they would arouse the prince's suspicions, and said that they would decide what to do with him as soon as they reached the palace.

When they arrived, the prince was locked up in a prison, and all the women came and told the princess that she was not to blame, and that it was written in her fate that she would be kidnapped.

Meanwhile, the merchant's *deo* sat near the huge boulder and wondered what to do. He thought: 'If I return empty-handed, what answer will I give to the merchant? He will say that I have lost the prince.' So with this in mind, he went to the kingdom of the girl's father and broke down the prison doors. Then he carried the prince outside the village and hid him in a deserted place. Having done this, he went to fetch the princess. He broke open the doors of her room in the palace and flew with her to the place where the prince was hidden. Then the prince and the princess sat on his back, and he flew with them to the merchant's house.

'Here is your friend the prince, and here is the princess whom he was looking for,' he said to the merchant. 'Now shut me up in my room. I don't want to see the prince again because he has deceived me two or three times and caused me great trouble, but by the grace of God we were saved.'

'What wrong has he done you?' asked the merchant.

'Ask him yourself, and now please leave me in peace,' replied the *deo*.

After locking the *deo* in his room, the merchant asked the prince what he had done and why the *deo* was so angry with him. So the prince recounted the whole story from start to finish. Then, when it was morning, the prince said to the merchant: 'Now I would like to return to my father's kingdom.'

The merchant became worried. 'Don't go, I beg you,' he said. 'As you know, your father is in love with this same girl, and either you will kill him, or he will kill you. You may both live with me, and whatever God provides, you are welcome to eat.'

But the prince insisted that he had to return home.

'If you are determined to go, I cannot stop you,' said the merchant, 'but I have a dog, and you must promise to take him with you wherever you go, and not to leave him for one minute.'

The prince and the princess bade farewell to the merchant and travelled to the kingdom of the prince's father, accompanied by the dog. The father was still sitting in the room that had been built for him, contemplating the picture of the beautiful princess. When the people came and told the king that his son had returned, bringing the woman in the picture with him, he shaved and gave his moustache a twist, and joyfully entered the palace and embraced the young couple.

'Have you brought her for me?' asked the king.

'No,' answered the prince, 'I have brought her for myself.'

'Give her to me,' commanded the king.

But the prince said that such a thing was impossible. So the king left the palace and told some bandits that he would give them three thousand rupees if they would murder his son. They went to the palace and called to the prince: 'Please come out. We have just learnt about your marriage and have come to congratulate you.'

When the prince came out, the bandits greeted him, and then invited him to go hunting with them in order to celebrate. When they were at a great distance from the village, they suddenly surrounded him.

'Are you going to kill me?' asked the prince.

'Yes,' they replied. 'Your father has paid us to kill you.'

'What will you gain by killing me?' said the prince. 'If you spare me, I will give you as much money as you want.'

The bandits consulted together and decided that they would not kill the prince. Instead they would pluck out his eyes and leave him in a ditch, and this is what they proceeded to do. They plucked out the prince's eyes and threw them on the ground; then they pushed him into a ditch.

Fortunately, the dog witnessed all this and noticed where the bandits had thrown the eyes. So when the bandits had gone, he ran all the way to the merchant and started to bark and tug at his clothes. Then the dog led the merchant to the spot where the prince was lying.

Several times the prince had stood up and attempted to walk, but each time he had tripped, screaming in pain. When the merchant reached the prince and took him by the arm, the prince wondered who it was. 'Who are you?' he asked.

'Don't worry. I am the merchant, your friend.'

The merchant and the dog pulled the prince out of the ditch and, after the merchant had wrapped the eyes that had been plucked out in a handkerchief, they travelled to his house.

In the meantime, the king was prowling round the princess. 'Your husband has abandoned you, so now you will have to marry me,' he said.

'If you are such a bad man that you want to marry your son's wife,'[3] replied the princess, 'then I agree, but I shall first wait for my husband for one year, and if he still does not return, then I shall marry you.'

The king did not believe that she meant what she said, and every day he bought her new clothes to wear, and day and night he begged her, but she repeated that he would have to wait for one year.

When the merchant arrived at his house, he went straight to the *deo*'s room, and said: 'Brigands have plucked out the prince's eyes and I have brought him with me.'

'If he had died, it would have been better,' said the *deo*. 'Why did you bring this troublesome person to me?'

'Please remember, whatever you do is for my sake,' said the merchant.

The *deo* agreed. 'For your sake, I shall help you, but this time I shall not take him with me. Give me a leather water-bag, and I shall go to my kingdom and bring back some water from the well of Zamzam. We will wash his eyes with that, then put them back in their sockets and bandage them for forty days, and he will recover his sight.'

The merchant gave the water-bag to the *deo*, and the *deo* went to his kingdom and soon returned with the sacred water of Zamzam. They washed the prince's eyes and put them back in their sockets and bandaged them, and after forty days the prince had regained his eyesight.

As soon as the prince had recovered, he said to the merchant, 'Now I would like to return to my father's kingdom.'

The merchant became worried: 'If you go this time, I warn you, they will finish you off.'

But the prince insisted. So the merchant agreed. 'If you are determined to go, I cannot stop you,' he said, 'but take my sword and, as soon as you arrive, kill your old father. Do not postpone killing him for one minute. He is an old man, after all, but you are young and deserve to live.'

On his arrival, the prince entered the palace. When the king saw him, he tried in vain to escape, but the prince jumped on him and killed him with his sword. Thenhe and the Princess of the Tower lived happily ever after.

26

Prince Bahram

In Search of Gulandama

There was once a king who had everything that he could possibly desire except a son. One day, when he had finished holding court, he returned home and lay down to rest in the courtyard. A fakir, who happened to be passing, looked into the courtyard and saw that the king was lost in thought. 'In the name of Allah, be charitable,' he cried. The king called one of his maidservants and ordered her to give the fakir some food. The woman went and returned with a basket filled with grain. She handed the basket to the beggar, but he refused to take it. She was surprised, and said: 'You asked for charity, so why do you refuse to accept this wheat?'

'I do not want charity,' replied the fakir.

The maidservant went back to the king, and said: 'The fakir refuses to accept charity.'

'Perhaps it is not sufficient,' said the king. 'Give him more grain.'

The woman added more grain to the basket and handed it to the fakir, but again he refused to take it. The king heard this, and addressed the fakir: 'Do you have some reason to reproach me that you decline my offer of charity? At first I thought that the servant hadn't given you enough grain, so I asked her to give you more; she filled the basket to the brim, yet you still refuse to take it.'

'Your Majesty, the truth is I haven't come for charity,' replied the fakir. 'I have come to meet you.'

The king invited him into the guest-house. 'Tell me, what brings you here?' inquired the king when they had sat down.

The fakir answered: 'As I was passing, I saw you resting in the courtyard, and I wondered what was on your mind.'

The king explained: 'Fakir, God has given me everything that I could possibly desire except a son.'

The fakir said: 'I shall pray to God to grant you a son, and I shall return after one year. If by then you have a son, you must promise to give me a reward.' The king agreed and the fakir left.

The story is quickly told, but a long time passed; and a year after the fakir's visit the king's wife gave birth to a son. The prince was named Bahram.

Three days after the prince's birth the fakir knocked on the door, and said: 'Tell the king that I've come to claim my reward.' The king invited the fakir into the guest-house and entertained him with great hospitality.

In the evening the king wondered what reward would please the fakir. He thought about it all night, and finally decided to grant whatever request he might make.

In the morning the fakir said: 'May I have my reward, so that I can go on my way?'

'Whatever you ask shall be granted,' replied the king.

'If I were to ask for your kingdom, would you give it to me?'

'Yes,' agreed the king, 'I am even willing to give you that.'

'Then give me your kingdom.'

The king willingly repeated three times: 'I grant you my kingdom and from today you are king.'

'Are you certain that you are willing to part with your kingdom?'

'Yes, absolutely,' replied the king without hesitation.

'I accept your reward,' said the fakir, 'and I believe that you are willing to give me everything you possess. You may keep your kingdom, and may God bless you.' With these words, the fakir left. The king called after him, but he continued on his way without turning back.

Time passed, and the young prince who was called Bahram grew up to be a handsome young man. His tutors taught him for fourteen years, after which he thought: 'I have everything in the world that a person could desire; therefore I have no further need of education,' and he began leading a life of leisure. Every day he used to go out hunting on horseback, leaving at dawn and returning at dusk.

One day his father said to him: 'Bahram, when you go hunting, you should be escorted by servants. It is not only fitting for a prince to have an escort but it is also necessary that you should have a bodyguard. In future, you must take 50 men who have been trained to fight brigands. But,' he added, 'do not injure or wrong the poor.' The prince agreed. One of the 50 men was a man named Aurang, and the prince appointed him as his vizier.

Next day the prince, accompanied by his guards, went hunting in the jungle. When they had travelled some distance, they saw a post in the ground, to which was attached a note. The prince took the note, read it, and handed it to his vizier.

'Read what is written here,' he ordered.

'You have just read it,' said the vizier, 'so tell me what it says.'

'It is written that if any man goes beyond this point, he does so at his own risk, because a man-eating tiger lives there.'

Hearing this, the vizier said: 'Prince, let us take another route. Why should we put our lives at risk for no good reason?'

The prince answered: 'We must go on. How can we turn back now for fear of a tiger?'

The vizier grew worried. 'If the tiger harms you,' he said, 'I don't know how I shall answer for myself when I meet your father.' But as the prince insisted on going ahead, he was forced to agree: 'I cannot stop you, but, in case you should come to any harm, please give me some evidence that I tried to persuade you to turn back so that your father does not hold me responsible.'

The prince quickly scribbled a note for his father and gave it to the vizier. Then he went on ahead. After he had covered some distance, the man-eating tiger emerged from the shadows and blocked the way. But when the beast pounced, the prince lifted it up with his bare hands and threw it on the ground with such force that it died immediately. Then the prince called to his guards: 'Come, take this tiger to my father, and tell him that his son, the prince, has killed it with his bare hands.' The guards carried the dead tiger from the jungle to the palace and laid it before the king in accordance with the prince's instructions.

'Who killed this tiger?' inquired the king.

The guards answered: 'Your son is so strong that he killed this tiger with his bare hands.'

The king ordered that a large dinner should be prepared and given to the poor, to thank God for having saved his only son from the man-eating tiger and for having endowed him with so much strength. He also ordered that another fifty men should join the prince's bodyguard.

Next morning the prince went out hunting with his new bodyguard of a hundred men. It was decided that the man in front of whom their quarry appeared should hunt it and kill it without any help from the others. While they were in the jungle, a deer appeared in front of the prince. He pursued it alone, but was unable to catch up with it, so that by the evening he had travelled a long way from the place where he had left his guards. So he said to himself: 'I am tired; I shall spend the night here, and find my way back in the morning.' He tethered his horse, placed his sword and scabbard beneath his head, and lay down to sleep.

They say that smoke from a fire can be seen from afar offat dawn, just as light from a fire can be seen from afar off at night. When the prince awoke at dawn, he saw a thread of smoke rising in the distance. He thought: 'Perhaps there are some houses over there. I shall go and find someone who can tell me the way to my father's kingdom.' He rode in the direction of the smoke and arrived there by midday.

When he reached the spot, he saw 80 empty *charpoys*. Nearby there were 80 posts for tethering camels. The smoke was rising from a narrow ruined tower. The prince entered the tower, and there he saw a beautiful statue. No sooner had he set eyes on it than he fell in love with the girl in whose image it was made. An old man with a white beard crouched in a corner, watching over the fire from which smoke was issuing. The prince was so blinded by his love that he did not notice the old man.

'Don't touch that statue,' shouted the old man as the prince was about to pick it up. Then the old man invited him to sit down. The prince sat down and asked the old man in whose image the statue was made.

The old man began his story: 'In the olden days I was a merchant, and I used to travel with my goods to many different countries. One year I took some merchandise to China. I happened to arrive in one of the cities on the very day that the Princess Gulandama was due to remove her veil. It was the custom in that country for the princess to wear a veil that she would remove once a month. When she appeared in public, and revealed her face, she was so beautiful that it was impossible for any man to look upon her without being captivated by her beauty. When I saw her, I immediately fell in love with her. I returned to the inn where I was staying, and sold all my goods at half their original price. Then I paid all my servants and divided the remaining money into three portions. The first portion I distributed in the name of Allah; the second portion I gave to my inheritors; and the third portion I kept for myself.

'In that city there were many skilled craftsmen. I asked one of them to make for me a likeness of Gulandama out of wood. I paid him handsomely for his work. Next I went to a tailor and a goldsmith, and ordered the fine clothes and expensive jewellery that the statue still wears today. Then I travelled for many years until I came to this spot. I had this tower built for myself, and I bought 80 camels and hired 80 servants. The camels are rented out to carry goods to different countries. The profits are divided among my servants, except for what I need for food and drink. I myself remain here with the statue.'

When the old man had finished his story, the prince said: 'Tell me the way to that city in China. I want to go and win the hand of Gulandama.'

'O foolish youth,' said the old man, 'many men have tried to win her hand, but to this day no one has succeeded.'

The prince grew impatient: 'Old man, keep quiet and just tell me the way.' The old man rose to his feet and pointed towards the east, and the prince rode off in that direction.

On the way the prince passed a garden that belonged to six brothers. These brothers were powerful *jinn*. That day they had left their sister, Sarasa, to take care of the garden during their absence. Seeing a *charpoy* in the garden, the prince dismounted, sat down, and allowed his horse to graze. When Sarasa saw him, she prepared some food and told the servant to give it to him: 'A traveller is sitting on the bed in the garden. Take this food and encourage him to eat it. When he has finished, tell him to leave at once for the love of Allah, because if my brothers return and see him there, they will kill him. They don't even allow insects into their garden.'

The prince had fallen asleep when the servant came bringing the food. The servant woke him up, and gave him the food and the message from his mistress. The prince listened to the message, and then inquired: 'Why should anyone wish to kill me?'

The servant explained: 'This garden belongs to six brothers who take such care of it that even mosquitoes are forbidden to enter; and you have allowed your horse to roam about in it.'

The prince was not afraid: 'Let them threaten to kill me. We'll see what happens.'

'The traveller refuses to leave the garden,' reported the servant to his mistress.

Sarasa then came herself and pleaded with him: 'For the love of God, leave this garden. If my brothers find you here when they return, they will certainly kill you.'

'Let them come,' answered the prince. 'If they are so cruel, they must have killed many innocent people. I shall fight them and avenge the death of their innocent victims.'

When she continued to beg him to leave, and he still refused, she grew angry and said, 'You deserve to be killed.' Then she went home and prayed: 'Please God, let my brothers return home late tonight, so that they don't see this young man and put him to death.'

After a short time the six brothers returned. When they saw the prince and his horse in the garden, the eldest brother summoned the others to a *jirga,* or council. The eldest said to the youngest, 'Find the traveller and cut off his head.' But as soon as the youngest brother raised his sword, the prince lifted him from his horse, bound him hand and foot, and left him under a tree. After some time the eldest brother called the second brother, and said: 'Our youngest brother hasn't returned; he may have been killed. Go and see what has happened.' But as soon as the second brother appeared, the prince caught him and bound him hand and foot. After some t ime the eldest brother sent the next brother, and then the next, and in this way the prince was able to tie up five of the brothers.

Then the eldest brother charged at the prince, wielding his sword and shouting, 'Prepare to meet your fate.' The prince caught hold of him, dragged him from his horse, and tied him up beside his five brothers. He then drew his sword, and was on the point of putting them all to death when the sister intervened: 'Wait, don't kill them.'

'Why not?' asked the prince.

'Have you forgotten the advice that your father gave you when you were leaving home not to injure or wrong the poor?'

'How do you know what he said?' he inquired in amazement.

'I know because I was there,' replied Sarasa.

'But they are rich, not poor,' said the prince.

'They are poor because they are in your power,' said Sarasa. 'Therefore you should forgive them.'

The prince finally agreed: 'Normally I would never have forgiven them, because they must have harmed many innocent people, but since you showed me hospitality without knowing who I was, I cannot refuse your request.' Then he mounted his horse and went on his way.

Sarasa tried to untie the knots of the rope binding her brothers, but could not. The eldest brother said: 'Call out to the traveller and ask him to untie us.' So Sarasa called out to the prince to help her untie her brothers. He thought: 'If I untie them, they will surely try to kill me, yet, in view of her hospitality, I cannot refuse her request.' So he returned and untied the six brothers. But when he didso, his suspicions were proved correct, for at once they all stood up and prepared to attack him.

'Beware!' cried Sarasa. 'Do not attempt to harm the traveller. Bow down and touch his feet, for he is your seventh brother.'

After much persuasion, they heeded her words and invited the prince to their house.

Now the eldest brother had a wife called Rueh Afza, and a *deo*, who had fallen in love with her, had kidnapped her. So he told the prince: 'We have an enemy. I have fought with him twice, but on both occasions I was defeated. Please help us.'

The prince agreed to help them, and next morning he said to them, 'Let us go and fight your enemy.'

They answered: 'He is not a weak adversary; we must rally our troops together.'

The prince cited the proverb: 'When there are too many butchers, the cow is not slaughtered.' And he said: 'There is no need to call anybody. I shall go alone.'

The six brothers did not contradict him. They conferred among themselves and came to a common decision: 'We shall make h im go in front; either he or the *deo* will be killed; whichever one dies, we shall stand to gain.' So they told the prince to lead the way.

They say that when the thief goes out to steal and approaches his target, fear gives him the urge to urinate. As they approached the *deo*'s house, the brothers, one by one, excused themselves to urinate. When the prince reached the house, and looked back, not a single brother was in sight. So he shouted: 'You are all cowards. If you don't dare face the *deo*, at least tell me which house he lives in.'

'It's the house with the big door,' answered one of the brothers.

The prince threw his weight against the door and broke it open. When he entered, he found the *deo* asleep on a wooden bed. Beside him lay a pile of stones weighing at least a hundred *maund*s on top of an iron cage. In this cage Rueh Afza, the eldest brother's wife, was imprisoned. When she saw the prince, she first laughed and then wept.

'Young lady,' said the prince, 'why did you first laugh and then weep?'

'I laughed because I was so pleased to see you,' replied the woman, 'and I wept because, if the *deo* wakes up, he will eat you alive.'

'Fear not, I have come to kill him,' declared the prince.

She warned him: 'Kill him now while he sleeps, otherwise it will be impossible.'

'No, I cannot do that,' he said. 'I shall wake him first, so people will not say he was murdered in his sleep.'

The prince approached the *deo*, caught hold of his legs, and shook him. As soon as the *deo* awoke, he sliced him in two with one stroke of his sword. Then he broke open the iron cage and freed Rueh Afza and took her back to her husband. When he had done this, he said to the six brothers, 'Now I must continue on my way.'

The brothers pleaded with him and begged him to stay, saying, 'You may sit on our throne and rule our kingdom,' but the prince would not accept. 'No,' he said, 'I have set out to win the hand of Princess Gulandama, and I must be on my way.'

'If you must go,' said the brothers, 'we can send some of our troops with you to guard you.'

But the prince refused, and told them: 'I must travel alone.'

As he was about to leave, the eldest brother pulled out a hair from his head and gave it to him. 'Whenever you are in trouble,' he said, 'and whatever the trouble may be, burn this hair, and I shall instantly come to your rescue. I have an army of attendants, and they will appear out of thin air if I give my word of command.'

The prince put the hair in his pocket and went on his way. After travelling for many months, he reached China and arrived at the city where Princess Gulandama lived. After paying a man to look after his horse, he bought an old blanket, wrapped it round himself, and inquired: 'Where do the fakirs live?'

The people pointed to the river on the outskirts of the city, and said: 'The fakirs live on the banks of that river.' The prince went and sat down with the fakirs, and asked them, 'When will Gulandama show her face?' They told him: 'She will show her face tomorrow, because it is almost a month since she last removed her veil.'

Next day the prince went into the town with the fakirs to catch a glimpse of Gulandama. Such was her beauty, when she removed her veil, that the prince became mad with love for her.

In the meantime, the hundred servants, who had been appointed to guard the prince while he was out hunting in the jungle, had been puzzled by his disappearance, and had informed the king: 'The prince pursued a deer in the jungle and was never seen again.'

'Go and find the prince at once,' ordered the king.

The guards went back to the jungle and travelled until they came to the ruined tower where the old man still sat, contemplating the statue of Gulandama. They asked the old man whether he had seen the prince.

'Yes,' he replied, 'the prince came here and saw the statue of Gulandama and fell in love with her. He has gone to China to win her hand.'

The guards asked the old man to return with them to the palace and recount what he had told them to the king. The old man accompanied them to the palace, and the king questioned him: 'Where is my son?'

The old man answered: 'Your son came to my tower because he had lost his way while out hunting. When he saw the statue of Gulandama, which I have in my possession, he fell in love with her and set off to China to win her hand.'

The king sent the old man away with a handsome reward, and ordered the hundred men of the prince's guard to go at once to China.

A month had already passed since the prince had first caught a glimpse of Gulandama, and she was about to reveal her face again. Thousands of people were moving towards the palace, and the prince joined the throng. But the prince was so strong that when he pushed with his right hand, a hundred men were knocked aside, and when he pushed with his left hand, another hundred were knocked aside. Princess Gulandama was sitting on the balcony of her palace, unveiled, watching the prince pushing thousands of people to one side or the other in his eagerness to reach the front. She said to herself: 'I must find out who he is.'

When it grew late, and the princess had once again covered her face, she gave a tray to one of her maidservants, and said to her: 'Go to the bazaar and ask the young men what tokens of love they are willing to offer me, so that I can tell how many of them are rich and how many are poor.'

This servant had such a good memory that she was able to remember the profession and the gift of each of the princess's suitors. The prince had offered his ring as a gift. It had his name engraved on it, and the stone was so precious that nobody in China could afford its price. That evening, when the servant was showing her mistress the gifts, saying, 'This gift is from a shopkeeper; this from a merchant,' and so on, the princess noticed the ring and asked, 'Who gave this?'

The servant answered: 'Among your suitors there is a fakir, and it belongs to him.'

'How can he be a fakir?' exclaimed the princess. 'From this ring it appears that he is a prince.'

'He may be a prince,' agreed the servant, 'but he is dressed as a fakir. Among your suitors there are many princes dressed as fakirs.'

The princess said to her servant: 'Go and give this man a message. Tell him that if there is any trouble in his kingdom, the princess is willing to send her army to assist him. Tell him to return home, and that if he requires any money, the princess will gladly offer it to him. But warn him not to imagine that if he waits, Gulandama will one day be his. Tell him that if he has this idea in his head, he is wasting his time.'

The servant went and delivered this message to the prince. He told her to convey the following reply: ' I have no need of your army or your wealth, but I need you, and one day I shall win your hand.' When the princess heard this, she thought: 'It would seem that he is a special person.'

Next day there was much agitation in the city because King Bayzad, who was also in love with Gulandama, had besieged the city with his army. People were whispering among themselves, saying that the army of Gulandama's father was too weak, and that they would be defeated, and that Gulandama would be captured. When the prince heard what the people were saying, he took out the hair that Sayfun had given him, and that night he burnt it. In the twinkling of an eye Sayfun appeared before him, and inquired, 'What can I do for you?'

The prince replied: 'King Bayzad is about to attack and destroy this city and kidnap Gulandama.'

Sayfun reassured him: 'Tonight we shall defeat his army. You wait here.' After some time Sayfun returned and told the prince, 'We have defeated King Bayzad's army and we have brought him to you alive.'

The prince then cut off King Bayzad's head and fixed it on a lance in front of the palace with an inscription.

In the morning news reached the emperor that King Bayzad's army had been vanquished in a single night, and that he would no longer have to prepare an army to face him. 'How was he defeated?' he inquired.

Those of King Bayzad's army who had survived said: 'We cannot explain how the army was defeated. At night a sudden blazing light appeared in our midst, and when it vanished, most of our men lay dead on the ground.'

The emperor suggested that a sorcerer had conquered King Bayzad's army. But nobody knew.

When the emperor's soldiers took down King Bayzad's head, they read the inscription: 'The person who destroyed King Bayzad's army is Prince Bahram.'

'He should be congratulated for having saved us,' said the emperor, when he read these words, and he gave instructions to his soldiers to search for Prince Bahram. The soldiers looked everywhere, but could not find him.

Meanwhile, the princess had summoned the fakir and had said to him: 'I order you to return to your kingdom at once. Haven't you heard what happened to King Bayzad? He came to conquer this kingdom, and to kidnap me, but Prince Bahram sent his army from the skies and destroyed him.'

The prince replied: 'No prince could have come from the skies and defeated an army such as that of King Bayzad. It is the deed of a fakir such as myself. It was I who defeated the army of King Bayzad.'

The princess laughed: 'This is not possible, you have no dagger or sword; you are just a fakir. King Bayzad was attacked by a whole army. Where is your army?'

'I will show you,' said the prince. He took the hair from his pocket and began to burn it. Sayfun appeared in a flash and stood before him, waiting for instructions. 'Go and fetch the army that defeated King Bayzad and his men.' The prince had no sooner uttered these words than a vast army had appeared out of thin air, accompanied by Sayfun's sister, Sarasa, and his wife, Rueh Afza.

'What can I do for you?' asked Sayfun.

'Go to the emperor,' replied the prince, 'and ask him if I may marry his daughter.'

When Sayfun went to the emperor with the prince's proposal of marriage, accompanied by his wife and sister, the emperor replied: 'My daughter refuses to marry. You had better let her answer for herself.'

So Sarasa and Rueh Afza went to the princess, and said to her: 'Will you marry Prince Bahram?'

'Who are you?' asked the princess.

'We are his sister and sister-in-law,' they replied.

The princess said: 'My father is a widower. If Sarasa is willing to marry him, I will agree to marry Prince Bahram.'

So Sarasa and Rueh Afza returned and delivered the princess's message to Prince Bahram. When he heard it, he said: 'Sarasa is my sister, but she is not there to be given in exchange for the princess.'[1]

Sayfun then spoke: 'Give us your word of command, and we shall kill the emperor and kidnap the princess.'

'No,' said the prince, 'we must not harm them.'

'Then there is no alternative but for Sarasa to marry the emperor,' concluded Sayfun.

And thus it happened that Prince Bahram married Gulandama and Sarasa married the Emperor of China. The prince returned to his father's kingdom, and he and his wife led a happy life together.

How Gulandama Was Kidnapped by Toroban

There was a *deo* named Toroban who was in love with the Princess Gulandama. Prince Bahram had been married to Gulandama for four years when Toroban entered the palace and carried her away by force. At that moment the prince was in the mosque performing his prayers.

The prince fainted from shock on hearing the news. When he recovered his senses, he went to the king, his father, and told him, 'Toroban the *deo* has kidnapped my wife, and I am going in search of her.'

'Forget her,' said his father. 'You can marry another woman.'

'No,' answered the prince, 'I will not rest until I find her.'

The king gave his consent and offered his son some advice: 'If you go and meet the fairy Badrijamala, she may know where Toroban has taken your wife.'

The prince left his father's kingdom, and travelled for three months until he reached the garden where the *jinn* Sayfun and his brothers lived. Sayfun was disturbed to see the prince in such poor health, and said to him: 'You look weak and pale. What troubles you?'

The prince answered: 'Toroban has kidnapped my wife.'

'You wait here,' said Sayfun, 'while I go with my brothers to look for her.'

Sayfun left with his five brothers, and they searched for six months, but could not find the princess. So they returned home and told the prince, 'We have failed in our mission.' The prince thanked them and went on his way.

After travelling for two months, he met a large crow sitting on a tree. 'Peace be upon you,' he said to the bird.

'And peace be upon you also,' replied the crow. 'Who are you, traveller? Where have you come from? And what troubles you?'

The prince recounted how his wife had been kidnapped by Toroban the *deo*, and how he had set out in search of her, but still had not found her.

'Don't worry,' said the crow. 'I have six million friends at my service, and I shall order them to go in search of the princess.'

The crow and his friends set out to look for the princess. They searched for six months, but could not find her. So they returned and told the prince, 'We have failed in our mission.'

The prince then said to the crow: 'Please take me to the fairy Badrijamala, the wife of Sayf al-Mulk.'

'Wait until my friends have finished eating,' answered the large crow. When the crows had eaten, he ordered them to take the prince to the fairy Badrijamala.

The prince sat on the back of one of the crows, and a guard of five hundred other crows accompanied him to the garden where Badrijamala lived. They dropped the prince in the garden and returned home. No sooner had his feet touched the ground than Sayf al-Mulk appeared before him and spoke in an angry voice: 'Traveller, what brings you to this garden? Leave at once, or I shall finish you off with one stroke of my sword.'

'I am your guest,' said Prince Bahram. 'Why do you wish to kill me?'

'Who are you?' inquired Sayf al-Mulk.

'I am Prince Bahram,' he replied.

Sayf al-Mulk embraced him and invited him home. He introduced him to Badrijamala: 'This is my brother and friend Prince Bahram.' She was very pleased, and set about preparing food for her guest.

Then Badri said to Bahram: 'We heard that you married Gulandama. Did she bear you a son?'

The moment Bahram heard his wife's name, he began to weep, and told them, 'Toroban Deo has kidnapped my wife and I cannot find them.'

When Sayf al-Mulk heard this, he was filled with grief. 'If I were young,' he said, 'I would search the four corners of the earth and find her for you.'

'Don't worry,' said Badrijamala, 'I will search the four corners of the earth.'

Next morning Badri departed in her quest for the princess. She searched without ceasing for six months, but could find no trace of either Gulandama or Toroban. So she decided to return home, feeling extremely sad that she had been unable to help Bahram.

While she was passing through a forest, she met an old man who asked her: 'Why do you look so troubled? What makes you so sad?'

Badri answered: 'Toroban has kidnapped the wife of Prince Bahram, who is my husband's brother, and I cannot find them. I have searched the whole world.'

'Don't worry, Badri,' said the old man. 'I shall tell you where they are.' He continued: 'I was standing here in this forest when Toroban and Gulandama flew past. He was taking her to Mount Qaf. It is the highest mountain in the world and no one can reach its summit. Even if you did manage to reach the summit, Toroban's fort is impregnable. He is the king of the *deo*s and it is impossible to defeat him.'

Badri thanked the old man and set out on the long journey to Mount Qaf. When she finally reached the summit, she saw people there who were from her own tribe, and she said to herself: 'The old man told me that only *deo*s live here; he didn't tell me that I would find people of my own tribe. I'll go and ask them for help.'

She went and sat on the garden wall of one of their houses, and when the fairies saw her, the word soon passed round: 'Badrijamala is here.' She looked very pretty, for she was wearing a garland of flowers that had been gathered in her husband's garden. They all wanted to invite her into their houses, but Badri said firmly: 'I shall not come down and sit with you until you go and call your king.' So they all went and called the king.

When the King of the Fairies appeared, he said: 'Come down, Badri, and tell us what we can do for you.'

'Tell me,' she inquired, 'where is the kingdom of the *deo*s?'

'The *deo*s live on the other side of our kingdom,' replied the king.

Badri explained the purpose of her visit: 'Toroban, the king of the *deo*s, has kidnapped the wife of my husband's brother. How can I discover where he has hidden her?'

The king gave orders to five of his people: 'Go and find out where the Princess Gulandama is held captive.'

The five fairies flew to the kingdom of the *deo*s and sat on the wall of Toroban's fort. They saw that Gulandama had been locked up in an iron cage. They shouted to her: 'Gulandama, Badrijamala has come in search of you. Tell us what we should say to her?'

Gulandama answered: 'If she has really come in search of me, tell her to come to me herself.'

The five fairies returned and told Badri: 'Gulandama is alive and locked up in an iron cage. She is as beautiful as ever, and wants you to go and see her.'

'Please take me to her,' said Badri, 'but go slowly, because I have been travelling for two and a half years and I'm tired.'

They took Badri to Gulandama. The five fairies waited on the wall while Badri flew down and alighted on the cage. For some time she searched for the cage door, so that she could open it and take Gulandama back to Bahram.

'What are you looking for?' asked Gulandama. 'Hurry up,' she warned, 'because if Toroban comes, you won't even have a chance to talk to me.'

'I'm looking for the cage door,' replied Badri.

Gulandama then inquired: 'How long did it take you to come here?'

'Two and a half years,' replied the fairy.

'Toroban is so swift and cunning that he brought me here in one night,' said Gulandama. 'You see now that it is not so easy for me to escape; otherwise I would have run away long ago. Nobody but Bahram can save me. He is known all over the world for his bravery, so much so that when a child cries, the mother says, "Hush, hush, Bahram will come!" Even Toroban the *deo* is afraid of him. Please give this ring to him.'

Badri took the ring and returned with it to Prince Bahram. Bahram then mustered his father's troops and joined forces with Sayfun and Sayf al-Mulk. The three armies, supported by an army of crows, set out on the long journey to Mount Qaf. When they reached the mountain, an army of fairies joined them, and they waged a mighty war against the *deo*s. With the help of the crows, Bahram was able to enter Toroban's fort.

During the battle many were slain, including eighty thousand fairies and one of Badrijamala's own sons. Sayfun sent an urgent message to Bahram, who was inside the fort: 'Come quickly, we have lost the battle.' Bahram had already slain Toroban, and was considering how to set Gulandama free, when he received the message. So he ordered the crows to carry him at once to the battle-front. They took him and dropped him in the midst of the fighting. He was so strong that he fought with a sword in each hand. With each stroke of the sword he killed thirty or forty *deo*s, and in a short space of time he killed most of the *deo*s and the battle was won. The few *deo*s that survived ran for their lives.

Bahram gave all the treasure that he had taken from Toroban to the King of the Fairies, and returned home with his wife.

27

Hazrat Ali Sahib

One day the Prophet of God, Hazrat Muhammad, peace be upon him, was sitting on his prayer-mat in the mosque, and his four chief companions were standing behind him.[1] The Prophet turned his head towards Hazrat Ali Sahib, and said to him: 'There is an unbeliever who is the leader of a tribe in Khyber. Go and convert him to Islam. If he refuses to become a Muslim, then you may kill him.[2]

When the Holy Prophet had finished speaking, Hazrat Ali Sahib mounted his horse and rode to Khyber with his army. Upon his arrival, he sent a message to the unbeliever: 'Embrace Islam, or prepare for a holy war.'

When the unbeliever received the message, he held council with his friends, and they advised him: 'You have nothing to fear: you are a champion, and you have a large army to back you. So prepare for war.'

Next morning the two armies confronted each other on the battlefield. They fought all day and many unbelievers perished. In the evening the infidels withdrew to their fort for the night. Next morning they sallied forth once again, and their leader said to Hazrat Ali: 'Today I shall compete with you in single combat and only one of us will leave the battlefield alive.'

'As you please,' answered Hazrat Ali, 'but make haste.'

Both men were equally matched in strength. When the unbeliever charged at Hazrat Ali with his sword, the latter protected himself with his shield, and when Hazrat Ali retaliated, the unbeliever raised his shield in defence. This exchange of attacks and counter-attacks occurred four times. In the fifth round Hazrat Ali lost his temper. He leapt from his horse on to his opponent's horse, seized him round the waist, and shouted: 'Repeat after me, "There is no God but Allah and Muhammad is the Messenger of Allah,"[3] or prepare to die at the point of my sword.' The unbeliever still refused to become a Muslim, so Hazrat Ali slew him with his sword.

They say that when the leader of an army dies, his followers become cowards and flee. When these infidels saw that their leader had been killed, they all fled from the battlefield.

Now the unbeliever had a beautiful daughter named Khyberay, who was stronger and more skilled in the art of war than her father. After receiving news of her father's death, she sent a message to Hazrat Ali: 'Do not leave. Tomorrow I shall meet you on the battlefield to avenge my father's death.'

When Hazrat Ali received the message, he thought to himself: 'It would suit me better if she could come and wage war at once.' But since she was a woman, he could not go to her house and challenge her to a fight. So he had to be patient, and that evening he lay down, covered himself with a sheet, and went to sleep.

Next morning Khyberay arrived on the battlefield at the head of a large army. When she saw Hazrat Ali, she thought to herself: 'He is a young man. Therefore, if I compete with him in single combat, and he approaches me, he will become nervous, and I shall be able to kill him.' Then she turned to Hazrat Ali, and said: 'We shall not use swords; instead we shall wrestle hand to hand.'

'I am ready to fight in whatever way you wish,' he replied.

They began to wrestle hand to hand, and each time Hazrat Ali picked up Khyberay and threw her on the ground, she dug her feet into the earth up to her knees, so that he wasted much of his strength pulling her out. Every time she threw him to the ground, he also dug his feet into the earth up to his knees, so that she wasted much of her strength pulling him out. They continued to wrestle in this manner for a long time until the hard earth of the battlefield became as soft as sand. So much dust was raised by the combatants that people could no longer stand and watch.

They say that there were only two occasions when Hazrat Ali appealed to God for strength. This was the second. The first was when he had met an old woman by the roadside with a basket of cotton. The basket contained only four *seers* of cotton and appeared to be very light, but when the old woman asked Hazrat Ali to help her place the basket on her head, he was unable to lift it, even though he used 200 *maunds* of strength, because, to test him, God, in His omnipotence, had made the basket so heavy that it contained the weight of the whole world.

'My dear boy,' said the old woman, 'if you cannot lift the basket, leave it.'

'Respected mother, I shall try a second time and, by the grace of God, I shall lift it.' Having said this, he applied 400 *maunds* of strength, but still he could not lift the basket. 'Move aside,' he said, dismounting from his horse, 'this basket possesses some supernatural power.' But after applying all his strength, he was only able to lift the basket to his knees.

At that moment God spoke to him: 'Place the basket on the ground immediately. I was merely testing your strength.'

Hazrat Ali was disappointed. 'God, I wish you had blessed me with more strength,' he said, 'so that I could have lifted that basket with one hand.'

Now, while Hazrat Ali was wrestling with Khyberay, he thought: 'What prevents me from overpowering her? She must possess some supernatural power.' Foreseeing that she would defeat him, he cried in a loud voice, 'Allahu Akbar, God is Great!' So mighty and loud was the cry that many of the city ramparts collapsed and many pregnant women miscarried through fear. After this shout, Khyberay lost her strength and began to tremble, and Hazrat Ali picked her up once again and threw her to the ground with great force. At that moment she admitted defeat, and he asked her, 'Which do you choose, Islam or death?'

The girl answered: 'Don't imagine that you defeated me through your own strength; you defeated me with the cry of "Allahu Akbar". I shall declare my faith in Islam, but you must teach me what to say, and when I have done so, you must marry me.'

'I cannot marry you,' protested Hazrat Ali, 'I already have many wives.'[4] But Khyberay caught him by the hand and said, 'You must come home with me.'

Hazrat Ali went to her house and they were married. After several days he took leave of her: 'I must return home now. The Holy Prophet will be waiting for me.'

'All right,' she agreed, 'but I don't know when we shall meet again. Perhaps you could give me a token of remembrance.'

Hazrat Ali had a handkerchief in his pocket and a ring on his finger with his name engraved on it. These were the only spare things that he carried. The ring was so valuable that it was worth more than Khyberay's kingdom, and it was very special because it fitted whichever finger it was placed on. Hazrat Ali gave the handkerchief and the ring to Khyberay, and then returned to Arabia.

A year passed, and Khyberay gave birth to HazratAli's son. She thought: 'If I were able to send a message to Hazrat Ali, informing him of the good news, he could give the baby a name.'

They say that when a son is born, the men should name the child, and when a daughter is born, the women should name the child. So Khyberay summoned the barber, and said to him: 'Go to the blessed city of Medina and ask for Hazrat Ali. When you meet him, tell him that in Khyber a son has been born to him, and ask him to give the child a name.'

The barber left for Medina, and as soon as he arrived, he asked one of the citizens, 'Where can I find Hazrat Ali, the Prophet's companion?'

The man answered: 'He travels abroad most of the time, waging war against the unbelievers, but when he is in Medina, he can always be found in the mosque.'

When the barber entered the mosque, he saw the Holy Prophet, peace be upon him, seated on his prayer-mat. His four chief companions, Hazrat Umar, Hazrat Abu Bakr, Hazrat Uthman and Hazrat Ali, were sitting behind him. The barber immediately recognized Hazrat Ali from Khyberay's description of him. He gave his salaams to the assembled company, and then quietly approached and sat down beside Hazrat Ali, and whispered in his ear: 'In Khyber a son has been born to you, and the mother has sent me as a messenger to report the good news and to ask you to give him a name.'

Hazrat Ali was very pleased to hear the news. He turned his face to the Holy Prophet, and said: 'Respected Prophet, please suggest a name for my son.'

The Prophet answered: 'I give him the name of Muhammad Hanifah, and may God grant him the strength of a hundred men.'

Hazrat Ali entertained the barber with great hospitality. Then the barber took his leave and returned home to Khyber, and told Khyberay, 'You must name your son Muhammad Hanifah.'

Time passed, and Muhammad Hanifah grew up to be a strong young boy. One day, while he was playing, he and another boy started quarrelling. The boy slapped his face, so he took hold of the hand with which the boy had slapped him and pulled it off. Then he slapped him back with the hand with which he had been slapped. At this the boy began to cry and ran to his parents, saying, 'You are a bastard; you don't have a father; and I'll tell my parents to kill you.'

Muhammad Hanifah went and stood by his mother, and said: 'Mother, one of the boys called me a bastard and said I had no father. Is that true? If not, tell me, where is my father?'

Khyberay looked at her son and saw that he was covered in blood. 'My son,' she said, 'your father is alive, but he lives far away, and even if I were to tell you who he is, you would not be able to meet him.'

'Where does he live?' asked Hanifah.

She answered: 'He lives in the blessed city of Medina, and he is as well known in those parts as the moon which lights the night sky.'

'I shall go and meet him,' said Hanifah, 'so I can see for myself whether what you say is true.'

Khyberay tried to reason with him: 'You cannot go: you are young and some harm may come to you on the way.'

'I will go,' said Hanifah, 'and if what you say is a lie and I don't find him, I shall return to kill you.'

'If you insist, you may go,' said Khyberay, 'but take this handkerchief and this ring which once belonged to your father.' She put the handkerchief in her son's pocket in such a way that it could still be seen, and placed the ring on his finger.

When Hanifah reached Medina, he was very hungry. The only crop cultivated in that region was the fruit of the date palm, and palm trees grew on all sides. Now it so happened that on that day Hazrat Ali had gone out with his sons Hasan and Husayn, and had told them to stand under a palm tree while he climbed up and threw down some dates. When Hanifah saw dates dropping from the tree under which the two boys were standing, he went up to them and, holding their hands behind their backs with one hand, began eating the dates with the other.

'Father, father,' cried Hasan and Husayn, 'this stranger has eaten all the dates you threw down, and he wouldn't allow us to eat any.'

'Stranger, you are welcome to eat some dates,' shouted Hazrat Ali, 'but you must also allow the children to eat some.'

As there were no more dates on the ground, Hanifah released the children. But as soon as Hazrat Ali dropped more dates to the ground, he again held the children with one hand and ate the dates with the other. Once again the children screamed and complained to their father. So Hazrat Ali climbed down the tree, and said to Hanifah: 'I did not forbid you to eat the dates, but I told you to share them with my sons.'

Hanifah answered: 'When your sons reach home, they will receive more food to eat, but do you know how many days I have gone without food?'

Hazrat Ali threw his hands in the air: 'How do I know how many days you have gone without food?'

Hanifah imitated Hazrat Ali's gesture, and again protested: 'Your sons will be fed at home, but I don't know when I shall get my next meal. So stand aside and let me eat.'

'Who is this young man who dares speak to me with such impertinence?' thought Hazrat Ali, and he gave Hanifah a slap. The slap was so powerful that, had another man been in his place, he would have been buried in the ground. But the slap had no effect upon Hanifah, who gave a slap in reply. At this Hazrat Ali was filled with rage. He picked up Hanifah and threw him on the ground, and when he was on the ground, he knelt on his chest and raised his hand to kill him. To protect himself from the blow, Hanifah lifted the palms of his hands. During the struggle the ring had turned round, so that the engraving of Hazrat Ali's name now faced him.

'Who are you?' asked Hazrat Ali, when his eye fell on the ring.

'You do not know me,' said Hanifah.

'Where do you come from?'

'From Khyber,' he replied.

Hazrat Ali thought to himself: 'With the slap that I gave him I could have flattened a mountain, and I threw him on the ground with equal force. His bones must surely be smashed to pieces.' So he quickly rose to his feet. As soon as he did so, Hanifah also leapt to his feet.

'Are you injured?' asked Hazrat Ali.

'No, I'm all right,' replied Hanifah.

Hazrat Ali now knew for certain that this was his son Hanifah. So he lifted him lovingly on to his shoulders and held Hasan and Husayn by each hand and took them home.

When the mother of Hasan and Husayn saw them returning home, she said to herself: 'This must be the son of one of my husband's other wives,' and she was filled with jealousy because he was carrying Hanifah on his shoulders, whereas her own children were walking; and the pressure of her jealousy was so great that her head split in two. Hazrat Ali immediately put Hanifah down, and placing one hand on each side of his wife's head, he pressed the two parts together again. The head was in good shape, but the join remained in the middle. It is said that women part their hair in the middle in remembrance of this event.

Hazrat Ali said to his wife: 'You have no reason to be jealous. This is my son Hanifah. He is a brave boy, and if anyone attempts to harm your sons, he will protect them and take revenge on their behalf.' Then, after begging God to forgive him for striking his own son, he went to the mosque to recite some prayers of thanksgiving. He was grateful to God that Hanifah had arrived safely. If he had fallen into the hands of the unbelievers, he would undoubtedly have been put to death, for in those days the unbelievers were ruthless.

Hazrat Ali remained absent for four or five days. When he returned, he told Hanifah: 'This is your house. You may eat, drink, and do as you please, but do not go far from here. If you do, you must ask my permission.'

Hazrat Abu Bakr and Hazrat Uthman both had two sons, and they used to play with Hanifah. One day, while the five of them were on their way to the mosque, they said to Hanifah: 'The jungle near here is an excellent place for hunting. Our fathers do not allow us to go there, but since you are a guest, Hazrat Ali will give you his permission.'

So Hanifah went and spoke to his father: 'I wish to obtain your permission to go hunting.'

Hazrat Ali bent his head and thought: 'I have many enemies who are unbelievers, and if any of them chanced to meet my son in the jungle, they would surely kill him. Yet I cannot refuse because he is a guest. I shall therefore entrust him to God's care.' So he said: 'You can go, but take your friends with you.'

'What did he say to you?' asked Hanifah's friends, as they were returning from the mosque.

'He has given his permission,' replied Hanifah, 'and has asked me to take all of you with me.'

The five young men mounted their horses and started on their way.

Meanwhile, Hazrat Ali summoned his slave, and said to him: 'The boys have gone out hunting. You too must accompany them, lest the unbelievers try to do them some mischief.' The slave hurried out of the mosque and joined the young men. With him the hunting party was now six.

In the jungle where they wished to hunt there was a princess named Zaytun, who was the daughter of the King of Haram.[5] This girl was renowned for her beauty, and she had reserved the jungle for herself. She and her forty companions used to go to the jungle in the morning and return home in the evening. If they caught any man in the jungle, they would ask him to drop his weapons and leave the jungle at once. If he did not obey promptly, they would put him to death.

When Hanifah and his five friends entered the jungle, they met the princess and her forty companions. 'How dare you enter my jungle!' said the princess. 'Drop your weapons, give me your horses, and leave my jungle immediately.'

'It would be cowardly of me to hand over my horse and weapons,' answered Hanifah. 'As long as I live, I shall refuse to do so. Besides,' he added, 'the jungle belongs to all men, and everyone has a right to hunt here.'

The princess grew angry and struck him with her sword, but Hanifah warded off the blow with his shield and the sword broke. Then she raised her spear, which was fifty feet long, and hurled it at his chest. It pierced his chest and he fell to the ground. Then her forty companions said to Hanifah's friends: 'Leave your horses and weapons and go on your way, or else you will meet the same fate.'

The slave had meanwhile concealed himself behind a tree, and when he saw what had happened, he rode away as fast as he could and hid deep in the jungle. As Hanifah's friends refused to hand over their weapons, they were captured and bound up in ropes. Thinking that Hanifah was dead, the princess left him lying where he was.

Zaytun returned triumphantly to her father, and told him: 'I have killed the son of Hazrat Ali and captured his friends. If you give me your permission, I shall go to Medina and seize Hazrat Ali, and have him locked up with the other four prisoners, so that they can all be hanged together.'

'Congratulations!' exclaimed the king. 'You have performed a brave deed which will make me famous among the unbelievers. If you really have the power to capture Hazrat Ali and bring him here, you must go at once.'

As soon as the princess and her companions had left the jungle, the slave came out of hiding, and thought: 'I shall rub Hanifah's hands and feet for some time, and if he does not revive, I shall carry him home to his father.' So he approached Hanifah, who still lay unconscious on the ground, and rubbed his hands and feet. The young man sat up. 'What happened to me?' he inquired. 'Why was I lying on the ground?'

The slave explained: 'The princess Zaytun struck you with her spear, and you fell to the ground. She thought that you were dead, but you had only been knocked unconscious. Your friends are now her prisoners, and she plans to execute them.'

'We must return home at once,' said Hanifah.

When Hanifah arrived at Hazrat Ali's house in Medina, he discovered that his mother, Khyberay, had also just arrived, and when she saw her son, she asked the slave: 'What have you done with my son? When he left Khyber, he was as fresh as a flower, and now he is pale and all covered in mud. Did you feed him properly? Did you burden him with too much work?'

After the slave had finished recounting what had happened in the jungle, Khyberay addressed her son: 'Your father is renowned for his courage. In every corner of the world, people tremble at his name. Yet you lost to a woman with a single spear and allowed your friends to be taken captive. It would have been better had you died fighting.'

Hearing these words, Hanifah was filled with indignation, and said to the slave: 'Bring me a horse and a sword.' Then, before departing, he turned to the slave and said: 'I swear upon my life, in the name of Allah, that I shall not return to Medina until I have rescued my four friends, and I swear not to leave a single stone standing in the city of Haram. Tell my mother to pray to God to give me strength.'

When the slave reported these words to Hanifah's mother, she thought to herself: 'He is only a young man; I had better help him in his struggle with the unbelievers.' So she set out in the same direction as her son. But no sooner had she entered the jungle than she came face to face with the princess Zaytun.

'You are trespassing on my land,' said the princess. 'Drop your weapons, give me your horse, and leave the jungle immediately.'

Khyberay answered as her son had done: 'The jungle belongs to all men, and everyone has a right to come here. As long as I live, you will not strip me of my weapons.'

Hearing this, Zaytun struck at her with her sword, but Khyberay warded off the blow with her shield, and the sword broke. So Zaytun hurled her spear at Khyberay. It pierced her and she fell to the ground.

'Bind her hands and feet,' said Zaytun to her followers, 'and tie her to the back of my horse. We shall drag her behind us all the way to Medina, and she will be dead by the time we arrive.' They bound Khyberay's hands and feet with ropes, and tied her to the back of Zaytun's horse.

Meanwhile, Hanifah, who had travelled by a different route, arrived at the same spot. Seeing his mother, he rode up to her, unsheathed his sword, and severed the ropes that bound her.

'Young man,' cried Zaytun, 'you had no right to set free my prisoner.'

'This is not your prisoner,' replied Hanifah. 'This is my mother, and you have wounded her. You will suffer for this.'

Zaytun recognized him, and said: 'You are the same young man whom I struck down with my spear yesterday, and now you have the audacity to confront me again.'

'You were lucky then,' he said, 'but now we shall see who is the winner.' And while she was still preparing to make a charge, he rode up to her, caught her round the waist, and hurled her to the ground. Then he ordered Zaytun's companions to drop their weapons. When they had obeyed his order, he approached his mother and examined her wound. This sight so filled him with anger that he returned to where Zaytun had fallen, and would have killed her had his mother not intervened: 'Don't kill her. Ask her to embrace Islam, and then you can marry her and she will be my daughter.'

Hanifah turned to Zaytun, and asked, 'Are you willing to embrace Islam?'

'Yes,' she answered, 'but you must teach me how to declare my faith.'

He told her to repeat, 'There is no God but Allah, and Muhammad is the Messenger of Allah.'

She repeated the profession of faith and became a Muslim. Then Hanifah turned to his mother and saw blood flowing from her wound, and again he wanted to kill Zaytun, but his mother cried: 'Don't kill her. She will be your wife and my daughter.'

'But what shall we do with her?' asked Hanifah.

'We shall take her back with us to Medina,' replied his mother.

'I cannot come with you,' said Hanifah. 'I have sworn, in the name of Allah, to rescue my friends and to reduce the city of Haram to dust.' Then he thought: 'My mother will be all alone with these forty-one women, and they may try to kill her.' So he said to his mother: 'Before sending you to Medina with these women, I shall tie their hands behind their backs.'

'No,' said his mother. 'They have all embraced Islam, and they will do me no harm. But if you tie up their hands and our enemies see us, they are likely to do us some mischief.'

'Mother, I'm going a long way away,' insisted Hanifah, 'and I don't know when I shall return, and if I don't bind their hands, I shall be worried about your safety.' So he tied their hands behind their backs and sent them on their way to Medina, and he himself rode towards the city of Haram.

Now it so happened that a Jewish king had fallen in love with Zaytun. He had asked Zaytun's father for her hand in marriage, but he had replied that his daughter was free to marry the man of her choice. So the Jewish king often used to come to the jungle

251

with the intention of kidnapping Zaytun, and once a year he would do battle with her. He had already fought with her twice and had been defeated on both occasions, and now it was the third time that the king lay in wait with his army. He saw Khyberay, followed by Zaytun and her companions with their hands tied behind their backs, and he immediately recognized Zaytun and she recognized him. He rode up to Khyberay and inquired: 'Who are these women whom you have tied up?'

'This is the daughter of the King of Haram,' replied Khyberay, 'and these are her companions. My son has just defeated her in battle and she has become a Muslim. I am taking her to Medina, and she will be my son's bride and my daughter.'

'I have been in love with her for many years,' said the Jewish king, 'and I have spent a lot of money pursuing her, and today I find her as a captive. Leave her with me and go on your way.'

'That is out of the question,' replied Khyberay. So he smote her on the head with his sword and she fell from her horse.

Khyberay then prayed to God: 'O Allah! Do not let me die in this jungle. At least give me the strength to reach Medina and die there, because if I were to die in the jungle at the hands of a Jewish king, Hazrat Ali's good reputation would be sullied.' God granted her prayers: there was a hurricane, and the sky grew dark, and God sent the angel Gabriel to carry Khyberay swiftly to Medina. All this occurred within the blink of an eye.

The Jewish king took Zaytun and her companions to his kingdom, and ushered them graciously into a magnificent palace built of glass.

'Now you must marry me,' he said, addressing Zaytun.

'You can go and bury yourself,' she replied. 'I shall never marry you. If my hands were free, I would punish your insult.'

The king pleaded with her, but his words made no impression upon her, so he grew angry and told his guards: 'Take the princess and her companions, and lock them up in prison.' The guards took Zaytun and her companions and threw them into prison, but in their haste, they forgot to deprive them of their swords.

Feeling dejected, the Jewish king went and sat in hisgarden. An old woman was tending the flowers, and the king told her, 'Go and fetch me some water, I'm thirsty.'

'You are very angry and your body is hot,' replied the old woman. 'If you drink cold water, it will do you harm. Instead I shall go and milk the cow and bring you some fresh milk.'

'It doesn't matter what it is, but bring it quickly,' said the king.

So the old woman went to fetch some milk. But when she felt the milk, she was surprised to find that it was cold. She therefore decided to heat it before bringing it to the king. While she was sitting by the fire, warming up the milk, she fell asleep, and in her sleep God showed her a vision of heaven and hell.

The Prophet Muhammad was seated on his throne, surrounded by angels. He was sending the good people to heaven and the unbelievers to hell. When her turn came, the angels bound her arms in chains of fire. 'Take me to the Prophet,' she said, 'I shall tell him that I have done no wrong.' When she was brought before the Prophet, the latter addressed her as follows: 'Your sins will be forgiven on condition that you promise to free the forty-one women imprisoned by your king, and on condition that you change your faith and become a Muslim.' Hearing this, the old woman recited the words 'There is no God but Allah, and Muhammad is the Messenger of Allah,' and promised to set the women free.

At that moment the old woman awoke, and there was neither heaven nor hell, but she said to herself: 'I have promised the Holy Prophet to free those women, and I must keep my promise. First I shall have to kill this king.' She pushed her finger through the skin of cream that had formed on top of the milk, and put some poison through the hole. Then she stirred the milk with a twig of the deodar tree, and took it to the king. The king drank it and died instantly. Then she went to the prison and said to Zaytun: 'I am going to untie you and set you free, so prepare to do battle.'

When the old woman untied Zaytun and her companions, there was much noise and excitement. The king's guards heard the noise and rushed to the prison to try to prevent the prisoners from escaping, but Zaytun cut off the head of every guard who approached, and her companions did the same, and in this way about nine hundred men were killed. Zaytun and her companions were now free to make their escape. As the old woman had joined them, they now numbered forty-two.

After travelling some distance, Zaytun turned and addressed her companions: 'I wish to propose a plan of action, and I want your frank opinion about it. Instead of going to Medina, which is very far from here, we should return to the city of Haram and help my husband to defeat my father, for my husband is very young and my father's army is very powerful.' Her companions all agreed with the plan, so they set out for the city of Haram.

Hanifah, in the meantime, had already reached the city of Haram and had sent a message to the king: 'I have come to rescue my friends. So prepare for war.' Having received this message, Zaytun's father commanded his army to repel the enemy. Without the help of an army, Hanifah fought alone until dusk, killing many of the king's men. The survivors returned to the city. Next day the king's army sallied forth once again, and again they fought until dusk. Many more of the king's men were slain, and the survivors withdrew into the city.

On the third evening the king assembled his court and sought the advice of his ministers: 'This young man has killed most of my best men, and if he continues at this rate, he will slaughter us all. We must therefore think of a trick to capture him.'

The vizier thought of a cunning trick: 'The men should return to the battlefield that same evening, and dig a pit about a hundred feet deep, and camouflage it with leaves and branches.

In the morning, when our army advances, one of our men will challenge Hanifah to compete in single combat. This man will strike at Hanifah and then run towards the pit. Knowing where the pit is, our man will be safe, but Hanifah and his horse will fall into the pit, and we shall block the opening to prevent him from escaping.'

The King of Haram was so pleased with the plan that he imagined that he had already captured Hanifah. He sent so many men to the battlefield that the pit was dug in next to no time, and many of them never had a chance to do any digging. They covered the pit with leaves and branches, and carried the earth elsewhere.

In the morning the king himself led his men into battle. He ordered his biggest and strongest warrior to hurl a spear at Hanifah and then run towards the pit. When the man struck Hanifah with his spear and fled, Hanifah galloped after him. His horse's hind legs sank into the pit, but its front legs were on solid ground, so he used all his strength to make the horse leap to safety. As the horse was leaping, he was thrown off and fell into the pit in a standing position. But he had so much strength that, as soon as his feet touched the bottom of the pit, he jumped high into the air, and by the time the unbelievers had gathered round to block the opening, he had already escaped. However, in this huge leap, he had expended so much energy that the lower half of his body beneath the navel was dead.

When the unbelievers saw him land, they retreated and fired arrows at him from a distance. Hanifah also had a bow and a quiver of arrows, and every time he fired an arrow, a hundred men were killed. He fought on like this until dusk, firing arrows in all directions. The unbelievers were amazed at the number of men he could shoot with one arrow, and wondered how they would capture him.

Suddenly, from the direction in which Hanifah had turned his face, Zaytun arrived, and he said to himself: 'I left Zaytun and her companions with their hands bound behind their backs. I wonder whether she has killed my mother, for if she has, I shall not spare her life.'

When the unbelievers saw Zaytun, they thought: 'She is the only person who is able to defeat Hanifah.' So they all dropped their weapons and went home.

Zaytun and Hanifah looked at each other for some time. She could see from his face that he had endured great suffering. His whole body was pierced by arrows. 'They have completely destroyed you,' she said; 'only your tongue is intact.'

'As long as my tongue works, and my hands work, and I still have breath in my body,' he replied, 'I will not spare the lives of any of these infidels.'

'Come,' she said, 'I shall take you home and tend your wounds.'

'Forget about my wounds. Tell me what happened after I had tied up your hands and those of your companions. How did you return to Medina? And what has become of my mother?'

After sending her companions to fetch a *charpoy*, which would serve as a stretcher, Zaytun knelt down beside Hanifah and began removing the arrows from his body. Then she said to him: 'I am now a Muslim and I shall always support you,' and she proceeded to recount her adventures from the time of her meeting with the Jewish king who waylaid them in the jungle until her arrival in the battlefield.

Meanwhile, the unbelievers approached their king, and said: 'We left Zaytun to fight Hanifah, but it appears that she has become a Muslim and is helping him.' Hearing this, the king gave orders that his daughter should be barred from entering the palace. Zaytun's companions returned with this news and brought a *charpoy* with them.

When Hanifah heard this, he said: 'Take me to King Imran and he will cure my wounds.'

18. Afghan Footsoldiers (Rattray, pl. 5)

19.   Afghan Warriors in a Cave (Atkinson, tp)

20. Chief Executioner (Rattray, pl. 14)

21. Fortress of Alimasjid and the Khyber Pass (Rattray, pl. 13)

'That is not possible,' said Zaytun. 'King Imran is an old enemy of our family, and if I accompany you, he will have us put to death. Tell me how he became your friend.'

Hanifah explained: 'He denied the truth of Islam and we fought against him. One day he fell into a well and I rescued him, and thus he became a Muslim and my friend.'

When Zaytun heard this, she agreed to take Hanifah to King Imran. They placed him on the *charpoy* and set out on the journey.

After travelling some distance, Hanifah gave a loud groan. Zaytun ordered the servants to put the bed down, and then asked, 'Why did you groan like that?'

'I did not die, nor did I fulfil my vow to save my friends, and now I don't know whether I shall ever recover and have the strength to save them.'

'Is that all that is troubling you?' asked Zaytun.

'Yes,' answered Hanifah.

Whereupon Zaytun ordered sixteen of her companions to take Hanifah to the kingdom of King Imran, while she herself returned with the other twenty-five to her father's kingdom. When she arrived, she and her companions went straight to the prison and released Hanifah's friends. However, as soon as they left the prison, they were confronted by an army of a thousand unbelievers. So she said to Hanifah's friends: 'You had better escape on your own and leave me and my companions to fight these infidels. You can slip unnoticed through the crowds and make your way back to Medina.'

Hanifah's friends escaped, but they had travelled only four or five miles when they were stopped by a regiment of unbelievers. Suspecting that they were either thieves or escaped prisoners, the soldiers seized them and locked them up in a nearby prison.

In the meantime, Zaytun and her companions fought valiantly against the army of unbelievers. Whenever she raised her sword, they scattered in all directions. Thus they escaped from the city of Haram and rode to the kingdom of King Imran. When they arrived, Hanifah inquired, 'What happened to my friends?'

'I freed them from prison,' replied Zaytun, 'but I don't know whether or not they reached Medina.'

Hanifah's health was deteriorating day by day. The best physicians in the land had been summoned to his bedside, but they could do nothing. He used to cry out in pain, and if anyone heard that cry, that person's heart was cut like a piece of wood by a saw.

One day Hanifah spoke to the people who had gathered round him: 'All of you must leave my room and let me be alone, because when I am surrounded by people, I cannot give vent to my grief. It is only by crying aloud that I shall be relieved of my burden; either my heart will break and I shall die, or else I shall recover.'

'It is difficult for us to leave you alone,' said Zaytun, 'but if you insist, we shall do as you say.' So they left the room, and Hanifah began to wail aloud.

Now it so happened that at that moment Sabspari, the daughter of the King of the Fairies, was flying over the palace with her friends. She had seen Hanifah when he was a baby in his cradle and had fallen passionately in love with him. From time to time she used to come with her friends to look at him. When she heard his cry, she said to her friends: 'I can hear a man crying in pain. Go to the palace and find out what is wrong with him.'

When the fairies entered the palace and saw Hanifah lying on the bed, they immediately recognized him. They returned to Sabspari, and said: 'It is the same young man whom you used to watch when he was a child in Khyber, and whom you were looking for today.'

When Sabspari heard this, she told them: 'Go and fetch him, and we shall take him with us to our kingdom.' The fairies picked up the bed on which Hanifah was lying and flew with it to their kingdom.

When this happened, the cries of pain ceased, and Zaytun thought that Hanifah must have died. She entered his room with King Imran, and, to her amazement, she discovered that both he and his bed had vanished. All that remained were his shoes. Imran picked up one shoe and Zaytun picked up the other, and they began beating themselves on the head and wailing in sorrow.

Then Zaytun said to King Imran: 'It is difficult for me to remain here without my husband. Tell me, should I go to Hanifah's parents or return to my father?'

Imran answered: 'A good and virtuous woman may remain a widow for a hundred years. But your husband has not died; he has simply disappeared. Be patient. Go to Medina and wait with his parents. If you receive any news of him, please inform me, and if I receive any news of him before you, I shall inform you.' Then he added: 'I shall send my guards to escort you, and you can take as much wealth as you desire.'

'I don't need more than a hundred rupees for the journey,' she replied, 'and I don't require any guards to protect me. I can protect myself.' So saying, she bade King Imran farewell.

When Zaytun reached the blessed city of Medina, she said to the old woman who was with her: 'Go to Hazrat Ali's house, and tell him that his son Hanifah defeated and captured the princess Zaytun, and made her a Muslim, and married her. Inform him of Hanifah's illness and his mysterious disappearance, and tell him that Zaytun is now outside the gates of the city and asks permission to enter his house. Otherwise, she will return to her father's kingdom.'

Soon after entering the city, the old woman met Hazrat Ali in the street. At once she guessed it was him. When they were face to face, Hazrat Ali moved aside to let her pass, and she stood where she was and addressed him: 'Are you Hazrat Ali?'

'Yes,' he replied. 'Is there something you wish to say to me?'

The old woman repeated Zaytun's message. When she told Hazrat Ali the news about Hanifah, he was very distressed and wondered what to do. They say that this occurred eight days after the death of the Prophet Muhammad, peace be upon him, and Hazrat Ali thought to himself: 'Had the Prophet been alive, I would have gone to him and he would have told me where to find my son, and I would have been able to go and rescue him.' Then he said to the old woman, 'You wait here,' and he went at once to the grave of the Holy Prophet and recited some prayers.

While Hazrat Ali was praying, the Prophet came to him in a vision, and said: 'Do not be afraid, for your son is alive. He is with a fairy princess, named Sabspari. She is in love with him and has taken him to her kingdom to cure him. Send Zaytun with some of your companions to her kingdom. The journey will take seven years and they will pass through the kingdoms of seven kings. On no account must they kill the seventh king, because his kingdom is separated from the kingdom of Sabspari by a river and he is the only person who can tell them how to cross it. They will encounter many hazards on the way, but they will arrive safely.

'Before introducing herself to Sabspari, Zaytun should put on her finest clothes and jewellery, but she must leave her head uncovered. Sabspari will say to her: "You look very beautiful, but why is it that your head is uncovered? Is it the custom in your country to go bare-headed, or do you not have a veil?" To which Zaytun should answer: "My veil is with you. You have taken it from me. If you return it to me, my head will be covered; and if you do not return it, you will be condemned on the Day of Judgement for covering your head with my veil and leaving my head uncovered."[6] Sabspari will then return Hanifah to Zaytun. But he will still be sick, and only Sabspari knows how to cure him. Therefore he should not leave the kingdom of the fairies until he has fully recovered.'

On hearing these words, Hazrat Ali thanked the Prophet, and then said to himself: 'I wonder where the old woman is.'

Meanwhile, the old woman said to herself: 'Hazrat Ali still hasn't answered my message. I shall stand and wait, and he will eventually come, even if it means waiting for a week.' So when Hazrat Ali returned, he found the old woman waiting for him.

'You are very intelligent,' he said. 'I was wondering where I would find you.'

'I knew you would definitely return,' she replied, 'because you hadn't answered my message.'

Then Hazrat Ali said to her: 'Go and tell Zaytun that I shall come to her, bringing my followers with me, and that she must go with them to the kingdom of Sabspari to find Hanifah. Tell her that a fairy princess is in love with Hanifah and has taken him to her kingdom in order to cure him.'

When the old woman reported this news, Zaytun was very pleased, and said: 'Now I shall find him, wherever he is.'

Hazrat Ali chose four hundred of his bravest followers and appointed Shahzad as their leader. 'Go with the princess Zaytun,' he commanded, 'and bring back my son Hanifah. Take care that Zaytun comes to no harm. At night you yourself must guard her tent.'

Zaytun set off to the kingdom of Sabspari, accompanied by Hazrat Ali's followers. They travelled for seven years and passed through the kingdom of seven kings, and it took one year to cross each kingdom. These seven kings were brothers.

When they reached the first kingdom, they went to the king and said: 'We are your guests and would like to spend the night here.'

He answered: 'I don't know you and you cannot spend the night here.'

So they killed him, and composed a letter from him to his brother in the neighbouring kingdom, saying: 'These people are my guests. Please entertain them with great hospitality and give them everything that they require.[7]

When they reached the neighbouring kingdom, they presented this letter of introduction to the king, and said: 'We shall have dinner and spend the night here.'

The king answered: 'Neither do we offer hospitality, nor do we receive hospitality.'

When he said this, Zaytun killed him and wrote a letter of introduction from him to his next brother. He too refused to help, and so in this way Zaytun killed six of the brothers, and they reached the kingdom of the seventh brother. Once again they presented a letter of introduction from the last brother, and the seventh king said: 'Neither do we offer hospitality, nor do we receive hospitality. But tell me, is there anything I can do for you?'

'We are going to the kingdom of Sabspari,' replied Zaytun, 'and we want you to help us cross the river.'

'How can I help you cross the river?' asked the king.

'Tell the people of your realm to collect wood and build a raft, because we know that you are skilled in this art.'

The king ordered his men to collect wood and to build a raft. When it was ready, Zaytun said to the king: 'You must also come with us.'

'No,' he answered, 'I cannot come with you, because I am at war with our neighbours and it would be dangerous for me to go.'

Zaytun explained: 'We are on our way to claim what belongs to us by right, but we do not intend to wage war.'

The king was eventually persuaded to join them, and they all climbed on to the raft. When they reached the far bank of the river, they moored the raft and pitched their tents near the water's edge.

Sabspari's father had recently died and the fairy princess now ruled the kingdom. Receiving news that some people had landed in her kingdom, Sabspari said to her vizier: 'Go to the people who have pitched their tents on the bank of our river, and ask them whether they have come to make war, so that we can prepare to meet them.'

When the vizier arrived at the encampment, Zaytun was in her tent and Shahzad was guarding her. The vizier attempted to enter Zaytun's tent without greeting Shahzad, but before he could take a single step Shahzad pulled him back and inquired, 'Who are you?'

'I am Sabspari's vizier,' he replied.

'First greet us politely and request to see Zaytun, and then we shall meet you,' said Shahzad.

So the vizier started afresh by exchanging salaams with Shahzad and then requesting to see Zaytun. Shahzad asked him to wait and went to Zaytun, and said to her: 'Sabspari's vizier has come and would like to meet you. Should I allow him to enter?'

'No,' replied Zaytun. 'First, I must change out of the male dress that I am wearing into the gorgeous clothes which Hazrat Ali gave me. I was like a man and I must become a woman again. Tell the vizier to lead the way; you follow him, and I shall walk behind you. Warn him not to look back, or else I shall cut off his head with my sword. Also tell your followers not to look at me.'

When Shahzad had left the tent, Zaytun combed her hair, perfumed her body, and put on her finest clothes and jewellery, leaving her head uncovered. Then she came out of her tent, and followed the vizier and Shahzad to Sabspari's palace. When they arrived, the fairy princess was seated on her throne. She took Zaytun by the hand and gestured to her to sit down beside her. At this point Zaytun turned to the vizier and Shahzad, and said: 'Now you can look at me with my permission.'

Then Sabspari addressed Zaytun in the manner foretold by the Prophet: 'You look very beautiful, and you are wearing such fine clothes and jewellery, but why is it that your head is uncovered? Is it the custom in your country to go bare-headed, or do you not have a veil?'

'No,' cried Zaytun, 'my veil is with you. You have taken it from me. If you return it to me, my head will be covered; and if you do not return it, you will be condemned on the Day of Judgement for covering your head with my veil and leaving my head uncovered.'

Sabspari answered: 'You must be looking for your husband. He is your veil, is he not? I kidnapped him, and brought him to my kingdom, and locked him in a dungeon; and I haven't seen him since then, because I know that if I visit him, he will cry in pain and beg me to cure him. If I cure him, I shall be dishonoured, because when he comes out, people will say that I have been keeping a lover.'

When Zaytun heard this, she began sobbing: 'Seven years have passed. He must be dead by now.'

'He is not dead, I assure you,' said the fairy princess. 'My guards have been instructed to look after him, and had he died, I would have been informed.'

Sabspari took Zaytun down to the dungeons. Hanifah was on the same bed on which he had been lying when Sabspari and her friends had carried him away. His wounds had turned septic and his whole body was swollen. Zaytun flung herself into his arms, but Sabspari took her by the arm and made her sit down: 'Don't worry, I shall cure him for you. Now that you are here, I am no longer afraid for my honour.' Then she told the vizier to go and find her the roots of a certain plant that only grew in her kingdom. When the roots were brought, Sabspari rubbed them on Hanifah's body, and she also gave him a drink made of the juice of these roots.

Day by day Hanifah's health improved. After three months of treatment, he had completely recovered, and had regained his strength and his ruddy complexion.

'Tell me whether you feel fully recovered,' said Sabspari, 'because if a single drop of pus remains in your body, you will fall ill again.'

'I feel very well,' said Hanifah.

Then Sabspari took Hanifah's hand in her right hand and Zaytun's hand in her left, and she joined them together, and said to Zaytun: 'Here is your veil. You may cover your head.'

So Hanifah, Zaytun, and Hazrat Ali's followers bade farewell to the fairies and set off on their homeward journey, accompanied by the king whose kingdom was across the river. Whenever this king passed in front of Hanifah, Hanifah would turn his face the other way.

'Why do you turn your face the other way?' asked Shahzad. 'This king has been of great service to us.'

'He is a scoundrel,' replied Hanifah, 'and you will see what tricks he will play on us as soon as we disembark on his side of the river.'

'How can you say that!' exclaimed Shahzad. 'It was he who helped us to cross the river.'

'In this too he had a purpose,' answered Hanifah.

When they reached the other bank of the river, the king held the raft while Zaytun and the followers of Hazrat Ali climbed ashore. Hanifah had one foot on the shore and the other on the raft. At that moment he drew out his sword and cut off the king's head. When both his feet were on dry land, he picked up the head and body of the dead king and threw them into the river. Shahzad rushed up to him, and asked, 'Why did you kill him?'

Hanifah explained: 'I killed him because I knew he was about to destroy the raft, and had he done so, nobody in future would have been able to cross the river, since only he would have known how to build such a boat. Now others can learn the skill of making rafts by copying this one and improving on it.'

'In that case,' said Shahzad, 'you did well to kill him.[8]

They say that the rafts that we see today are an imitation of and an improvement on the raft built by that king.

Thus they continued on their way to Medina. As they approached the wall of the city, crowds of people flocked to welcome them. Hanifah looked around him, but could not see his four friends, so he thought: 'Perhaps my friends are angry with me, since they did not come to greet me.' While this thought was running through his mind, somebody told him that his friends were still in prison. So he said to himself: 'I am glad I didn't enter Medina, otherwise I would have broken my vow.' He told Zaytun, Shahzad and the others to enter the city, while he himself rode towards the city of Haram,

He sent a message on ahead of him to the King of Haram: 'Prepare for war, for I have come to rescue my friends.' When the King of Haram received this message, he told his men: 'We shall fight with him to the death; we shall either kill him or be killed by him.'

They fought on the battlefield for three days and three nights. Once again the unbelievers had set a trap for Hanifah. They made him pursue them towards a deep ravine that they had covered over and skilfully concealed, and Hanifah and his horse fell into it. Then all the unbelievers rode up and down the edge of the ravine, shouting, 'Kill him! Kill him!'

Hanifah rode as fast as he could, but the ravine was long and deep. He travelled along it for three months, and then said to himself: 'It is too long. I shall have to turn round and ride back.' God saved him, because had he come out at the end of the ravine, the unbelievers would have killed him. He rode back down the ravine, and travelled for three months, but finding no way out, he thought that the hour of his death had come.

So he drew up his horse and prayed to God: 'O Allah, it is very difficult for me to escape from here. By some means inform my father that I am in danger, so that he will come and rescue me.'

God listened to his prayer, and through His supernatural power caused some drops of blood to appear on Hanifah's face, and these drops fell upon the face of Hazrat Ali as he lay asleep in the mosque in Medina. When he lit a match and saw that it really was blood, he suspected that his son was either dead or in serious danger. So he rose at once and mounted his favourite horse Duldul, which ran faster than the wind, and prayed to God to transport him to the battlefield where Hanifah was fighting. God granted his prayer: the horse took a leap into the air, and when it next touched the ground, he found himself in the battlefield.

'Hanifah, where are you?' he shouted.

'Father, I am in this ravine,' replied Hanifah, 'and there is no way out.'

'I shall lower my whip,' said Hazrat Ali. 'Grip your horse with your legs, and catch hold of the whip with your hands, and I shall pull you out.'

Hazrat Ali gave the whip such a tug that Hanifah and his horse landed a long way off. By the time Hanifah had reached the scene of battle, his father had slain most of the unbelievers.

'Father, what should I do?' asked Hanifah.

'My son, if there are any infidels still alive, you may kill them,' replied Hazrat Ali, 'and then you must take the lead and show me the way to the prison, so that we can rescue your friends.'

When they reached the prison, Hazrat Ali broke down the door and freed Hanifah's friends. Then he asked his son, 'What other vow did you make?'

Hanifah answered: 'I swore that I would not leave a single stone standing in the city of Haram.'

So Hazrat Ali told Hanifah to push on one side of the city, while he pushed on the other side, and with each push, a hundred walls collapsed. Thus the city of Haram was razed to the ground.

'In future,' said Hazrat Ali to his son, 'don't go anywhere without my permission.'

Hazrat Ali and Hanifah returned to Medina, and there was great rejoicing when they rejoined their wives and family.

28

The Simurgh

nce there was a gigantic bird, called the Simurgh, which nested on the emerald mountain of Qaf at the very edge of the world. Every year when she laid her eggs, and the eggs hatched, a big black cobra used to come and devour her young.[1]

This happened for many years until the bird could tolerate it no longer. So she went to the Holy Prophet, peace be upon him, and said to him: 'In my country I have an enemy who comes and devours my little ones every year. Have mercy on me and save my offspring.'

'Where have you come from?' inquired the Prophet.

'From Qaf, the furthest and highest mountain in the world,' replied the bird, 'and I have journeyed for three months to come and visit you.'

The Holy Prophet turned and addressed Hazrat Ali, the Tiger of God, who was seated beside him: 'Go with this bird, slay the serpent and return by this evening.'

So Hazrat Ali and the Simurgh set off for the mountain of Qaf. When they reached the serpent's den, the serpent caught sight of Hazrat Ali. Taking a deep breath, it swallowed him in one gulp, with his unsheathed sword still in his hand.

Hazrat Ali was trapped in the cobra's stomach, but he gave a loud cry, 'Allahu Akbar, God is Great,' and leapt out by ripping the serpent's throat with his sword. As soon as he was out, he severed the serpent's head from its body and placed it before the bird. 'Now you may live in peace,' he said.

Then the huge bird flew off and came back with the tastiest fruit that she could find on the mountain of Qaf, and placed it before Hazrat Ali as a sign of her gratitude. Hazrat Ali took the fruit with him to the holy city of Medina and distributed it there. He returned to the Prophet by that same evening as he had been instructed to do.

VI

Comedy and Farce

29

The Woodcutter

here was once a poor woodcutter who used to go to the forest every day to cut wood. He would sell the wood in the bazaar, and with what he earned he and his wife managed to make ends meet.

One evening the woodcutter had called at his friend's house, and was sitting in the guest-quarters listening to the conversation of those who had gathered there, when someone turned to him and remarked: 'It is from God's hands that we receive our daily bread, and God sends us food from heaven.'

That whole night the woodcutter pondered over these words. Finally he said to himself: 'If God sends us food from heaven, what need have I to go to the forest to earn my daily bread.' Next morning, instead of going out early to cut wood, he lay on his bed.

'It's getting late,' said his wife. 'Why are you not going out to cut wood?'

'God sends food from heaven,' replied the woodcutter. 'That's what I've been told. So why do I need to go to the forest to cut wood and carry it on my back and sell it in the bazaar?'

His wife pleaded: 'You must go, because even if I borrow money from the neighbours to buy us enough food for today, tomorrow we shall have to repay the money, and then what shall we do on the following day?'

The wife borrowed some money from the neighbours, and grumbled to herself: 'If a tenant-farmer dies, his wife does not become a widow until a year has elapsed, because she has enough stocks of food to last her for a year; whereas if a poor labourer dies, his wife becomes a widow that very evening.'

Then, once again, the woodcutter's wife addressed her husband: 'Go to the *Khan* [the lord or landowner] and beg him to give you some land. We shall cultivate it, and even if it produces nothing, at least we should be able to get a loan on it.'

The woodcutter agreed, and went to the rich landowner's guest-house. There he sat and waited. When the *Khan* entered, he stood up and said: 'Sir, you haven't asked me what I've come for.'

The *Khan* gave him two curses: 'Tell me, what have you come for?'

'I have come to beg you to give me a piece of land to cultivate,' replied the woodcutter.

The *Khan* took pity on him, and said: 'I have some fallow land near the river. Take it.'

The woodcutter had no idea what the land was like. 'What happened?' asked his wife as soon as he returned home. He answered: 'I asked the *Khan* for land to cultivate, and he has given me some land near the river. On my way back I approached various people and made inquiries about the land, and they all told me that it's very good land. It's about ten *jaribs*.'

'Hurry up. What are you waiting for?' said his wife. 'Go and borrow a pair of bullocks, and ask some men to help you to plough and cultivate the land.'

So the woodcutter asked some men to help him and asked them to lend him their bullocks. They agreed. One of them was a very clever farmer who offered him some advice. Now in those days the landlords often used to give seed to their tenants, and the tenants in return would have to give the landlord half their produce at harvest time. So the farmer said: 'Go and ask your landlord for melon seeds. If they grow well, you will have a good field of melons, and if not, then it's not written in your fate.'

The woodcutter went and obtained some melon seed from the *Khan*. Then he and his helpers ploughed the land and sowed the seed and flattened the earth with a harrow. It was a good year and there was no shortage of rain; and the woodcutter had such a big crop of water-melons that it was unbelievable. Every day he went out early in the morning and returned late in the evening. The whole day would be spent supervising the work on the land.

One day he announced to his wife: 'We must go and live on the land, because it is a long way for me to travel each day.' So they built a wooden hut and began living on the land. Everybody used to come and buy melons from them, and they would earn between ten and twenty rupees a day. But they spent all the money and saved nothing.

One day the *Khan* was informed by one of his friends that his land near the river had produced a large crop of melons. So he thought to himself: 'I shall take half the produce of the land and the woodcutter can keep the other half, as is the custom between landlords and tenants.' He called the woodcutter and told him: 'You can give me half the produce of the land which you have cultivated.'

The woodcutter did not know that this was the custom. He and his wife had already sold half the melons and had spent the proceeds. They had saved nothing. The woodcutter was very worried, but his wife said to him: 'Go and fetch a donkey and two or three sacks. We shall put five to ten melons in these sacks, and you can take them to the king. If the king is pleased, he will give you a handsome reward. You can then give some of this money to the *Khan*, and we shall keep the rest.'

So the woodcutter left his house and went to the donkey-keeper, and said: 'I would like to borrow a donkey.'

'What will you do with it?' asked the donkey-keeper.

'I wish to take a gift to the king,' he replied.

The donkey-keeper lent him a donkey and some sacks. The woodcutter returned to his orchard and chose ten of his best melons. He placed them carefully in the sacks, loaded them on the donkey's back, and took them to the king. He did not know the king's name, nor had he ever seen his face.

The king had gone for a walk and was just returning when he saw the woodcutter approaching the palace. The top of the woodcutter's head was bald through years of carrying wood on his head.

'Tell me, baldhead,' shouted the king, 'what are you carrying on your donkey?'

'Are you blind? Can't you see that I am carrying a gift?' replied the woodcutter, little suspecting that he was addressing the king.

'Who is the gift for?' asked the king.

'For the king, of course,' answered the woodcutter.

Then the king inquired: 'Why are you taking a gift to the king?'

'I'm a poor man,' he replied, 'and if the king is pleased with my gift, he may give me a reward.'

'Suppose he doesn't give you a reward?' suggested the king.

The woodcutter cursed aloud and boasted: 'I'll give him a good thrashing.'

All this time the king had been walking behind the woodcutter. He now overtook him and walked on ahead. But the woodcutter had his eyes fixed on the ground, and he failed to recognize that it was the same man as the one who had been walking behind him. The king addressed him once again: 'Tell me, baldhead, where are you taking those water-melons?'

The woodcutter answered: 'Can't you see that I'm taking a gift to the king? I'm a poor man, and he may give me a reward.'

'Suppose,' said the king, 'that he doesn't give you a reward?'

Again the woodcutter began to curse loudly.

They say that in the olden days people would always repeat a question three times in order to be sure of the answer. So the king went round behind the woodcutter and again overtook him, and asked: 'Where are you taking those melons?'

Not realizing that it was the same man, the woodcutter answered: 'I am taking them to the king. I'm a poor man, and he may give me a reward.'

'Suppose,' said the king, 'that he doesn't give you a reward?'

Again the woodcutter began to curse loudly.

The king returned to his palace, and after seating himself on his throne, he issued instructions to his guards: 'There is a bald man who has brought some water-melons for me on a donkey. As soon as he comes, bring him before me.'

The king was in a furious temper. He had different methods of punishing those who offended him. These included death by immersion in boiling water or boiling oil, death by hanging, death by the stroke of the sword, and death by being burnt alive. He thought to himself: 'When the bald-headed man is brought before me, I shall order that he be put to death by whichever method first comes to mind.'

When the woodcutter entered the king's presence, he dropped the melons on the floor. Then the king thought: 'If I ask him again where he is taking his melons, he will curse me and thus dishonour me in front of my own people, and even if I have him put to death, this will not wipe away the stain of dishonour. But if I don't ask him, how can I punish him for no apparent reason.' So he turned and said to his vizier: 'Take this man to the treasury, and fill up all his sacks with gold, and then get rid of him.'

The vizier took the woodcutter to the treasury and filled his sacks with gold, and said to him: 'Now be off with you!'

Then the vizier thought to himself: 'If people start bringing gifts to the king, and if he treats them all in the same way as he has treated this woodcutter, the treasury will soon be empty, and I shall be blamed for offering the king bad advice.' So he went to the king and complained: 'You should have given the bald-headed man a few gold coins, instead of filling up all his sacks.'

'Why?' asked the king.

The vizier explained: 'We gave him sacks of gold. Now we shall have to give sacks of gold to everyone else who brings you gifts, and if this continues, your treasury will soon be empty.'

The king was not convinced: 'Although we gave gold to this man, we needn't give gold to every petitioner.'

'But we have set a bad example,' said the vizier, 'and I am determined to make him return the gold.'

'If you take the gold back,' warned the king, 'he will come and report you to me, because he knows you, and I shall be forced to punish you, and I would hate to do that. It is best if we leave him alone.'

'No, I shall recover the gold,' insisted the vizier.

'If you insist,' said the king, 'but don't do it by force; you will have to think of a ruse.'

The vizier buckled on his sword and rode off in pursuit of the woodcutter. 'Baldhead, wait!' he said, when he had caught up with him. 'I have a question to ask you. If you give me the correct answer, you can take the gold with you. If not, you must return it to me.'

'I'm in serious trouble,' thought the woodcutter. 'How will I ever be able to answer the question correctly?' Then he turned to the vizier and said: 'What is your question?'

The vizier asked: 'Where is the centre of the world?'

At that moment the woodcutter's donkey urinated. So the woodcutter answered, pointing to the round pool of urine: 'This is the centre of the world. You will find it by measuring right to left and near to far.'

'Baldhead, you are absolutely right,' said the vizier, and the woodcutter proceeded on his way.

'I must think fast,' thought the vizier, 'or the king will lose his gold.' So he rode after the woodcutter and caught up with him, and said: 'Baldhead, I shall ask you another question. If you can answer it, you can take the gold. If not, you must return it.'

'What is your question?' said the woodcutter.

'Which side is God's face on?'

The woodcutter took his turban-cloth and wrapped it round the stick that he carried in his hand. Then he set fire to the sheet and held it up in the air. The flames burnt it on all sides.

'What are you doing?' inquired the vizier.

'Can you see which side the flames are on?' asked the woodcutter.

'The flames are on all sides,' replied the vizier.

The woodcutter explained: 'Like the flames, God's face is on all sides. He is not a creature like us with a face on only one side.'

'Baldhead, you are absolutely right,' said the vizier, and the woodcutter proceeded on his way.

The vizier said to himself: 'I shall try once more to recover the gold.' So he rode after the woodcutter and caught up with him, and said: 'I shall ask you the third and final question. If you can answer it, you can take the gold. If not, you must return it to me.'

'What is your question?' asked the woodcutter.

'It is well known that God takes from one man and gives to another. But how does He do it?'

The woodcutter replied: 'I can answer this question only on condition that you take off your clothes and give them to me, and wear mine instead.' When the vizier and the woodcutter had exchanged clothes, the woodcutter continued: 'Now give me your horse and your sword, and take my stick.' The vizier obeyed. Then he asked the vizier to hold his horse steady while he loaded his sacks of gold on to it. Then, after mounting and buckling on the sword, he rode away.

'You still haven't given me your answer,' screamed the vizier.

'Be quiet!' shouted the woodcutter in reply. 'Don't you see that God has given me the fine clothes of a vizier and has given you the cheap clothes of a labourer. This is how He takes from one man and gives to another. Go home with your donkey, and if you say another word, I'll finish you off with my sword.'

The vizier thought to himself: 'I had better not argue with this fool, or else I shall perish at the point of my own sword.' So instead of going to the king, he went home.

In the meantime, the king had been waiting in his palace, hoping that the vizier would soon return with his gold. After some time he began to suspect that the vizier had absconded with the gold. So he gave instructions to a servant: 'Go and fetch the vizier. Tell him that I want to see him immediately.'

When the servant arrived at the vizier's house, the vizier was lying on his bed brooding over his misfortune.

'The king wants to see you immediately,' announced the servant.

The vizier rose to his feet and went to the king, and the king inquired: 'Well, did you recover the gold from the bald-headed man?'

'No,' replied the vizier. 'I tried to trick him into returning the gold by asking him three questions. He not only answered them correctly but he tricked me into giving him my clothes, my sword, and my horse.'

The king then admitted: 'I too was forced to give him all that gold. He is such a foolish man that I was afraid he would curse me in my court-room in front of my own people and thus dishonour me. Go to him. Tell him to return your horse and your sword, and tell him that when he has spent the gold which I gave him, he can come back for more.'

The vizier went to the woodcutter, and said: 'Give me back my horse and my sword. The king says that when your gold is finished, you can come back for more.'

The woodcutter gave back the vizier his horse and his sword, and he and his wife lived comfortably ever after.

30

The Swindlers

swindler was once walking round the bazaar in Kabul, boasting in a loud voice: 'I am the biggest swindler in the world; I can pick someone's pocket in a second without him even knowing.'

Boasting in this fashion to every shopkeeper in the bazaar, he came to a shop where a serious man was sitting. When the serious man heard the swindler singing his own praises, he said: 'Is that the way a real swindler talks? What sort of a swindler are you? The most famous swindlers live in Hindustan,[1] and nobody can compete with them.'

The swindler could not believe that anyone in his profession could possibly be greater than him. So he decided to go and see for himself. He set out from Kabul and travelled on foot until, after many days, he reached Hindustan. There he made it known that he wished to meet a famous Hindu swindler, and the people informed him about a certain individual. They told him his name and the name of the village where he lived. When he reached the house, he called out his name. But the Hindu swindler happened to be away at that time, and his wife shouted in reply: 'My husband is not at home. Who is it?' There was no answer.

The swindler from Kabul was disappointed not to find his rival at home, and since his wife had not informed him of her husband's whereabouts, he decided that the only thing to do was to stand in front of the door and wait.

The wife said to herself: 'Let me peep round the door to see who it is, and if it is a relative, I shall invite him in.' When she peeped round the door, she immediately realized that he was a swindler, and she guessed that he had come to compete with her husband. So she said to him: 'Come inside. My husband will be back soon.' He entered the courtyard of the house and sat down on a *charpoy* under the shade of a tree.

After some time, the Hindustani returned home, and when he saw the stranger, he immediately realized that he was a swindler who had come to compete with him. He shook hands with him and sat down.

While waiting for the Hindustani, the Kabli swindler had already glanced carefully round the house. He wondered: 'What should I take to cover my expenses on the homeward journey?' He had not found anything worth stealing, except half a *seer* of flour and one old silver drinking-bowl covering the water-jar. Since he had seen nothing else of any value, he had decided to take the old drinking-bowl.

The Kabli swindler kept eyeing the drinking-bowl, and the Hindustani said to himself: 'This Kabli will certainly try to steal my silver bowl. It would not be fair play to remove it; but in order to save it, I must put it in a place where it is visible and yet cannot be stolen.'

That evening the wife said to her husband: 'We only have half a *seer* of flour. That is more than enough for both of us. But what shall we do now that we have a guest to entertain? The neighbours will not lend us any money.'

'Prepare whatever you have,' replied the Hindustani, 'and our friend will share it with us.'

So the wife kneaded the flour and baked two flat loaves of bread. She placed one in front of her husband and the other in front of the guest. The Hindustani made his wife sit with them, and the three of them ate together. When they had finished eating, the Hindustani said to his wife: 'We have only two *charpoy*s. You can prepare my bed for the guest, and when we have finished talking, I shall go to the village guest-house and borrow an extra bed.'

The wife prepared a bed for the guest by placing a mat on her husband's string bedstead – for in the olden days a mat was used instead of a mattress. Then she prepared her own bed. The Hindustani and the Kabli talked late at night until the Kabli fell asleep. Then the Hindustani went to the village guest-house and borrowed a bed for himself. He placed his bed underneath the clothes-line. Having done this, he filled the silver bowl with water and tied it to a piece of cloth and hung it from the line. He was well satisfied because he thought that the Kabli would never dream of looking for the bowl there. And even if he did find it, there was no danger of it being stolen.

In the middle of the night the Kabli woke up. He immediately looked in the direction of the earthenware jar, but the silver bowl had vanished. He was puzzled and wondered where the Hindustani had hidden it. He searched the whole house. In distress he looked heavenward and saw it dangling from the clothes-line. He said to himself: 'Before I touch it, I must make sure that the Hindustani hasn't put some water in it. If he has, and if anyone were to touch it, water would fall on his face and wake him up.' When he looked inside the bowl, he discovered that it did indeed contain water. So he went to the hearth and picked up some ashes; and little by little, he dropped the ashes in the bowl until all the water had been absorbed and the bowl was dry. He was then able to take the bowl without waking the Hindustani.

After stealing the silver bowl, the Kabli swindler said to himself: 'I must hide this somewhere, so that I can easily collect it before leaving.' He left the house and walked down the road. After passing three or four houses, he reached a ditch containing dirty water. He thought: 'What's the use of going any further! I shall turn the bowl upside down and press it into the mud at the edge of the water so that no one can see it. Tomorrow morning, when I am passing this way, I shall wash it and take it with me.' So he hid the bowl in the mud and returned to the house. Then he lay down on his bed and fell asleep.

Later that night the Hindustani awoke. Looking up, he noticed that his bowl had vanished. He rose from his bed and went over to where the Kabli was sleeping. He touched the hem of the Kabli's baggy trousers and felt that one trouser-leg was wet. So he left the house and went straight to the ditch. With his foot he probed around at the edge of the water until he came across the bowl. He picked it up out of the mud and washed it, and when he returned home, he put it back on top of the earthenware jar.

Next morning, when the Kabli awoke, he was surprised to see the silver bowl lying on top of the water-jar, and he said to himself: 'This swine must have seen me leaving the house, and he must have followed me to the ditch.'

When the Hindustani awoke, he saw that the Kabli was gazing at the silver bowl, and he said to him: 'Please be frank with me and tell me what is in your heart. You wish to steal that silver bowl, but you haven't a chance. Every time you try, your schemes will be frustrated; and even if you succeed, it will not be of much use to you. I bought it for my wedding, and it's very old now, and would only fetch one-sixth or one-eighth of its original price. Besides, if it were stolen, it would be no great loss. I would simply go to the potter and buy an earthenware bowl to drink

out of. In short, by stealing the bowl, you will gain nothing and
I shall lose nothing. You cannot achieve anything on your own:
you need two hands to clap. If we combine our forces, we can
earn thirty thousand rupees by this evening. Fifteen thousand
will be yours and fifteen thousand will be mine.'

'Where is this money?' inquired the Kabli.

The Hindustani answered: 'It's not just lying in a heap
waiting for us to collect it. We shall cheat certain people and
extract the money from them. When you tell a lie, I shall back
you up and make it seem the truth; similarly, when I tell a lie,
you must make it seem the truth.'

The Kabli agreed with this plan, and the two swindlers set off
together. When they had travelled some distance, the Kabli again
inquired: 'Where is this money?'

The Hindustani explained: 'In a village near here a rich
landowner has just died. So I shall tell his son that his father
owed me thirty thousand rupees. When I claim this amount, he
will not believe me, and we shall start quarrelling; but if you are
a true swindler, you will make him believe the claim.'

The Kabli smiled confidently: 'I shall be so successful at
convincing him that you will remember it for the rest of your
life, and rest assured that the sum of thirty thousand rupees is
already ours.'

So they went to the village and made inquiries at the
graveyard: 'Which is the grave of the rich landowner who died
recently?' The villagers pointed to it.

'I shall bury you here,' said the Hindustani to the Kabli, 'and
then I shall tell the *Khan* that his father owed me thirty thousand
rupees, and if he refuses to believe me, I shall tell him to go to his
father's grave and ask if it is true; and when the son comes and
asks if it is true, you must answer from the grave, "Yes, it is true,
I owe him that amount."' The Kabli nodded his head in
agreement.

To one side of the grave they dug a hole, and the Kabli climbed into it. The Hindustani covered him with a sheet, and on top of that he placed some earth and stones so that no one would know that he was buried there. Then he went to the *Khan*'s guest-house.

Many people had come to the guest-house to invoke God's mercy for the dead man. The Hindustani entered and sat down amidst the relatives who had gathered there. 'Let us pray to God to forgive Arbab Sahib for his sins,' he said, and they all recited some prayers.

The Hindustani did not know which of those present was Sher Ali Khan. So he waited for one of the mourners to rise to his feet and take his leave of the dead man's son. At that moment a man entered the guest-house and approached one of the men who had been praying, and said: 'Sher Ali Khan, may God give you patience, and may your father be rewarded in paradise.' After saying this, the man left.

Then the Hindustani stood up and made an announcement: 'I want to say something. If I am wrong, then you can call me a sinner. If I am correct, then you are bound to agree with me. It is entirely for you to judge.'

The people answered: 'Say what you have come to say.'

The Hindustani spoke in a solemn voice: 'Arbab Sahib and I were very close friends, so much so that each was willing to lay down his life for the other. Last month Arbab Sahib came to my house and asked for me. Hearing his voice, I quickly came out and inquired, 'Is everything all right?' He answered: 'Please give me a loan of thirty thousand rupees and I shall return it to you after several days.' Since I had the money on me, I gave it to him without hesitation. I then invited him to sit down and have some tea, but he was in a hurry and left without wasting a moment. As he was leaving, he said to me: 'Don't bother to come and fetch the money; I'll send it to you.' So I naturally agreed. Today, quite by chance, I discovered that Arbab Sahib had died; so I came to pay my respects, and to find out whether he had mentioned anything about my loan in his will, because it's not a question of a hundred rupees or two hundred rupees or even a thousand rupees, but thirty thousand rupees, and that's a large sum of money.'

'He never mentioned anything about this sum of money to me,' said Sher Ali quickly. 'I cannot just hand out thirty thousand rupees like that.'

'If my claim is legitimate, then you will have to give me the money,' said the Hindustani. 'I shall give the *Khan*'s son two chances, and I shall give myself only one.'

'What do you mean?' the people asked.

He explained: 'They say that the dead don't speak, but I am willing to go with him to his father's grave, and there he should ask his father whether or not he borrowed money from me. If there is no answer, then I shall no longer insist, and if the answer is no, then, of course, I shall withdraw my claim. But if the answer is yes, then you must give the money to me.'

The people agreed with this proposal: 'The dead don't talk; and if, in this case, the dead man really does say yes, then Sher Ali Khan is bound to admit that your claim is fully justified.'

So they all went to the cemetery, and the Hindustani told Sher Ali Khan to stand at the foot of the grave and ask his father about the unpaid debt. Sher Ali went and stood at the foot of the grave. 'Father,' he said, 'do you owe this Hindustani any money?'

'Yes, my son,' replied the Kabli swindler from his hiding place beside the grave, 'I owe him thirty thousand rupees. I am on my way to paradise, but because I have failed to repay this debt, the gates of paradise are closed. You must therefore settle this debt as soon as possible so that the gates will open for me.'

When the people heard these words, they said: 'Sher Ali, you must pay the money at once, or else your father will be prevented from going to paradise.' Then, because they had heard a dead man speak, they appealed to God for protection and forgiveness.

Among those present was a village elder who offered his advice: 'Since Arbab Sahib is dead, everyone should assist him by giving whatever he can afford, so that we can repay this man's loan.'

The majority of the mourners were wealthy men. So some offered five thousand rupees, others ten thousand rupees, and so on. When everyone had contributed something, they counted the money and found that it came to well over thirty thousand rupees. Sher Ali gave thirty thousand rupees to the Hindustani, and he wrapped up the rest of the money in his turban-cloth and took it home.

The Hindustani then purchased a horse and two large sacks. He filled the sacks with his ill-gotten earnings, mounted the horse, and rode off. As he was passing the graveyard, he said in a loud voice so that the Kabli would hear: 'Everybody can go to hell. I got the money I came for and now I'm taking it home.'

When the Kabli heard this, he quickly climbed out of the grave, shook the earth from his clothes, and went in pursuit of the Hindustani. Then he paused and said to himself: 'The Hindustani is a swindler and we gained this money through swindling. Therefore it's no good using force. I shall have to win my share from him by guile.'

So he went to the bazaar and bought a pair of new shoes. Then he took a shortcut, which enabled him to overtake the Hindustani. He dropped one of the shoes on the road and hid himself. When the Hindustani came upon the shoe, he stopped and looked round to see if anybody was in sight. Seeing nobody, he dismounted and examined the shoe. He then searched for the other of the pair, but could not find it. 'If I were to go to the bazaar and find the pair to this shoe,' he thought, 'it would cost me as much as a pair of shoes. But since I have plenty of money,

I might as well buy myself some new shoes.' So he mounted his horse and continued on his way.

'Now is my chance,' thought the Kabli, when he saw that the Hindustani had left the shoe, instead of picking it up. He went on ahead and dropped the other shoe on the road, and then climbed into a tree to hide. When the Hindustani reached the spot where the Kabli had dropped the second shoe, he exclaimed: 'O, this is a pair to the shoe I came across earlier!' So he dismounted and ran back to fetch the first shoe.

The Kabli, in the meantime, climbed down from the tree and mounted the horse and rode off with the money. When the Hindustani returned with the first shoe in his hands, he saw the Kabli riding off with the money, and he said to himself: 'How on earth did the swine manage to rise from the grave? Now he has run off with the money, but I am determined to get my rightful share.' So he began pursuing him.

The Kabli arrived at a crossroads, and thought: 'If I go straight on, the Hindustani will follow me. So I shall leave the road here and cut across the fields and rejoin the road later.' As he was crossing the fields, he met a farmer who had just finished stacking his sheaves of corn. He was saying aloud to himself: 'I shall sell this stack for thirty rupees, and this for forty rupees,' and so on. Hearing this, the Kabli thought: 'I shall buy a stack and hide in it.'

'How much are you selling this for?' he asked, pointing to a stack.

'I've already promised them all to someone else,' replied the farmer.

'I just need it for a short time,' insisted the Kabli.

The farmer agreed.

'How much do you want for it?' asked the Kabli.

'Twenty rupees,' replied the farmer.

The Kabli gave the farmer twenty rupees, and said: 'You must try, as best you can, to cover me with corn.'

The farmer did as he had been asked, and threw corn over the Kabli and his horse until they were hidden from sight.

When the Hindustani arrived at the crossroads, he thought: 'I bet that cunning swindler has left the road, hoping that I would lose track of him.' And he too turned off the road into the fields. There he met the farmer, who was still chuckling to himself, because he thought it funny that the stranger should ask him to throw corn over him. When the Hindustani saw him chuckling to himself, he inquired: 'Which stack did you sell today?'

'That one,' replied the farmer, pointing to the one in which the Kabli was concealed.

The Hindustani offered to buy it: 'I'll pay you twenty-five rupees for it, because last night a holy man appeared to me in a dream, and told me that I should buy a stack of corn, and that I should burn it, and that when I had done this, my poverty would cease.'

The farmer said to himself: 'I shall sell it, because I have nothing to lose. The man who is hidden inside it will be burnt to death, so he will not be able to incriminate me.'

As soon as the Hindustani had bought the stack of corn, he set fire to it and cried: 'He who hides from his friends will be burnt.' The Kabli heard this, but at first he did not realize that the stack was on fire. When he felt the heat of the flames and heard the noise of burning, he sent the horse out of the stack, and then ran out himself, shielding his eyes with his hands. The Hindustani caught hold of the horse and extinguished the flames with a stick. Then the two swindlers came to an agreement that they would share the money half and half.

'My house is close by,' said the Hindustani. 'We shall go there and share out the money.'

So they went to the Hindustani's house and unloaded the sacks of money from the horse. The Kabli expected the Hindustani to say, 'Come, let us share the money,' and the

Hindustani expected the Kabli to say, 'Come, let us share the money.' But the days passed, and neither of them said anything. Whereupon the Hindustani called his wife and said to her: 'Tonight I shall pretend to be dead, and you must spend the whole night weeping, and in the morning you must bury me. If we are lucky, the Kabli will go away quietly, but if he does ask for the money, you must say to him: 'Why didn't you ask my husband when he was alive?' When you are sure that he has left, then dig up the grave and help me out.'

In the middle of the night the Hindustani's wife began screaming and tearing out her hair: 'O my husband is dead! What am I to do?' When the neighbours heard her wailing, they came to offer prayers for the dead man. Then the wife asked them to prepare the grave.

The Kabli, meanwhile, had been listening to all this drama. In the morning, after taking a look at the dead man, he said to the wife: 'Your husband and I were great friends, and we decided among ourselves that if he died first, I would do something for him before he was buried, and if I died first, then he would do the same for me. Since your husband is dead, I must fulfil my promise.' Having said this, the Kabli went to the bazaar and purchased a cow for forty rupees.

The Hindustani's wife thought: 'Perhaps he will slaughter the cow and cook it and give the meat to the poor on behalf of my dead husband.' But instead, the Kabli brought the cow and made it stand beside the *charpoy* on which the dead man was lying. He took a piece of rope from the bed, and tied one end to the dead man's foot and the other end round the cow's neck. Then he took a stick and hit the cow hard to make it run.

When the cow began to run, it dragged the Hindustani behind it. The wretched man was dragged over thorns and hard ground, but still he pretended to be dead. At the end of the day the Kabli said to himself: 'I still haven't succeeded in making this swine come alive. I shall therefore alter my tactics.' By this time the cow had reached the graveyard. The Kabli untied the rope and set the cow free. Then he concealed himself in an old grave and waited, while the Hindustani lay on the ground pretending to be dead.

In the meantime, a band of six thieves passed by. They had been informed that a rich farmer had sold his crop and had hidden the money in a certain room. These thieves were on their way to steal the money when they tripped over the Hindustani, who was still lying in the graveyard. They realized, on closer inspection, that it was the body of a man, and thought: 'Somebody has murdered this man and has then dragged him here. That is why there is a rope round his neck.'

One of the thieves came forward and gave the dead man's body a kick, and said: 'Respected martyr, I'm going to commit a theft, and if I'm successful, I shall break your mouth open and extract every tooth from it.'

The next thief came forward and gave him a kick, and swore: 'I too am going to commit a theft, and if I'm successful, I shall sever your head from your body.' And so each thief stepped forward and vowed to do something to the dead man if the theft went well.

Then they went to the rich farmer's house and stole all his money. On their way back they stopped in the graveyard to unload their loot. The leader of the group said: 'We really ought to show our gratitude to the respected martyr for making our robbery such a success.'

So the first thief went to look for a stone with which to break open the dead man's mouth; while the second, who had sworn to sever his head from his body, began to urinate over him. The first thief returned with two wooden pegs used for tethering cows. He placed one of them inside the dead man's mouth and started hammering it with the other. When it began to hurt, the Hindustani screamed: 'A thief! A thief! Catch him!'

'Wait! I'm coming,' shouted the Kabli from the grave where he was hiding.

When the thieves heard the first voice, and then the second, they were terrified and said: 'This man really is a martyr, and the dead are rising from their graves to assist him, so we had better run for our lives.' The thieves fled, leaving all the stolen money behind. Whereupon the Hindustani jumped to his feet and grabbed the money, and said: 'It's mine.'

'It's not yours,' intervened the Kabli. 'If it hadn't been for me, the thieves would never have run away. I shouted from the grave where I was hiding, and they thought that the dead were rising from their graves and coming to your rescue. That's why we should both share the money.'

The Hindustani agreed, and each of them picked up three bags of money and carried them to the Hindustani's house. Then the Hindustani said: 'If we go on like this, one of us will kill the other. Therefore the wisest thing to do is for each of us to take his fair share and go his separate way.

So the Hindustani and the Kabli divided the money equally among themselves, and the Kabli left the house and set off on his journey home.

31

The Barber's Son

Once upon a time a barber's son said to his father: 'Today I shall go and pay my respects to my father-in-law.'

The father answered: 'Give him my greetings too. But, since you are travelling alone, go straight there and take care not to lose your way.'

They say that barbers have no intelligence because they belong to a menial tribe. The son thought his father had said: 'Follow a straight path, or else you will lose your way.' He put on his best *shalwar kameez* and set off on his journey. After following a straight path for some time, he bumped into a tree. When he looked up and saw the tree, he said to himself: 'If I turn to the right or to the left, I shall stray from the straight path which leads to my father-in-law's house, so there's only one solution: I shall have to climb the tree and come down the other side.'

It was winter and the days were short. The barber's son had to climb the tree with great care for fear of dirtying his new clothes or tearing them on a branch. Therefore it took him half the day to climb the tree. When he reached the top, he said to himself: 'It took me half the day to get up here and it will take another half to come down on the other side, so I shall have no time left to reach my father-in-law's house.' He therefore decided that the only solution was to lie on his stomach and slide down a branch. But when he lay on a branch, it broke under his weight, without falling to the ground, and he was left dangling from the branch. He then concluded that to reach the ground, he would have to wait for a gust of wind. But he also kept a lookout for any passer-by to whom he could appeal for help.

A *kuchi* , a nomadic Pashtun, happened to pass by with his four camels. He had just been to the market to sell molasses and was returning home. As he and his camels passed beneath the tree, the barber's son called out to him: 'Help me down for the love of God!'

The nomad looked up. 'How can I help you? I cannot reach you.'

'I'll show you,' said the barber's son.

The nomad agreed: 'Tell me and I'll do my best to help you, since you have requested me in the name of God.'

The barber's son explained: 'Bring one of your camels and make it sit under the branch from which I am hanging. Then you should mount the camel and make it stand up. Once it is standing, you can raise yourself into a standing position and catch hold of my waist, and I'll let go of the branch and we'll both fall safely on to the camel's back.'

The nomad caught one of his camels and made it sit directly under the branch to which the barber's son was clinging. Then he mounted the camel and made it stand up. Then he too rose to his feet and took hold of the barber's son by the waist. 'My master has safely climbed the tree,' thought the camel, after glancing over its shoulder. So it strode off to join its companions.

Finding himself hanging in mid-air from the barber's son's waist, the nomad was furious and began uttering words of abuse: 'If you had been a creature endowed with any intelligence,

you wouldn't have been hanging in a tree in the first place. I'm
sure you have nothing in your house to lose,' he grumbled, 'so
it's all right for you to be hanging here. But look at me. My
camels will be lost because there's nobody to catch and tether
them.'

As the branch to which they were clinging was already partly
broken, the extra weight soon caused it to snap in two. The
nomad fell to the ground and broke his leg, and the barber's son
fell safely on top of him. The barber's son got up quickly,
straightened his clothes, and continued on his way.

'Wait! Come back and help me,' shouted the nomad. 'It's all
because of you that my leg is broken.' The barber's son returned
and the nomad said to him: 'Go to the nearest shop and buy
some oil to rub on my leg. Then I can bandage it and go home.'

'I haven't a *paisa* on me; I'm a crow from hell,' said the
barber's son.

The nomad took out one rupee from his pocket, and said: 'Go
and fetch the drinking-bowl which is tied on the camel's back
and get some mustard oil.' The barber's son untied the drinking-
bowl and walked to the nearest shop.

When he arrived, he gave the shopkeeper one rupee and asked
for some mustard oil. In those days oil was very cheap and one
seer of mustard oil cost only two *anna*s. The shopkeeper filled
up the drinking-bowl with seven and a half *seer*s of oil, and then
said to the barber's son: 'There's no room for more oil and you
have one *anna*'s worth left. What should I do with it?'

The barber's son lifted the bowl, turned it upside down, and
pointed to the small hollow underneath: 'You can put the
remainder of the oil here.'

'Look what you've done!' screamed the shopkeeper. 'You've
spilt fifteen *anna*s' worth of oil. You're the biggest fool I've ever
set my eyes on.' But he poured the one *anna*'s worth of oil into
the base of the bowl, and said: 'Now go on your way.'

The barber's son brought the bowl upside down to the nomad. 'How much did you pay for this?' asked the nomad, when he saw how little oil there was.

'One rupee,' replied the barber's son. Then he added, turning the bowl the right way up: 'There's more on the other side.'

The little oil that he had bought for one *anna* spilt on the ground, and the nomad cursed him: 'You are as stupid as a donkey. Otherwise you wouldn't have been hanging in a tree and you wouldn't have put me to so much trouble.' With the palms of his hands, the nomad picked up some of the oil that had spilt on the ground and rubbed it on his broken leg.

They say that those who belong to the menial tribes are not trustworthy. The barber's son did not wait to help the nomad, but continued on his way. With great difficulty, the nomad limped to his camels, mounted one of them, and went home, grumbling to himself.

32

The Shepherd

There was once a shepherd who had a thousand sheep. One evening there was a fair in his village. People from all the neighbouring villages had come to take part in the celebrations. The shepherd had also gone. The celebrations continued throughout the night, and at dawn everyone made their way home.

The shepherd looked up at the stars as he was returning home, and said to himself: 'It will soon be morning. If I go to sleep, I am so exhausted that I shall never be able to wake up on time; and if I don't take my sheep to graze, they will die of hunger. I shall set out now with my sheep, and by the time we reach the hill where they graze it will be morning.' So he took his flock to the hill, and while the sheep were grazing, he spread his turban-cloth on the grass and fell asleep.

Next day the shepherd slept. At dusk he still had not woken up. The sheep thought to themselves: 'He must have gone to sleep. We had better start on our homeward journey.' So they left the shepherd and began to make their own way home.

Time passed, and the shepherd, who had been sleeping on one side, felt the need to turn over. As he did so, he awoke and discovered it was growing dark. He quickly rose to his feet, picked up his turban-cloth, and looked around for his sheep, but could not find them. Still half-asleep, he took two steps forward, stumbled, and nearly fell. He thought to himself: 'On the one hand, I have lost my sheep; on the other hand, I am still sleepy. I really ought to do one thing at a time. Either I should search for my sheep, or I should go to sleep. My sheep must have strayed far away by now,' he argued, 'whereas my sleep is readily available. Therefore first I shall satisfy my desire to sleep.' Once again he spread his turban-cloth on the ground and fell asleep.

When half the night had passed, he woke up feeling cold. He got up and set off down the hill where his sheep had been grazing. On the way he saw a farmer ploughing his fields. He went up to him and greeted him in the traditional way: 'May you not feel tired.'

Now the shepherd and the farmer were both somewhat deaf, and the farmer thought that the shepherd was inquiring about the price of one of his bullocks. So he replied: 'I bought it for twenty-eight rupees.'

The shepherd was bewildered. He said to himself: 'What is the meaning of this? I never asked about the price of his bullocks.'

After the farmer had ploughed one furrow, he turned his bullocks and returned to the spot where the shepherd was standing. The shepherd addressed him again: 'I said, "May you not feel tired." I didn't inquire about the price of your bullocks.'

When the shepherd had first greeted the farmer, the bullock on the left was nearest to him, but now, after one furrow had been ploughed, the one on the right was nearest to him. So the farmer thought that he was inquiring about the price of the second bullock, and said: 'It cost me thirty-five rupees.'

The shepherd tried to explain: 'Please, I don't want to buy your bullocks, so why are you telling me what they cost? All I said was, 'May you not feel tired.''

'I am not selling my bullocks,' said the farmer.

The shepherd repeated: 'I said, "May you not feel tired." I don't want to buy your bullocks.'

The farmer replied angrily: 'On no condition will I sell them to you.' He was annoyed because he thought that the shepherd was insisting on buying his bullocks. 'Please leave me in peace and go on your way,' he said, raising his right hand to his brow in a gesture of despair.

The shepherd thought that the farmer was indicating the direction in which his sheep had gone. So he went in that direction and found his flock grazing there. He inspected them and found that one of the ewes had broken a leg. He thought: 'It will be difficult to take this lame sheep home with the flock, so I shall give it to someone as a gift. Since the farmer was kind enough to show me where to find my flock, I shall give it to him, instead of to the mullah. The farmer can use it for milk.'

When the farmer saw the shepherd bringing the lame sheep, he thought: 'This shepherd is now going to accuse me of injuring his sheep. No doubt he has come to claim some money in compensation. Today is an unlucky day for me. God alone knows what further misfortune is in store for me!'

The shepherd approached the farmer and thanked him: 'I am grateful to you for telling me where to find my flock. One of my sheep has injured its leg and cannot travel with the flock, so you may keep it for milk.'

'I didn't injure your sheep,' replied the farmer, 'and therefore I refuse to pay any money in compensation.'

The shepherd grew angry, and said to himself: 'Come what may, I shall leave this sheep with him.'

When the farmer saw that the shepherd was losing his temper, he said to himself: 'Come what may, he will claim damages for the sheep, so it is best if we go to the mullah and allow him to settle the dispute.' So he suggested: 'Let us both go to the mullah and he will decide which of us is right.'

As the shepherd himself was somewhat deaf, he understood the farmer to say, 'Let us take the sheep home and set matters right.' So he willingly agreed to accompany him.

It so happened that the mullah had just had a quarrel with his wife. When she had hurled abuse at him, he had left the house in anger and had sought refuge in the mosque. He was sitting in the mosque thinking to himself: 'I lead the congregation in prayer and yet my wife has the audacity to insult and abuse me. I shall throw her out of my house to teach her a lesson.'

While he was considering the quarrel that he had had with his wife, he saw the farmer and the shepherd approaching with a sheep. He thought: 'Perhaps my wife has sent this delegation because she regrets her rudeness towards me. She must have sent this sheep as a sign that she seeks my forgiveness, but I shall not accept it.'

When the shepherd and the farmer entered the mosque, the shepherd spoke to the mullah: 'I had lost my flock of sheep and this farmer told me where to find them. Therefore, as an act of charity and a sign of my gratitude, I offered him this sheep, but he refuses to accept it.'

The mullah, who was himself hard of hearing, replied: 'This sheep is not acceptable to me, nor am I willing to accept her delegation, so please go on your way.'

The farmer then addressed the mullah: 'I didn't injure his sheep, nor did I know where his flock was, and he is claiming money from me for no good reason.'

An intelligent man had meanwhile entered the mosque and had overheard the conversation. He said to himself: 'All three of them appear to be stupid, so I shall take advantage of the situation.'

He approached the shepherd, and said: 'Leave the sheep with me, and I'll clear up the misunderstanding with the farmer and give it to him. You had better stay with your flock, or else they will again get lost.'

When the shepherd had gone, he turned to the farmer, and said: 'Go and return to your ploughing. You are not to blame.'

When the farmer had gone, he turned to the mullah, and said: 'Don't trouble yourself. This matter doesn't concern you.' He then took the sheep and went home laughing.

33

The Weavers

There was once a very pious man who lived in a village called Sursak. It was in this same village that all the weavers used to live. Weavers belong to one of the menial tribes, for they are the makers of cloth. It is said that they are cowards and lack common sense.

On Big Eid, the feast of *Loe Akhtar*, the pious man sacrificed a sheep in accordance with Islamic practice. He then gave some money to a friend and told him to buy another sheep. Since the friend was unable to find anyone in the village willing to sell him a sheep, he travelled to the city. There he continued to search until he found a shopkeeper who had a sheep. He approached the shopkeeper, and said: 'Will you sell me your sheep?'

The shopkeeper had bought the sheep for himself for three rupees and had no intention of selling it. But not wishing to give a straight refusal, he decided to demand such a high price for it that the man would be unable to pay and would leave him in peace. He therefore said: 'I'll sell it to you for ten rupees.' This was more than three times the amount he had paid for it.

Without hesitation, the man gave the shopkeeper ten rupees and took the sheep. The shopkeeper was surprised, but could say nothing. So he consoled himself by reflecting: 'I have made a profit on this sale, and now I shall buy myself another sheep.' The pious man was very pleased when his friend returned with the sheep. He looked after it with great care. Everyday he used to give it grass and water. Thus a year passed and the sheep became fat and strong.

In a nearby village there was a shepherd who used to bring his flock to Sursak for grazing. One day a lamb from the flock lagged behind, and its mother went in search of it. This sheep wandered through the village of Sursak saying 'Bha! Bha!' calling for its lost little one. When the pious man's sheep heard the bleating, it broke free of its halter and stood in the doorway of the house, with only its head sticking out, waiting in the hope of hearing the bleating again so it would know which way to run to join the flock.

Meanwhile, a weaver happened to be passing the doorway with his loom and spinning-wheel. When the weaver saw the pious man's sheep, he thought at first it was a demon, but when, on closer inspection, he saw the black wool and horns, he concluded that it must be a sheep. So to shoo it away, he muttered: 'Dus!'

The sheep was as big and strong as an ox, and hearing the word 'dus,' a word that sheep find offensive, it grew angry. It ran towards the weaver, lifted him on its horns, and tossed him across the street. The man quickly picked himself up and ran for his life, warning other members of his tribe: 'Today he is my enemy, but watch out, because tomorrow he'll be your enemy.' The sheep walked in the opposite direction and joined the flock.

This weaver then summoned all the other weavers in the village. Having assembled their weapons, in other words, their spindles and distaffs, they decided that, instead of pursuing their enemy, they would fortify their own position. They remained where they were, one behind the other. At the very back crouched the weaver who had been tossed by the sheep.

They wa ited for some time and nothing happened. The weaver who was at the very front suddenly took fright. He got up and quietly moved to the back. The next one did the same, and the next, until the weaver who had been tossed by the sheep was at the front and their whole line of defence had receded. When he looked up, he saw several sheep approaching. One of them stopped to relieve itself. Mistaking the dark droppings for bullets, the weaver became even more terrified and wondered how his men could compete with such a powerful enemy.

Meanwhile, some hounds approached the flock of sheep from the rear. When the sheep saw them, they took fright and began to run in all directions. 'They are attacking us from all sides,' shouted the weavers, and each man abandoned his position and fled for his life with the sheep in hot pursuit.

One weaver continued to run until he reached a nearby village, and he was followed all the way by one of the sheep. As he was looking over his shoulder to see how far behind the sheep was, he fell headlong into a dried-up well and the sheep came tumbling after him. He found himself at the bottom of the well with the sheep trampling over him.

'We do not consider you our enemy,' said the weaver, pleading for mercy. 'The other weaver, who is a relative of ours, forced us to fight against you. He is a foolish man who takes offence very easily. If you spare me, I shall prove my goodwill by making you some cloth.'

Eventually the shepherd arrived and lifted his sheep out of the well. When the weaver had climbed out of the well, he decided to remain and live in the little village not far from that spot. The other weavers, who had run to other villages to save theirlives, some a long way off and some nearby, settled down in those villages. That is the reason why weavers are no longer to be found in one village, but scattered in many parts.

34

Nasruddin, the Holy Man

One day a peasant called Nasruddin had a quarrel with his wife. He took his bullocks out at dawn and ploughed all morning. At noon he unharnessed his bullocks from the plough and sent them home. He followed them to the doorstep, but because his wife was angry with him, he hid near the door instead of entering.

When the bullocks reached the house, the peasant's wife gave them water to drink and hay to eat, and then waited for the return of her husband. But he did not come. She waited all afternoon until the evening, and still he did not come. All this time the peasant had been hiding near the door, planning to enter the house while his wife was not looking.

In the evening the wife took out some flour. She kneaded it and covered it and put it aside. Then she began to prepare the meat that she had bought from the butcher. All this time her husband had been watching her. When she had finished preparing the meal, she sat down and waited, looking at the door, hoping that her husband would soon come home.

The peasant kept standing up and peering into the room to see what his wife was doing. While he was doing this, his wife saw him. When he realized that his wife had seen him, he entered the house. 'Wait! Don't move!' he said. 'I have become a holy man and I can read the hearts of men.'

So she questioned him: 'What is underneath the kneading trough?'

As the peasant had been watching his wife from the door, he answered: 'You kneaded the wheat flour and put it in a dish and placed the trough over the dish.' Then the peasant inquired: 'Would you also like to know what is cooking in the pot?'

'Yes,' she replied.

'Meat,' he said. Then he repeated three times: 'I have become a holy man.'

The wife picked up her earthenware jar and went to the well to fetch water. She met her friends there and said to them: 'Something strange has come over my husband. When I turn to one side, he says, "Keep quiet! I have become a holy man." When I touch my hair, he says, "Keep quiet! I have become a holy man."' Thus the news that the peasant Nasruddin had become a holy man soon became common gossip.

The holy man had now given up working on the land and used to sit in his house. One day, a farmer, who was one of the king's tenants, had to go to the mill to grind his corn. It was a night's journey, and he told his wife before leaving home: 'I am going to the mill. Take care that nobody steals our bullocks while I'm away.'

The wife thought: 'It's hard for me to stay awake and keep watch, so I shall work all night instead.' She lit a kerosene lamp and began separating the fluff from the cotton-seeds. She called the women of the neighbourhood and invited them to join her: 'Come and sit with me, and do your work here, while I keep watch during my husband's absence.' The women came and worked until late into the night, and then took their leave and went home. The wife herself felt very tired.

Now one of the farmer's neighbours was Nasruddin. Only a few trees separated the two houses, and he had overheard the farmer telling his wife to guard the bullocks while he was away. He had hidden nearby, waiting for the farmer's wife to fall asleep. As soon as she did so, he came and stole the bullocks, and led them to a secluded place.

When the farmer's wife woke up and discovered that the bullocks were no longer there, she began to scream: 'My bullocks have been stolen! My bullocks have been stolen! What will I tell my husband?' The neighbours gathered round and tried their best to console her. 'Don't worry,' they said, 'you will find your bullocks.'

On his way back from the mill the farmer met a villager who told him the bad news. He was very angry with his wife, and said to himself: 'I had especially warned her to be vigilant, but instead she allowed them to be stolen.'

When the farmer arrived home, his wife recounted what had happened. He then began to beat her in anger, but the neighbours stopped him, and said: 'Don't worry, if you look for your bullocks, you will find them.' So he decided to go and look for them. He went from village to village, saying: 'My bullocks are white with dark patches; if you see them anywhere, please let me know.'

As he was returning home, one of the villagers said to him: 'You will never find your bullocks like that. You should go and call on Nasruddin the holy man. Give him some money and he will tell you who has stolen your bullocks.'

So he went to Nasruddin's house and shouted 'Hey, holy man!' three times.

'What's the matter?' asked Nasruddin.

'Please come out,' replied the farmer.

Nasruddin came out of the house. 'Is anything wrong?' he inquired.

The farmer explained: 'My bullocks have been stolen, and I have been told by the people of the village that you can help me find them.'

'How much would you pay me?' asked the holy man.

'Whatever you want,' replied the farmer.

'Very well, go and fetch me sixty rupees.'

The farmer went home and came back with sixty rupees. He handed the money to the holy man and the holy man told him where his bullocks could be found.

In the field that Nasruddin had mentioned the farmer found his bullocks. He untied them and returned home with them. On the way people asked: 'How did you find your bullocks?'

He answered: 'I gave sixty rupees to Nasruddin the holy man, and he told me where to find them.'

When the people heard this, they spread the word that Nasruddin had become a holy man who could read the hearts of men.

Now in that kingdom there was a king whose daughter possessed a very precious necklace. At night she used to take it off and place it beside her pillow. One day a friend of the princess, who was leaving the palace and returning to her father's house, saw the necklace and thought: 'I want to take this with me.' That night, when the princess was asleep, she stole the necklace and buried it in a hole that she had dug at the foot of the bed.[1] The princess was very upset when she awoke and found the necklace missing, and soon news of the theft had spread throughout the palace.

When the king heard the news, he summoned his vizier and said: 'Nobody is ever permitted to enter my daughter's bedroom, except for her friends. If the necklace has been stolen, it must have been stolen by one of them.'

'Yes,' agreed the vizier, 'we must lock them all up in the cells and torture them with the smoke of burning straw mixed with chillies, and I'm sure that this will make them talk.'

The king followed this advice. After locking up all his daughter's friends, he ordered his servants to kindle a fire made of straw and chillies. Fortunately, however, there was a good man in the palace, and when he heard what was happening, he said to the king: 'Why are you taking the lives of forty innocent girls? Why don't you ask Nasruddin the holy man? He should be able to tell you who stole your daughter's necklace. He has recently helped one of your tenants to find his stolen bullocks.'

Hearing this, the king sent his guards to fetch Nasruddin the holy man. They went to Nasruddin's house and shouted: 'Holy man! Holy man!'

'What's the matter?' inquired Nasruddin.

The guards explained: 'The king has sent for you, because the princess's necklace has been stolen. You told one of the king's tenants where to find his bullocks, so now you must come with us and find the necklace.'

Nasruddin became very worried and wondered what to do. He said to himself: 'I knew where my wife had put the kneaded flour and what she was cooking in the pot because I had been watching her. I knew where to find the farmer's bullocks because I myself had stolen them. But how will I ever be able to discover who stole the princess's necklace? The only way to save my skin is to enter the palace and take a ladder and escape over the back wall. Then I shall hide until the princess's necklace is found.'

So he entered the palace and took a ladder and began climbing over the back wall. But the king's guards saw him and shouted, 'Wait, where are you going?' Nasruddin realized that it was useless to try to escape from the guards, so he accompanied them and they took him into the king's presence.

'Holy man,' said the king, 'come and sit next to me. Somebody has stolen my daughter's necklace. Tell me, who is it?'

'I cannot tell you immediately,' replied Nasruddin, 'but I shall tell you in three days' time.'

The king became angry: 'What sort of a holy man are you if you need three days to tell me who stole my daughter's necklace?' He ordered his guards to lock him up in one of the cells, and said: 'I shall set you free after three days, when you tell me the name of the thief.' Then he ordered that all his daughter's friends should be set free.

Nasruddin did not know what to do. The first night passed; then the second. Finally, on the third night, the girl who had stolen the necklace came to Nasruddin and whispered: 'Come here, holy man.'

'What's the matter?' asked Nasruddin.

'I shall tell you where the necklace is hidden, but please don't mention my name,' said the girl.

'So it was you who stole the necklace!' said Nasruddin. 'If you hadn't come to me tonight, I would have told the king that it was you.' Then he asked: 'Where have you hidden it?'

She answered: 'God knows and you know, so why do you ask me?'

'I am asking you just to check whether you really know where it is,' said the holy man.

'I dug a hole at the foot of the princess's bed and hid it there,' confessed the girl.

'It's all right, my child,' said Nasruddin. 'When I tell the king, I promise not to mention your name.'

As soon as the girl had left, the holy man began screaming: 'Take me out of here. Take me out of here.' Although it was the middle of the night, the guards took him to the king.

'You are an odd sort of man,' he said, addressing the king. 'When I told you that I couldn't give an answer to your question immediately, and requested three days' grace, you had me locked up in a cell. Three days have passed, and I am now in a position to tell you where to find the princess's necklace. It is concealed in a hole at the foot of her bed.'

The king and the vizier went to the princess's bedroom and found the necklace in the place that he had mentioned. The king was so pleased with the holy man that he appointed him Chief *Imam* of the Royal Mosque. He took him to the mosque and asked him to lead the midday prayer. Nasruddin knew the prescribed times of prayer because these are known to every peasant, but he did not know his *namaz* (prayers) properly. The king had already made it known that the holy man would be leading the midday prayer, and had issued special instructions to his people to put on clean clothes and attend. Nasruddin told his assistant to give the call to prayer.

When all the people had gathered in the mosque, they began to recite the four customary *rakat,* or units of prayer, while the holy man began to recite the four obligatory *rakat.* His left hand was on his stomach, and his right hand was on his hip, instead of both hands placed palm downwards, the right palm over the left, and across the chest. After every bow the holy man tucked his baggy trousers higher, so that by the time he had finished reciting half the midday prayer, he had tucked in the left trouser-leg to well above his left knee, and he had started tucking in his right trouser-leg.[2] Since the holy man was leading the prayer, the people who were praying behind him followed his example and began tucking in their *shalwar*s. When the holy man reached the last words of the *Fatihah,* the first chapter of the Quran, 'and have not gone astray,' the people said 'Amen' and bowed.

'This is the best moment for me to escape,' thought Nasruddin, and he ran out of the mosque. However, believing it to be praiseworthy to follow the example of the Chief *Imam,* the people ran out after him. They were in such a rush to leave the mosque that the crowd pressed against the verandah wall, and as the wall was made of mud, it collapsed.

Glancing behind him, the Chief *Imam* noticed the king among the throng of devoted worshippers, so he turned back to explain why he had run away: 'While I was praying, I received a message from God that the verandah wall would collapse, so instead of reciting the prayer, I was preparing to escape and save my life. I said to myself: "I shall run, and if my followers are intelligent, they will follow me, and if they are not intelligent, they will remain where they are, and the wall will collapse on top of them." Your Majesty,' he added, 'I am pleased to say that you are intelligent and that you saved your life by following me.'

Nasruddin then ordered the people to rebuild the wall with wood and mud. While they were busily engaged in this work, he escaped and went on his way.

35

The Barber and the Farmer's Wife

Once upon a time there was a barber who had arranged that his only son should marry a girl in a neighbouring village. After some time the boy's parents died, and the boy decided that he would go and live with his future parents-in-law and work in their village. 'When I have earned enough money to pay the marriage portion [*mehr*], then I shall get married,' he thought. So he packed his barber's equipment into his leather bag and set off to the village where his parents-in-law lived.

After travelling some distance, he passed a farmer who was ploughing his fields with a bullock. 'May you not feel tired,' he shouted. The farmer did not answer. He was in a bad mood because that morning he had quarrelled with his wife. The barber greeted the farmer a second time, and then a third time. Receiving no reply, he went up to the farmer, seized his moustache, and cut it off with his razor.

When the farmer returned home that afternoon, his wife smote her breasts in anger. 'Who has insulted you and cut off your moustache?' she asked.

'Be quiet! Don't make such a noise,' he answered. Then he recounted what had happened: 'I was ploughing the fields this morning when Zaybaddin the barber passed. He greeted me three times, but I didn't reply because I was angry with you. He then lost his temper and cut off my moustache.'

When the wife heard this, she said: 'I shall go myself and take revenge on your behalf.' She changed into her husband's clothes and turban; then she took the plough handle and hid it in her *shalwar* trousers. 'Which way did he go?' she asked. The farmer explained to his wife that the barber was engaged to marry a girl in a neighbouring village and would be staying with his future parents-in-law.

The farmer's wife left the house and went in search of the barber. Running as fast as she could, she caught up with him. She first greeted him with the words, 'You are welcome,' which is what her husband should have said that morning, then asked, 'Where are you going?'

He replied: 'Both my mother and my father are dead, and I'm going to stay with the father of the girl to whom I'm betrothed.'

The farmer's wife, who was disguised as a man, said: 'I am also betrothed to a girl in that village. If you like, we could first visit my in-laws and have dinner with them, and then go to your in-laws.'

'No,' said the barber, 'we shall go at once to my in-laws.

Since the farmer's wife had been lying – for she had no in-laws in that village – she readily agreed. When they reached the house, the barber called out his father-in-law's name.

'Who is there?' shouted the father-in-law.

'I am Zaybaddin,' replied the barber.

The father-in-law turned to his daughter, and said: 'You had better go to your uncle's house so that Zaybaddin and his friend can stay here.'

The barber's father was considered a rich man, for he had several cows and goats. Zaybaddin and his companion were received with great hospitality. A chicken was slaughtered in honour of the guests and preparations were made for the evening meal. The mother-in-law mixed all the milk that she had from the cows and the goats, poured it into a clay dish containing some yoghurt, and left it in a cool place to set. She heated the clay oven and baked some wheat-bread. Then she took the chicken and cooked it with spices.

After the meal the farmer's wife, who was still dressed as a man, said to Zaybaddin: 'Let's go for a walk in the village.' So they both got up and went out.

'You are my friend,' she said to him, as they were strolling along together, 'and your in-laws have been extremely hospitable. They too are my friends. But we mustn't put them to any more trouble. So when we return to the house, I suggest you tell them that we can share a bed for the night; otherwise, they will have to borrow one from their relatives.'

Zaybaddin agreed.

'You must also ask them if we can sleep on the roof,' she added, 'because they only have one room, and if we sleep in that room, their daughter will have to spend the night elsewhere.'

When they returned to the house, the father-in-law said: 'We shall all go and sleep in the village guest-house.'

But Zaybaddin answered: 'My friend and I will share a bed on your roof.'

The father-in-law tried to dissuade them: 'It's winter. How can you two spend the night on the roof?'

The barber insisted: 'A quilt will be quite enough to keep us both warm. We don't feel the cold.'

The father-in-law agreed somewhat reluctantly and a *charpoy* was placed on the roof. When everyone had gone to bed, Zaybaddin and his companion climbed on to the roof. 'Which side should I sleep on, the right or the left?' asked the barber.

'Stay where you are,' replied the farmer's wife. 'You are my friend and you must keep watch all night. If you come any closer, I'll kill you,' she said, reaching for a plough handle concealed in her *shalwar*.

The barber was a coward, being a member of one of the menial tribes, and he remained where he was. Later that night it grew chilly, and the barber began to shiver. 'If you don't make room for me on the bed,' he threatened, 'I'll shout and tell my in-laws.'

'Beware!' said the woman. 'You told your in-laws that you don't feel the cold. You can't take back your word now.'

When half the night had passed, the barber's teeth were chattering with cold. 'Are you still feeling cold?' asked the farmer's wife.

'Yes, I am,' he replied.

'Go downstairs,' she said, 'and fetch the yoghurt that your mother-in-law has prepared. If you eat it, it will give you warmth.'[1]

'But how will I go downstairs without being seen?' asked the barber.

'I'll show you how,' she replied. After removing her turban and his turban, she tied the long sheets together. Then she tied one end of the rope that she had made round the barber's waist and lowered him to the room below. 'When your feet touch the ground,' she whispered, 'you must fetch the dish of yoghurt and place it on your head. Then you must give me a shout, and I'll pull you up on to the roof, and we'll both sit and eat yoghurt together.'

When the barber's feet touched the ground, he went to fetch the dish of yoghurt, and put it on his head, and shouted, 'Pull!' In the olden days the rooms in the village houses were generally three yards high and three yards wide. After his first shout, the farmer's wife pulled him up a yard. When he shouted a second time, she pulled him up a second yard. Then she took her end of the rope and tied it to one leg of the *charpoy*. Whereupon she retired to bed, leaving the barber dangling in mid-air. Again and again he shouted, 'Please pull me up,' but received no reply.

The barber's mother-in-law heard the shouts and woke up. When she saw someone hanging by a long white sheet from the roof with a dish on his head, she woke her husband and told him, 'There's a *jinn* in the house; quick, let's get out!'

They both rushed out of the house. 'What shall we do now?' asked the father-in-law.

'We must call the mullah,' replied his wife. 'He can perform special prayers to exorcise the evil spirits.'

The man ran all the way to the mullah's house and rapped on the door.

'What brings you here on such a cold night?' asked the mullah.

The man answered: 'There's a *jinn* in our house.'

The mullah was sceptical: 'How do you know it was a *jinn*?'

'Because it keeps screaming, 'Pull me up! Pull me up!''

The mullah thought to himself: 'It sounds as though some thieves entered this man's house and then managed to escape, leaving one of their companions behind, shouting for help and begging his friends to pull him up.' But he said to himself: 'I'll go with this man; at least I'll receive a reward for my services.'

The mullah accompanied the man to his house, and there he perceived the figure of a man hanging in mid-air with a dish on his head, shouting, 'Please pull me up! Please pull me up!'

'Do you have a stick?' asked the mullah, turning to his companion.

'No,' replied the man, 'but I've got an old *charpoy*, and its legs haven't been fixed yet.'

'Bring them to me,' ordered the mullah.

The man went and fetched them. After giving one of the legs to him and one to his wife, the mullah told them to stand at the door of the house and to beat anyone who came out. Then he entered the house, armed with the shepherd's crook that he used on such occasions. After much hesitation, he took one step forward and shouted, 'Go away!' He himself was shivering with fright, because he now really believed that the man was a *jinn*. Then he took another step forward and again shouted, 'Go away!' With the third step, he reached the hanging man, and he began reciting special prayers and striking him with his crook.

The barber wondered how on earth he could escape from the mullah. He decided to throw the dish of yoghurt at him. The dish hit the mullah's head and broke in two, spilling yoghurt all over his face. The mullah took fright. 'Help!' he shouted, and then ran away as fast as he could. But the barber's mother-in-law and father-in-law were guarding the door. Failing to recognize the mullah, they started striking him with their sticks. They struck him so hard that he fell unconscious to the ground.

Then the father-in-law lit a lamp to examine the face of their adversary. He was astonished to see his son-in-law dangling from the roof and the mullah lying unconscious on the ground. He was furious with his son-in-law: 'You swine, look at the trouble you've caused us. Thanks to you the mullah is now unconscious and the yoghurt dish is broken. If you wanted yoghurt, you could have asked us.'

Zaybaddin quickly recounted what had happened, and told them to climb on to the roof and catch the real culprit. Having rescued their son-in-law, they rushed to the roof. But it was too late. The farmer's wife had already escaped by jumping to the ground.

It was thus that the farmer's wife took revenge on the barber for the insult done to her husband.

The story went for Eid.
I came down through the deodar tree.
The story was distributed like roasted corn,
and I returned to my bed.

Folkloristic Analysis

1. Fate and Intelligence (AT 945, N141)

A story with the same basic plot was collected in Czechoslovakia: Luck and Intelligence take turns to enter a simple peasant, to prove which of them should make way for the other. When Luck enters the peasant, he is saved from the executioner's sword and becomes a prince; Intelligence concedes that Luck is superior to him. Stith Thompson included this Czech tale in his anthology, *One Hundred Favorite Folktales* (pp. 363–65). The incident of the snake in the Raja's turban and the collapse of the roof of the council chamber are both found in a much shortened version of our tale, 'Fate is Mightier than Wisdom' (154 words), recounted by a Brahmin of Gajadharpur, Mirzapur (*NINQ*, vol. 4, 1894–95, no. 26; Kang, no. 16). A different version is found in Raju Ramaswami's *Indian Fables* (p. 44). In this tale a minister proves to a king that luck exists by making a parcel of peas and diamonds and tying it to the ceiling. He then calls in two men, one a believer in luck, the other a believer in human effort. The former lies on the ground. The latter climbs up, eats the peas, and throws down the precious stones. The man of luck walks away with the diamonds.

2. The King and the Clever Vizier (AT 875D, H561.1.1.1, H561.5, H586, H587, J1111.4)

The clever minister in this story resembles Birbar, the Emperor Akbar's vizier, who appears in a number of tales from the Indian subcontinent, in particular the Kashmiri tale 'Why the Fish Laughed' (*Indian Antiquary*, vol. 22, 1893, 321–25; Knowles, pp. 484–90). The vizier fears that he will be put to death if he fails to discover why a fish that a fisherman was selling laughed at the princess. The vizier's son promises to solve the riddle. On the way he meets an old man who is puzzled by the young man's remarks and considers him a fool, but on his arrival home, his daughter explains them one by one. The enigmatic remarks about the living and the dead, the farmer whose corn has been grown on borrowed money, and the best method of crossing a stream resemble those found in our tale. Another Kashmiri version of the tale contains a close parallel with regard to the farmer's debt. The girl explains why the vizier's son asked her father if the corn was eaten or not: 'He simply wished to know if the man was in debt or not; because, if the owner of the field was in debt, then the produce of the land was as good as eaten to him; that is, it would have to go to his creditors' (Jacobs, p. 190). The vizier's son begins by suggesting that it would be more pleasant if he or his companion give the other a lift, meaning that they might exchange stories to beguile the time. It is a riddle that occurs in another tale of the same type, 'The Choice of a Wife,' from Bannu in the Tribal Areas (Thorburn, pp. 190–91). In our tale the idea of one man carrying the other has become associated with the crossing of the river. In most versions of this type of tale the girl marries the young man, but in our version the vizier simply agrees to become a guest in the old man's house.

3. *Sweeter Than Salt (AT 923, H592.1, L52, M21, N451.1, N534.4, N582, Z71.5)*

This story of a princess who compares her love for her father to salt has been found by folktale collectors in many parts of the world: England, Belgium, Germany, Austria, France, Italy, Sicily, Spain, Portugal, Rumania, Morocco, and India. The tale is probably of Indian origin, depending as it does on the opposition of sugar and salt. As sugar-cane is not indigenous to Europe, in European versions the metaphor of sugar is generally replaced by other types of food or other comparisons. Bread and wine are used in an Italian version (Calvino, pp. 172–75). At the end of the tale, in at least two Indian versions, the young princess serves her father dishes made with sugar and dishes made with salt. The king pushes aside the sweetmeats and eats with relish the food seasoned with salt (Stokes, p. 164; Swynnerton, *Indian Nights' Entertainment*, pp. 78–79). But in our tale, and in a tale reported by William Crooke from Mirzapur (Crooke, *Indian Antiquary*, vol. 22, 1893, 323–24), elaborate dishes without salt are set aside in favour of simple food containing salt. Thus the king learns through experience the truth of his daughter's words. In Crooke's version the princess is already married when she is banished from her father's palace, and it is her son who leads the old king to his mother's palace after obtaining, by means of magic, certain things that the king had seen in a dream.

This tale forms the basis of the story of Shakespeare's *King Lear*. It is recounted by Geoffrey of Monmouth in his *Historia Regum Britanniae* and is repeated in Holinshed's *Chronicles of England*, this being the likely source of Shakespeare's tragedy. It is precisely the archetypal nature of the plot that makes the play so powerful. Emmanuel Cosquin unfairly remarks: 'Shakespeare has in no way improved upon a very poor version of an excellent Indian tale' (Cosquin, p. 108).

A parallel to the episode of the two snakes and the hidden treasure occurs in 'The Story of Vickramadit' (Dracott, pp. 119–24), a tale combining elements of 'Sweeter Than Salt' with 'King Thrushbeard'. A princess says to her father, 'I am what I am through my favourable destiny, and not because I happen to be your daughter.' As a punishment, the king orders that she should be married to the poorest and most sickly person available. That person happened to be Vickramadit, a holy mendicant, who, in reality, was a great king. He had once taken pity on a snake and had allowed it to enter his throat to have a drink, and since that time it has refused to come out. Overhearing a conversation between this snake and another inhabiting a mound of earth, the girl discovers that the mound conceals vast treasure. One snake predicts that the other will be killed by a certain seed. The other replies that 'a woman will kill you by pouring boiling milk and butter over you'. Fulfilling these prophetic words, the girl kills the two snakes and becomes immensely rich, thus eventually proving to her father that she was correct. Another tale of the same genre (AT 923B) is 'The Princess who Got the Gift of Patience,' recorded in Mirzapur from a Muslim cookwoman (*NINQ*, vol. 2, 1892–93, no. 633; Kang, no. 65). This tale is also entitled 'Prince Sabar' (Day, pp. 119–31; Wadia, *Indian Antiquary*, vol. 16, 1887, 322–27; retold in Ramanujan, pp. 159–68). In this case the youngest princess is abandoned in the jungle because she tells her father that she has confidence in herself, instead of in him, or she is a princess because of her own good star.

4. The Gardener's Daughter (AT 888A, H461.1, H659.2.3, H1385.4, J1112, J1545.6, K1837, N9.1, R152, T11.1, T121.8)

There are several Indian versions of our tale about a clever and headstrong peasant girl who marries a king, whom she later rescues after he has failed to win the hand of a clever princess (AT 888A). Two tales from the Punjab are worth mentioning.

In 'The Story of Gholam Badshah and his Son Ghul' (Swynnerton, *Indian Nights' Entertainment*, pp. 313–30), the prince, as in Tale 19, has vowed never to marry, much to his father's displeasure. A girl who offers him a drink at the well taunts him, 'O you are the prince whom no one will marry!' The prince, after refusing to drink, vows to marry this girl, the blacksmith's daughter. His father disapproves of the match, but grants his consent, hoping that a bride of worthy rank will later be found. Like the gardener in our tale, the blacksmith is opposed to the match. His daughter delays the marriage for one year, and then outwits the king's ministers by challenging them to take some water-melons out of their jars without breaking the jars. After the wedding the prince whips his wife to punish her for her taunt at the well, and he whips her on repeated occasions. She defies him to marry a king's daughter and treat her in a like fashion. So the prince sets out to win the hand of a beautiful dumb princess. He plays chess with her and loses three times. As a result, he suffers the penalty, which is to become her groom. Worried by her husband's absence, the blacksmith's daughter goes in search of him dressed as a man (like the heroine of our tale). A rat that she saves from drowning informs her that the princess uses an invisible cat to win at chess. Following the rat's advice, the blacksmith's daughter distracts the cat and checkmates the princess three times. Then, with the rat's help, she tricks the princess into speaking three times before sunrise, this being the final condition which each suitor must fulfil. She herself weds the princess and selects her husband as her personal groom, still without revealing her identity. She later asks permission to visit her family, and exchanging some clothes with her groom, and taking his curry-comb and brush, she returns home. When the prince arrives home, accompanied by the dumb princess, boasting that he has won his bride, the blacksmith's daughter puts him to shame by producing his curry-comb, brush, and old suit of clothes.

In a Kashmiri version of this tale (Knowles, pp. 144–51, retold by Ramanujan, pp. 66–72), the husband of a blacksmith's daughter loses everything to a woman at a game of *nard*, a game played with counters, because her cat extinguishes the light whenever the game goes against her. The wife uses a mouse to distract the cat and wins back her husband.

In a Punjabi version of this tale (King, *Folk-Lore*, vol. 32, 1921, pp. 271–73), the prince already has six wives whom he beats with a slipper. The gardener's daughter tells the prince that, if she were his wife, she would not agree to being beaten; instead she would expect him to prepare her hookah. Hearing this, the prince marries her. She then agrees to being beaten if her husband will agree to earn his living, instead of depending on an allowance from his father. So the prince sets out to earn a living by trade. He meets a beautiful harlot with whom he plays chess. She cheats by using a mouse to alter the game in her favour. Thus the prince forfeits all his possessions and becomes a slave with the duty of replenishing the girl's hookah. The gardener's daughter, disguised as a man, plays chess with the harlot and recovers what her husband has lost by bringing with her a cat to frighten away the mouse. She then purchases the slave, her husband, and returns home. When she shows him the dirty clothes he had worn as a slave, he is so ashamed that he never again beats her.

In each story the peasant girl demonstrates to her royal husband that it was thanks to her that he was rescued and/or obtained another wife of royal birth, and in each case she does so by producing the uniform or implements of his menial occupation. In our tale, however, it is as a result of gambling with swindlers that the prince is stripped of his fine clothes and belongings; and the game of chess is replaced by a test of riddles. The penalty for failing the test would have been death if the princess had not intervened and made the prince her gardener and water-carrier. So, unlike the harlot who plays chess, her conduct is above reproach. Here we perceive, even more clearly, the superior wisdom of women and the triumph of egalitarianism in a tribal society where women and peasants are expected to remain subservient: a peasant girl becomes the leader of the prince's forty wives, and, in a befitting reversal of fortune, the arrogant prince whose wife is the daughter of a gardener is given the task of watering the princess's flowers.

5. *Sass Begum (AT 516A, H607.3, H611.2, J1112, Z175)*

A very similar use of sign language is found in a tale from Baluchistan, 'The Prince, the Goat-herd and Naina Bai' (Dames, *Folk-Lore*, vol. 4, 1893, pp. 287–88). While hunting, a prince sees a princess passing in a boat. Their eyes meet and they fall in love. She places her hand on her head to indicate that she lives in *Choti* (which means a lock of hair in Baluchi and Urdu), over her eyes to indicate that her name is *Nain* (eye), and on her arms to indicate that she is by caste or tribe a *churigar*, or maker of bangles. These signs are interpreted for the prince by his friend the goatherd.

This incident also occurs in 'The Prince and the Vizier's Son' (Swynnerton, *Indian Nights' Entertainment*, pp. 167–69), an amalgam of half a dozen tales. Here again a princess in a boat makes signals to a prince who has gone out hunting. The new vizier who accompanies the prince fails to interpret her gestures. So the prince's former favourite, whom he had assumed dead, because he himself had issued orders for his execution, explains: she put her hand to her forehead to indicate that her name is Chusma Ranee, or Eye Queen; she pointed to her heart, meaning 'If you visit my country, my heart shall be yours'; she touched the bowl because her home is Lotah (a bowl).

6. *The Clever Princess (AT 983, H 583.4.5, J81, J1112, P111)*

The plot of this tale, more than any other in the collection, depends on riddles. The riddle posed by the princess at the outset (and repeated in the middle and at the end of the tale) motivates the quest for an answer and creates suspense. The vizier's son, who has been brought up in the wilds by his wise mother, supplies the answer. Once again it is evident that, without female instruction, men are singularly lacking in wisdom. In the end the unfortunate vizier is executed, not because of his failure to solve the riddle, but because of his inability to recognize his wife's innocence.

In this riddle the knife symbolizes death and the melon symbolizes man. The same symbolism is found in a tale recently collected in Uttar Pradesh, 'The King of Delhi and the King of Turkey' (Beck, pp. 233–35). A Muslim wise man buys a melon, and, when asked by his wife what he has with him, replies, 'Today I cut off the head of a man.' The editor notes the obvious parallel between a large melon and a man's head, and then remarks that 'the same equation is sometimes made in Hindu shrines' where a gourd or a coconut may be sacrificed as 'a symbolic equivalent to the offering of the worshipper's own head' (Beck, p. 233). However, the general cultural context of our riddle is Muslim, not Hindu. Izrail, the angel of death, is one of the four archangels, and it is recorded in one of the sayings of the Prophet Muhammad that this world is a table or tray in the hands of the angel of death, from which man may eat what he wishes (al-Qadi, p. 29). Since man has freedom of choice, he will ultimately be judged on the basis of the choices he has made. Nevertheless, God alone will decide the hour of death.

The other riddles in the story are likewise concerned with the meaning of life and death, or with the metaphor of life (or life's pleasures) as a meal (or a drink). The peasant girl puts straw in the bowl of water that she offers to the vizier because, if he quenches his thirst in one gulp, he may die. She thus gives him a practical lesson in the need for self-restraint. By means of riddles, she reveals that her father is a gravedigger (he mixes earth with earth), her mother is a midwife (she separates earth from earth), and her brothers are irrigating a garden (they are trying to bring the dead to life). The riddles about grave-digging and midwifery are both found in 'The Choice of a Wife' (Thorburn, pp. 190–91), a Pashto tale mentioned above (Tale 2).

The king's daughter, like the peasant girl, attempts to communicate with her father in riddles. By placing an orange on a tray and cutting it in two, she had meant to ask her father if he would swear, on pain of death, not to reveal that he had visited her. The vizier's son explains the symbolic gesture and gives the appropriate response, which is to cut the orange in four, and so on. The boy keeps his pledge of silence, even when the cannon to which he is tied is about to explode, until finally the princess makes it known, by means of the broken pitcher of water, that he is released from his pledge. Thus the boy earns the princess's hand in marriage and becomes the vizier in his father's stead.

The central episode of the tale is the king's visit to the vizier's wife during her husband's absence. Like the king's daughter, she also uses the language of symbolic gestures. She boils eight eggs for her guests and paints them different colours. In this way she conveys the message that women may appear different, but in reality they are the same – they taste alike! The king feels so ashamed of his sinful intentions that he departs immediately.

This episode is a universal folklore type (AT 983): 'The Dishes of the Same Flavour'. There are several literary examples. In Boccaccio's *Decameron* (I, 5), the Marchioness of Monferrato teaches the King of France the same lesson by offering him diverse dishes, all consisting of chicken. Juan Manual's *El Conde Lucanor* (*Exemplo* 50) contains a very different version: the wife of one of Saladin's vassals agreed to comply with Saladin's desires if he would first tell her which is man's best quality and the fount of all virtues; after a long quest, he discovers the answer – a sense of shame – and is thus deterred from committing a sin.

The best-known example of type AT 983 is 'The King and the Vizier's Wife' in *The Arabian Nights* (Ranelagh, pp. 227–28). The vizier's wife sets 90 dishes of different kinds and colours before the king. He eats a spoonful of each and finds that they all taste alike. She then explains: 'In thy palace are ninety concubines of various colours, but their taste is one.' Hearing this, the king leaves in such haste that he forgets his signet-ring, which the vizier later discovers. After a year of estrangement between the vizier and his wife, the king is able to inform the vizier, by means of another parable, that his wife is blameless: 'Return to thy garden, O vizier, and fear nothing, for the lion came not near it.'

An Indian parallel to the above is 'The Clever Wife of the Merchant' (King, *Folk-Lore*, vol. 33, 1922, 122–24). In this tale, as in ours, the message is communicated by means of coloured eggs. A merchant tells his wife that if he does not return within two years, she may remarry. A day before the two years have elapsed, the merchant returns to find his wife in bridal dress. Despairing of her husband's return, like Penelope in the story of Ulysses, she has consented to marry the governor of the town. She now takes four eggs; she dyes one black, one yellow, one green, and leaves the fourth white. She asks the governor to break them separately. He does so, and the same substances, yellow and white, come out of each. After the meaning of the parable has been explained to him, the governor sends her home with gold pieces.

Finally, a Syrian tale entitled 'The Clever Minister's Daughter' may be mentioned (Bushnaq, pp. 354–55): a king tests his vizier with riddles which his daughter answers for him; when the vizier admits that it was his daughter who had solved the riddles, the king marries her.

7. The Greedy King (B470, B552, L419.1, Q42, V410)

The king who becomes a beggar (L419.1) and helpful fishes (B470) are common motifs in Indian folktales. In 'The Three Princes' (Knowles, pp. 203–8), a holy man advises a prince to buy corn and throw some of it into the sea every day. Later the king of the fishes orders the fish to repay the king's generosity by each giving him a ruby. A close analogue of this tale, 'The Baker and the Grateful Fish', was collected in southern Iran and translated from Bakhtiari (Lorimer, pp. 344–46). The huge bird resembles the Roc, or *rukh*, the fabulous bird in *The Arabian Nights*, which carries off elephants to feed its young, and there is also an obvious analogy between the Mountain of Diamonds and the Valley of Diamonds in 'The Second Voyage of Sinbad' in *The Arabian Nights*.

8. The Sin of Pride (AT 757, L412, L419.1, L432.3, N844.2, Q331, S411.3, T511.1)

The main motifs in this story are L412 (rich man made poor to punish pride), L419.1 (king becomes beggar), S411.3 (barren wife sent away), and T511.1 (conception from eating fruit [berry]). A mouse plays a similar role in 'Prince Half-a-Son' (Steel, p. 190): it eats half the mango of the youngest queen and she begets only half a son. In the Palestinian tale of 'Half-a-Halfling' (Muhawi and Kanaana, pp. 85–86), the husband eats half the mango. The Baluchi tale, recorded by Dames and discussed above with reference to 'Sass Begum' (Tale 5), begins in the same way.

9. The Two Viziers (J1111.5, K1218.1.8, K2100, Q302)

Although this particular tale is not found in any published collection, the trick devised by the Muslim vizier's daughter to punish the Hindu vizier for falsely accusing her father of accepting bribes is well known. It occurs in 'The Clever Wife of the Wazir,' told by Jagat Bihari Lal, Kayasth of Kasganj, Etah District (*NINQ*, vol. 5, 1895–96, no. 428; Kang, no. 105, pp. 205–06). A man who was formerly a vizier seeks employment in another kingdom. The vizier of that kingdom arranges that the ex-vizier should go in search of the exotic Rangtatiya bird so that he can seduce the ex-vizier's wife. The wife outwits the vizier in the same manner as the daughter of the Muslim vizier in our tale, except that she uses treacle and a sheet covered in pieces of coloured cotton. The king's couriers are instructed to fetch the strange bird and the king laughs when the identity of the bird is revealed. The vizier is dismissed and the ex-vizier takes his place.

Compare this with 'The Prince and the Vizier's Son' (Swynnerton, *Indian Nights' Entertainment*, pp. 195–201), where it is the king who is made an object of ridicule. The king commands his new minister to go into the wilds and bring back nothing, hoping to ensure that the minister will be absent for a long time. Meanwhile, the minister's wife has two vats constructed in adjoining rooms. One of these she fills with liquid glue, the other with the feathers of many birds. While the king is visiting the lady, the husband knocks on the door. The king, in panic, hides in the vat of glue, and is then led to the feathers. The husband attaches bells to the bird's ankles and puts a rope round its neck. Then he announces at the royal palace that he has brought nothing, little realizing that he has brought the king. The king, now bereft of his hair and beard, is thoroughly humiliated, and swears never to visit the lady again. Like the king in Tale 6, he has been taught not to covet another man's wife, whereas the moral of our tale, 'The Two Viziers', is that one should not make false accusations. Another version of the tale is 'The Gutrun-Goon Bird' (Bahadur, no. 23). Here the minister's wife transforms the king's wicked servant into an exotic bird, using treacle and gold and silver paper.

10. *The Lion of the Jungle (AT 156, B103.0.6, cf. B103.0.8, B381, B431.2)*

This tale combines the Grateful Lion type (AT 156) with the tale of 'The Sensitive Tiger' (Oakley and Gairola, pp. 252–54). The former is found in many parts of the world, whereas the latter is rare. In the Kashmiri tale published by Rev. E. S. Oakley in 1935, we find the following common elements: the man is travelling to earn money as a dowry for his daughter; the wild beast gives him treasure; the wild beast attends the daughter's wedding, but does not wish to alarm the guests; the beast's feelings are wounded; the story, like all fables, ends with a moral ('Sometimes words wound more than swords').

The best known version of AT 156 is the story of Androcles and the Lion, recounted *c.* AD 160 by Aulus Gellius in *The Attic Nights* (V, 14): Androcles, a Roman slave during the time of the emperor Tiberius, had taken refuge from the cruelty of his master in a cave in Africa. A lion entered the cave and showed him its swollen paw, from which he extracted a large thorn. When, years later, the slave was recaptured and thrown into the arena, the lion, now also a captive, displayed its gratitude by caressing him, instead of attacking him. George Bernard Shaw was inspired by this story to write a comedy entitled *Androcles and the Lion*, first performed in Berlin in 1912, combining the traditions of the miracle play and Christmas pantomime.

Apion Plistonices, a rhetorician of Egyptian or Libyan origin, who recorded this tale in Book 5 of his *Wonders of Egypt* (*Fragmenta Historiae Graecorum*, III, 510), claims that he personally witnessed this incident in the Roman amphitheatre. A. G. Brodeur suggests that the story was inspired by an actual occurrence, and then 'Apion supplied both motivation and decorative incident out of his fertile fancy' (Brodeur, p. 485). It is possible that a traditional folktale, which Apion may have heard as a child, provided a plausible explanation for an actual occurrence.

The formula of a man who delivers a lion from peril or suffering, and is rewarded by the lion's lasting gratitude, is not common in the Indian subcontinent. But Brodeur is wrong to say that it is unknown in oriental tales (Brodeur, p. 488). In several Indian tales it is used as a convenient device to spark off the narrative. But the lion is generally replaced by the native Indian tiger. In 'The Man Who Went to Seek his Fate' (Stokes, pp. 63–67) and 'How the Raja's Son Won the Princess Labam' (Stokes, pp. 151–63; Jacobs, pp. 3–16, 237–38), the main protagonist receives gold and jewels, or a promise of help, from a tiger as a reward for extracting a thorn. Similarly, in 'Sir Buzz' (Steel, pp. 9–15), a poor soldier, seeking his fortune, is asked by a tigress to take a thorn out of her paw. He does so, and is given a box that he is forbidden to open until he has travelled nine miles. Finding the box heavy, he opens it sooner, and is confronted by a one-span manikin of prodigious strength. The manikin, who flies like a bee, fetches food and brings about a meeting between the soldier and the Flower Princess. In a tale from Baghdad (Stevens, pp. 58–59), the grateful lion gives the youngest prince three magic hairs.

Our tale, unlike these tales of magic and adventure, is set within the framework of Pashtun society, and it expresses the traditional view of the universal scheme of things, namely that the lion's place is in the jungle and man's place is to live with his fellow creatures.

11. The Great Saint (D1719, R167, V220)

In Central and South-East Asia there are many tales concerning the miracles of Sufi saints, some more plausible than others. Two of the best-known collections are Persian literary works: *The Mathnawi* by Jalaluddin Rumi and the *Memorial of the Saints* by Farid al-Din Attar. This particular tale has not been traced.

12. The Saint of Baghdad (D1719, H1573, V220)

This is a contest in spiritual authority between a tribal elder of the *jinn* and a Sufi saint, perhaps Shaykh al-Junayd of Baghdad, about whom there are numerous anecdotes. The name Jabar evokes the notion of God's mighty power. For information on the well of Zamzam and Mount Qaf, see the Glossary.

13. *The Fakir and the Princess (E34, E121.4, Q421, T121.5.2, V113.0.1, V220)*

There is a legend that St Peter accidentally struck off the heads of the devil and an old man, whereupon he tried to repair the damage, but placed the heads back on the wrong bodies (AT 1169). Here, however, the beheading is not an accident: the fakir and the princess's brother both commit suicide, one to fulfil a sacred pledge, the other because he disapproves of his sister's marriage. The princess, through the miraculous power of the dead saint Loe Zwan, raises the two men from the dead, but the miracle has to be repeated because, in her haste, the heads were placed on the wrong bodies.

The origins of the tale are extremely remote. One version of it, 'The King and the Corpse,' was translated from an ancient Sanskrit manuscript (Van Buitenen, pp. 16–19), and it inspired Thomas Mann's novella *Die Vertauschten Köpfe*, which was the basis of the libretto of an American opera performed in 1957 (*ibid.*, p. 9). The non-Muslim character of the story is more evident in 'Barbil's Son' (Dracott, pp. 104–6), a tale from Simla in the Himalayas. In this case the man is a rajah's son, not a fakir, and it is while visiting a sacred stone that he meets the girl and offers his head in exchange for taking her as his bride. The second man is the young man's father, not her brother; and she is advised by the gods to marry the man with her husband's head. Note that Barbil is a deformation of Birbal, the emperor Akbar's wise counsellor, about whom there are many stories. Birbal was the only Hindu converted to the emperor's syncretic Divine Faith and it is said that he composed poetry in Hindi (Ahmad, pp. 180, 242). A brief Pashto version of the tale, 'The Story of Hazrat Khizr, the Woman, and the Two Heads,' was published in 1913 (Malyon, pp. 384–85). Two men are killed by robbers. The wife of one of the men is instructed by Hazrat Khizr, to replace their severed heads. When the heads are transposed, a quarrel ensues as to whom the wife belongs.

14. *Musa Khan Deo (F124, H1333.5, H1578.1, K1837, N844.2, P672.2, T111, T532.1.1.1)*

This type resembles the Quest for the Wonderful Flower (AT 467), except that it is a *deo*, or demon, who possesses the magic flower and a princess, not a young man, who goes in search of it. It illustrates two themes discussed in the Preface: the desire to produce a male heir and the duty to avenge an insult. The methods used to test the sex of the girl disguised as a man are especially interesting. In the Arab legend of Solomon and Bilqis (the Queen of Sheba), Bilqis sends 500 young girls dressed as men and 500 young men dressed as girls to test Solomon's wisdom. Solomon is able to distinguish between the men and the women by the way they wash their faces (Ranelagh, pp. 32–34). In 'Why the Fish Laughed', the man disguised as a female slave who is plotting to kill the king is discovered because he manages to jump across a pit, which none of the girls can do (Jacobs, p. 193).

15. *Khurram Deo (F611.3.2, H1233.6.2, R11.2.2, S146.1, T111, Z231)*

This is another tale of a liaison between a princess and a *deo*. In this case the marriage is really an abduction, since the princess is kept imprisoned in a cave. The hero is her son Khurram, a child of precocious and prodigious strength (F611.3.2). The ending is abrupt and unexpected. One wonders what he has done to deserve such a fate. Is he punished for the sins of his father?

16. *The Man-eater (AT 327C, AT 1120, G11.3, G11.6, G441, K526, K711.4, K764, Q467)*

This is a variant of type AT 327C (The Devil or Witch Carries the Hero Home in a Sack), but, like AT 1120, it ends with the witch being drowned, not burnt to death in her own oven. Stith Thompson believes that this type, like that of Hansel and Gretel (AT 327A), is of European origin, noting how popular it is in Norway and the Baltic states (Thompson, *Folktale*, p. 37). But examples of it have been found all over the world (Ralston, p. 168), including several from Sri Lanka and the Indian subcontinent, and one from Palestine. In most of the Indian and Sri Lankan tales there is a magic tree, producing fruit, bread or cake, which seems to serve the witch's purpose of fattening her victim for the pot. A millstone or a pestle is generally used as an instrument with which to kill the witch's daughter. Usually this is done by means of a ruse; the witch unwittingly eats her own daughter; and the boy, or young man, escapes by dressing up in the girl's clothes.

One of the best examples of the story was collected in Sri Lanka (Parker, vol. 2, pp. 269–79, in three versions). A Yaksani (female demon), or Rakshasi (ogre), makes a cake-tree grow. A youngster climbs it and eats cakes. The Yaksani asks him to throw her down a cake. He throws it down, but it falls in a heap of spittle. The second time, it falls in a heap of mucus; the third time, in a heap of dung. She tells the youngster to hold the cakes in his hands and mouth and jump into her sack. Having tied up the sack, the witch sets off home. She leaves the sack near a field where some men are ploughing while she goes off on some business. Hearing the boy's shouts, the ploughmen untie the sack and fill it with clods of earth. Then the boy returns to the cake-tree and continues eating. The Yaksani takes the sack home and tells her daughter to cook the boy. When the Yaksani later sees the boy eating cakes in the tree, she again begs him for a cake, and the same sequence of events is repeated, except that this time the boy fills the sack with rat-snakes. On the third occasion, the Yaksani takes the sack straight home and instructs her daughter to draw the blood and cook the flesh. The boy asks the girl to first let him comb her hair. As he does so, she falls asleep, whereupon he cuts her throat, drains her blood, and cooks her flesh. After that, he takes a rice-mortar, a pestle, and a grinding stone, and climbs a palm tree. While the Yaksani is eating her own daughter's flesh, he sings a song to attract her attention and kills her by dropping these heavy objects on her head.

This story is found among the aboriginal Kolhan and Santal tribes of Bengal (Bompas, pp. 464–65; Campbell, pp. 12–13). The chief difference is that the boy dresses up in the girl's clothes to make his escape, a detail also found in our tale. In the Santal tale of 'The Two Brothers, Jhorea and Jhore' the girl expresses her admiration for the young man's long hair. He tells her that it became long by being pounded. So she puts her head down so that he can pound it, and he kills her and puts her in the pot.

A similar trick is played on the vain and gullible girl in the Bengali tale of 'The Witch's Dinner' (McCulloch, pp. 206–11) and in 'The Witch and the Boy', a tale recorded by Crooke in Bulandshahr (Kang, no. 83, pp. 173–74). In the Bengali tale, the witch's daughter-in-law informs a herdsman that she intends to kill him, but before doing so, she wishes to know how his teeth are so beautiful. He advises her to fetch a kettleful of oil and a skein of flax. The girl lies down as bidden and places the flax over her teeth. Then the herdsman pours boiling oil down her throat and she dies. After changing into the girl's clothes, he cuts her up, and cooks her flesh, and serves it to the witch and her children. Later, while pretending to draw water from the river, he escapes by jumping in and swimming across. In 'The Witch and the Boy', as in our tale, the girl admires the boy's round head, and he explains that his mother shaped it with a mortar and pestle.

It is curious to note that the detail about the ploughman releasing the boy from the sack occurs in our tale and in the different versions of the Sri Lankan tale, but not in the other tales discussed. This exact motif also occurs in the English tale of 'Jack the Buttermilk' (Briggs, vol.1, pp. 322–23). The merchant's daughter, in a Palestinian tale of that title, tricks the dim-witted daughter of a female ghoul (*ghouleh*) into releasing her from the sack in which she is imprisoned; she then slaughters the *ghouleh*'s daughter and puts her in the cauldron (Muhawi and Kanaana, pp. 259–60).

17. *The Prince and the Fairy (D212, F302.3.1.4, F302.3.4.5, F320, F324.3, F375, H1385.4, M149.5, R152, T69.1.2, Z71.5)*

The motif of the seven princesses sought by seven princes (T69.1.2) is not uncommon. See a Syrian story, 'Father of Seven Sons' (Bushnaq, pp. 50–55). In an Indian tale, 'The Story of the Seven Princes' (Chilli, pp. 54–80), a king searches the world for seven brides, of equal beauty, talents and birth, for his seven sons, but is unsuccessful. So each prince fires an arrow from a high tower, vowing to marry a girl from the house where the arrow lands. The arrow of the youngest prince strikes a tree where a she-monkey sits. He later discovers that his bride is a fairy who has taken the form of a monkey in order to test him.

'The Brave Princess', a tale from Kashmir (Knowles, pp. 197–202), resembles our tale more closely than any other, although it lacks the above-mentioned motif. In this tale, as in ours, the prince and his new bride chance to camp in a garden that was a favourite resort of a company of fairies, and these fairies charm the prince into a death-like sleep. The princess assumes that he is dead until she overhears the conversation of two birds. She sets out in search of her husband and, following the directions of an old man, finds him asleep in a garden. When she removes a wand from under his feet and places it under his head, he awakes. The fairies quickly return and the princess hides in a hollow tree. Smelling the girl's presence, the fairies remove the prince to another place.

Later the princess finds shelter in the house of a *deo*, who believes that the girl is his daughter whom another *deo* had recently kidnapped. He teaches her some of his secrets: how to bring the dead to life and how to find what is hidden. She perceives that her husband is concealed in an ornament hanging from the ear of one of the fairies. She pretends to admire the ornament and persuades the fairy to lend it to her. Thus the princess recovers her lost husband. The *deo* approves of the match and a feast is given in her honour, attended by all the fairies, after which the young couple fly to the palace of the bride's father laden with gifts. Comparing this tale with ours, it is obvious that the King of the Fairies, who adopts the princess as his sister, performs the same function as the *deo*, but our tale is superior in its style and narrative technique.

18. *The Parrot and the Starling (AT 334 [2], AT 1510 [3], AT 1359 [4], A2494.13.11.3, B211.3.4, G11.3, G11.6, J1163, K1551.1, K2213.1, N771, N825.3, Q241, Q411.0.2)*

Tales about parrots are universally popular. The best-known literary masterpiece on the subject is the Persian *Tuti-Nama* (Book of the Parrot) by Ziya al-Din Nakhshabi (d. 1350 AD [751 AH]), completed in 1330, based on the Sanskrit *Sukasaptati*. This work is also in the form of a framework with inset stories: there are 52 chapters or 'nights'. Our tale contains only four inset stories. However, two stories in the *Tuti-Nama* are found elsewhere in our collection: the 'Story of the Merchant and his Wife' (Nakhshabi, 1st Night, pp. 7–15; *cf.* Tale 21); and the 'Story of the Emperor of China' (*ibid.*, 39th Night, pp. 242–46; *cf.* Tale 25). A simplified version of the work was written by Abul-Fadl ibn Mubarak for the emperor Akbar, and this version was later supplanted by that of Muhammad Qadiri in the seventeenth century (in thirty-five chapters), which was translated into Hindi, Bengali, Turkish, and Qazan Tatar. Some of these stories entered the cycle of the Punjabi folk hero Raja Rasalu (Temple, vol. 1, pp. 1–65). But, as far as I am aware, no version of our frame-story has been published before.

The four stories are skilfully introduced by the two parties in the dispute, the parrot and the starling, as parables to influence the judge's decision. In the first story, 'The Glittering Necklace', the mullah, who is the judge, is invited to compare the starling with a brave and impulsive princess who is attracted by things that glitter, but remains chaste and so preserves her honour. It is an unusual story, which we have not encountered elsewhere.

In the second story, 'The Man-eaters', the parrot likens the starling's conduct to that of witches who waylay travellers with the intention of devouring and robbing them. These creatures belong to the same species as the old lady in 'The Man-eater' (Tale 16), and the story falls into the broad category of type AT 334: Household of the Witch. Note that, as in so many folktales, it is the young girl, in this case the youngest sister, who has a soft heart and comes to a bad end as a consequence. It seems unjust that she should be sliced up and devoured. If the three princes had been men of honour, they would not have betrayed the secret of their escape, nor would they have abandoned the girl who had saved their lives! Also note two motifs which will be familiar to readers of Robert Burns's *Tam O'Shanter* (ll. 208, 216): escape from witches by crossing water; and the attempt by witches to prevent escape by grabbing the horse's tail.

In the third story, 'The Widow and the Missing Corpse', the starling compares the parrot to a widow who falls in love with a sentry in the graveyard and offers him her husband's corpse so that the king will not notice that the corpse of a thief is missing. The implication seems to be that the parrot is cunning and wishes to be rid of his wife so that he may remarry. This tale, which is really less apt than the others – since the widow and the parrot have little in common – belongs to a very famous type, the Matron of Ephesus (AT 1510), a type rarely found in the Indian subcontinent. It is told by the twelfth-century author John of Salisbury in his *Policraticus*. The best-known version is that of Petronius, in *The Satyricon* (cx–cxii), composed during the reign of the emperor Nero in the early decades of the first century AD. This version is the main source of the plot of several plays: George Chapman, *The Widow's Tears* (1612), J. M. Synge, *In the Shadow of the Glen* (1903), and Christopher Fry, *A Phoenix Too Frequent* (1946). Critics were shocked by Synge's play, regarding it as a hideous slander on Irish womanhood.

Comparing our tale with the version of Petronius, in our tale there is only one dead thief, who was shot dead, not crucified, and the widow has no maidservant. In Petronius there is a long account of the matron's inconsolable grief in the graveyard vault beside her husband's corpse. The lady, after several days' fasting, is persuaded to share a meal with a sentry who is guarding the bodies of some crucified robbers. Eventually the sentry wins the lady's heart and spends three nights with her locked in the sepulchre. Meanwhile, the parents of one of the robbers, perceiving that the vigilance of the watch has been relaxed, take their son's body down from the cross to perform the last rites. The sentry, fearing punishment for neglecting his duties, declares that the gloomy vault will soon enclose both the widow's husband and her lover, to which she replies, 'Rather would I that the dead should hang than send a living man to his death.' So she proposes that her husband's corpse should be nailed on the vacant cross. The removal of the husband's beard is a realistic detail not found in Petronius. This detail gives the story an extra twist and introduces the punchline: 'If she is prepared to do this to her dead husband, what will she do to me?' The sentry, we feel, was right to be mistrustful.

The parrot wins the dispute by recounting another story about the infidelity of women. This misogynistic tale, 'The Two Unfaithful Wives,' belongs to type AT 1359: The Husband Outwits Adulteress and Paramour. As in 'The Prince and the *Fakir*' (Tale 19), a poor man and a prince are united in friendship by their recognition that they are both cuckolds; in both there is the motif of the husband who returns secretly to kill the paramour (K1551.1).

19. *The Prince and the Fakir (AT 1359, K1551.1, N825.3, Q241, Q411.0.2, T381)*

The central motif in this tale is that of the virgin imprisoned to prevent knowledge of men (T381). A curious feature of this tale is the fakir's magic doll who betrays her owner by transforming herself into a girl and by transforming her doll into a young man. This links up with the next tale. The theme of the woman's adulterous affair with a black man is also found in tales 22 and 23 (*cf.* Muhawi and Kanaana, pp. 212–18).

20. *The Dancing Dolls (K1549.8, Q241, Q411.0.2)*

No analogue for this tale has been found.

21. *The Merchant and the Parrot (AT 243, AT 1422, A2493.26, B131.3, B211.3.4, J551.1.1, J1154.1)*

A version of this tale is recorded in ancient Sanskrit (Penzer, vol. 6, pp. 186–89). As mentioned above (Tale 18), it forms part of Nakhshabi's *Tuti-Nama* (Tales of a Parrot) and was incorporated into the cycle of legends about the Punjabi folk hero King Rasalu (Swynnerton, 'Four Legends,' 129–52; Temple, vol. 1, pp. 1–65). When the Queen entertains Raja Hodi while her husband Raja Rasalu is out hunting, the *maina* bird, or starling, and the parrot witness her infidelity. When the starling rebukes her, she wrings the bird's neck. The cunning parrot asks to be allowed to keep watch in case her husband should return, then escapes and finds his master and reports what has happened. The tale belongs to a universal type (AT 1422), an example of which is found among the Kota people who live in the Nilgiri hills in southern India (Emeneau, vol. 2, pp. 271–89). Our tale ends in a similar way to the Kashmiri tale, 'The Clever Parrot' (Knowles, pp. 312–20): a fakir's parrot is bought by a king, whose wife orders the bird to be killed or else she will die; the parrot arranges for the king to marry another woman, a princess who lives on a faraway island and who offers the parrot pearls and candy.

22. *Gul and Sanobar (B30, B365.0.1, B421, B552, H1233.6.2)*

The first part of this tale – about Sanobar's discovery that his horses are in a wretched condition because his wife has been out riding at night, his feigning sleep to find out where she goes, and his confrontation with the black man who is her secret lover – is found in a Pashto tale, 'The King's Tale and the Vizier's', collected among the Afridis in 1911 (Malyon, pp. 392–93). At this point the two tales diverge, because Sanobar does not succeed in killing the black man. Instead he becomes his prisoner. Later, with the help of his dog, he escapes, taking Gul with him, and the couple evade the social stigma they would have faced had they returned home by remaining on a remote island; and eventually, through the intervention of a merchant, Sanobar is persuaded to return to his father's palace, but Gul is left behind. There is a Pashto version of the tale in verse, edited by Talib Rashid, which has not been translated; and there is an elaborate and stilted reworking of the tale, combined with elements of the Prince Bahram legend, translated from Urdu in the nineteenth century by Garcin de Tassy (see Rashid and Garcin de Tassy in the Bibliography). The name Gul means rose, and Sanobar means a pine-tree. The bird whose young are saved by Sanobar is the Simurgh of Persian mythology (see Analysis of Tale 28, and the Glossary).

23. The Three Friends (AT 449 [1], AT 1358C [2], D10, D132.1, D141, D525, K1549.8, K1550.1.2, K1571, Q551.3.2.6)

As in 'The Parrot and the Starling' (Tale 18), there are several stories, in this case three, set within a frame-story. It is a story-telling competition between a king, a vizier, and a peasant. The aim is to tell an amazing, but true, story, and the prize is a diamond. The winner, in accordance with the law of poetic justice, is the poor peasant. All the stories involve magic, courtship, and infidelity.

The first story belongs to a well-known type (AT 449), known as the Tsar's Dog, or Sidi Numan, which is found in *The Arabian Nights*. The basic plot is as follows: an unfaithful wife, who practises witchcraft, transforms her husband into a dog; a magician, or sorceress, disenchants him and gives him advice how to transform the wicked wife into a mare, a mule, or a donkey. The tale has been recorded in many countries, including India, Turkey, Arabia, Hungary, Lithuania, Finland, Poland, Scotland, Ireland, and France. This type is combined with another (AT 1358C), namely that of the husband who discovers adultery and eats the food prepared for the lover. The Pashto tale mentioned above with reference to Gul and Sanobar (Malyon, pp. 392–93) is an example of AT 449: the man is transformed into a black dog by the woman's magic spell; a witch disenchants him and gives him some magic dust with which he transforms the woman into a mule; he gives the mule to a potter with instructions to ill-treat her.

24. The Shy Prince (D1980, J1112, N771, T15)

This a charming tale of romantic love in which, once again, women, in this case the princess and the vizier's wife, show themselves to be superior to men in cunning and practical common sense. The prince overcomes his shyness by means of a magic amulet that makes him invisible. I have not found a close analogue. But in 'The Perfumer's Daughter' (Thornhill, pp. 15–66), a fairy marries a prince on condition that she should wear seven veils, and that she should leave the palace each day at sunset and spend the night in her father's house. After four months the prince falls ill and says that he will never recover until he sees his wife's face. This he succeeds in doing after receiving from a fakir a magic ring that makes him invisible.

25. The King's Dream (B421, D1381.11, D1520.17.1, D2121.5, H1381.3.1.2.1, N813, R41.2, S165, T11.2, T11.3, T381)

Many traditional Indian folk motifs are found in this tale, but again no exact parallel has been identified. It is not uncommon for love to be inspired by a dream or a picture. In 'The Artist's Stratagem' (Wadia) and 'The Story of the Prince and the Wazir's Son' (Swynnerton, *Romantic Tales*, p. 317), the prince falls in love with an unknown princess when he sees a painting of her.

26. Prince Bahram (AT 400 [2], B242.2.1, B451.4, D1421.1.9, D1475.5, D2074.2.2, F124, F145, F320, F375, F628.1.1.1, H1385.3, N771, N774.3, N813, N815, N844.2, R11.2.2, R151.1, T11.2.1, T548.1, V410)

This is a Pashto prose version of the Persian tale of 'Bahramgor and Dilaram' ('Heart's Delight'), which Saeed Khan Baba also knew in verse. Another version of the tale, recited by 'the Minstrel Faiaz', was published in 1875 by the British Assistant Commissioner in the Punjab under the title *The Ballad of Shahzadah Bahram and Gul-Andama* (Plowden, pp. 209–59). This translation sounds extremely stilted because Plowden gave it the form of an English ballad, using self-consciously poetic diction. Here is a brief sample:

> O mantle-clad! in truth art thou my (faithful) swain
> Prov'd 'tis that thou art true, and no-wise false (to me).
> Now to thee will I the Door of Candour ope:
> The Truth will I to thee right truly tell (my love!)
> The arrow of thy love is buried in my inmost breast:
> Since (first) the day I gaz'd upon thy (disguised) form. (ll. 531–33)

Plowden's ballad includes most of the narrative elements in the first part of our tale: an account of the birth and education of Bahram, son of Kishwar, the Lord of Rum [Persia], an interview with his father in which he vows to abstain from oppressing the poor, his combat with the tiger and pursuit of the deer, his meeting with the old man who has a marble statue of Gul-andama, daughter of Fagh-fur, the Emperor of China, his journey to China, his combats with Saifur and his brothers, the intervention of their sister the fairy Sarasia, his combat with the demon Afrad to release the captive fairy Ruh Afza, the gift of the magic hair which will bring help when burnt, his arrival at the town of China, beseiged by Bahzad, Prince of Balghar, his disguise as a dervish, his routing of Bahzad's army with the help of the fairy host, his proud inscription over the head of Bahzad, his first sight of Gul-andama when she makes her monthly public appearance, his offer of a precious ring as a token of love, Bahram's father's search for his lost son, and the marriages of Bahram with Gul-andama and Sarasia with Fagh-fur.

However, in our tale, there is no exchange of ornate love-letters, nor does Bahram's father send an embassy to China. The sequence of events is also slightly different: Bahram does not witness a battle outside the walls of the town of China upon his arrival, nor does he have to wait until he has slain Bayzad before catching his first glimpse of the princess. The detail of the smoke that leads Bahram to the old man may have been suggested by the description of the dark smoke in the sky, caused by vapours issuing from the mouth of the sleeping *deo* whom Bahram kills. Some of the names are the same. But it is not stated in our tale that Saifur is the King of the

Fairies; he is a *jinn* and the eldest of six brothers. The names of the others are not given. In Plowden's ballad the others are named Shamas, Kamas, Samel, and Kamel; it is Shamas, not Saifur, who gives Bahram the magic hair; and Ruh Afza is not Saifur's kidnapped wife, but a maiden who at the end becomes his wife. The narrator Faiaz seems to have been conscious of the fact that in Persian Bahram may either refer to the planet Mars or to an angel. For this reason the Chinese vizier says that Bahram inhabits the clouds and came with a host of angels (ll. 340–41).

It is interesting to compare these Pashto versions of the legend with two tales from the Punjab: 'The Faithful Prince' (Steel, pp. 22–28) and 'The Story of Prince Bairam and the Fairy Bride' (Swynnerton, *Indian Nights' Entertainment*, pp. 342–47). In Swynnerton's tale the prince is hunting deer when a demon king, named Safeyd, descends from the mountains of Khwa Qaf in the form of a snow-white horse and carries off the prince with whom he is enamoured. In Steel's tale the prince is transported to Demonsland by the demon Jasdrul in the form of a golden deer. Jasdrul is the youngest of three brothers; the second is named Nanak Chand and the eldest Safed. The first gives the prince a magic wand to protect him, the second gives him magic antimony to make the far near and the near far, the third a magic cap which will make him invisible. Temple judiciously notes that Safed is 'a corruption, or rather, an adaptation to a common word – *safed*, white – of the name Saifur for the demon of the older legends of Bahramgor (Steel, p. 207). This interpretation is corroborated by the nature of the three gifts which the prince receives from Safeyd in Swynnerton's tale: 'his invisible cap, some of King Solomon's antimony, and one of his own hairs' (p. 345).

In Steel's tale, the princess Shahpasand (King's Delight) – a variant of Dilaram (Heart's Ease), Hasan Bano (Lady of Beauty), Ghulab Bano (Lady Rose) or, as in our tale, Gulandama (Rose Princess) – inhabits the Emerald Mountain (Koh-i-Zamurrad). Temple suggests that this may refer to 'the celebrated Green Mount in the Winter Palace at Pekin' (Steel, p. 207). This is unlikely because in the other tales that we have been discussing the fairy princess lives in the mountain of Qaf, an emerald mountain range which, according to ancient Islamic cosmologists, surrounds the earth (see the Glossary).

'The Perfumer's Daughter' (Thornhill, pp. 15–66), mentioned above in connection with 'The Shy Prince' (Tale 24), opens in the same way as 'Prince Bahram': while pursuing an antelope, the prince and the minister's son, without knowing it, enter the region of the North, where astrologers had warned that the prince should not go. They arrive at a walled enclosure, which they enter by climbing a tree and find themselves in a beautiful garden. They learn from the gardener that the garden belongs to the perfumer's daughter, with whom the prince falls in love by hearsay; and it later transpires that she is a fairy.

The motifs with which 'Prince Bahram' opens are all common in Indian tales: the child born in answer to prayer (T548.1), the fakir as helper (N844.2), adventures from pursuing an animal (N774.3), sometimes an enchanted animal, such as a deer, boar, or bird (N775), the strong man who kills a tiger single-handed (F628.1.1.1), and love through sight of a statue (T11.2.1). The curious incident of the prince's encounter with the old man who has a statue of the princess is not found in Swynnerton or Steel (except that the demon Jasdrul takes the form of a little old man), but it is an important part of Plowden's Pashto ballad; and it is also the central episode of a very brief tale, entitled 'The Prince and Khizar Deo,' collected by William Crooke, told by Ramnandan Lal, village accountant of Kon, in Mirzapur, near Benares (*NINQ*, vol. 4, 1894–95, no. 52). The old man has transformed the beautiful lady into a stone idol. All representational art, especially portraiture, is considered by Muslims to be potentially idolatrous. This is why the Taliban leaders, influenced by Wahhabi puritanism, eventually decided to destroy the Buddhist statues at Bamiyan.

The burning of the hair serves the same magic function as the burning of the Simurgh's feather in the Persian epic romance of Zal and Rustam: the Simurgh offers one of her feathers to the young prince and tells him that, if he is ever in trouble, he must burn it and she will come to the rescue. In a Santal tale, the hero, Lelha, summons the Indarpuri Kuri (Celestial Maiden) by taking one of her hairs in his hand and asks her to send an army four times greater than the one he is facing (Campbell, p. 87).

27. *Hazrat Ali Sahib (AT 369, F141.1, F302.3.1.4, F320, F375, F611.3.2, H94, H1216, H1381.2.2.1, H1385.4, N731, N731.2, Z231)*

In many parts of the Muslim world, especially in Shia areas, tales are told about the heroic exploits of the Prophet Muhammad's son-in-law Ali ibn Abi Talib, but few of them have been published in English (Knappert, vol. 1, pp. 238–68). He is especially venerated in Afghanistan because his tomb is in Mazar-i-Sharif, although other traditions have his body interred near Kufa at the twon of Najaf. This tale belongs to the type AT 369 (The Youth in Quest for his Lost Father). Muhammad Hanafiya was the youngest son of Ali by his second wife Khawla, a woman of the tribe of the Banu Hanifah, who had been brought as a prisoner to Medina after the battle of Aqraba. He was born in 16 AH. Although he did not have the blood of the Prophet in his veins, the Shias regarded him as the Prophet's rightful successor after the violent and untimely deaths of Hasan and Husayn, the sons of Fatimah, and some spread the belief that he was the hidden Imam who would return to defeat the enemies of his family and restore justice before the Day of Resurrection (Knappert, vol. 1, pp. 306–11).

The storyteller has confused the battle of Aqraba with the more famous battle against the Jewish stronghold of Khaybar in 628 AD (7 AH) and gives the name Khyberay to Hanifah's mother, a name appropriate for an Afghan heroine on account of its association with the Khyber Pass. There is also no evidence that Khawla fought in battle. The whole story bears little relation to historical reality.

Hazrat Ali's physical and amorous conquest of a beautiful giantess, which symbolizes the conversion of the Afghan people to Islam, is the subject of a Pashto legend in verse which was translated in the nineteenth century (Masson, pp. 151–58). In this version the giantess, named Bul Shinwari, who 'suffers no stranger to pass through her land', throws a rock at Hazrat Ali; he seizes her by the waist and holds her between the earth and the sky until she acknowledges the one true God; he assures her that there is no shame to be vanquished by the Lion of God; he marries her and gives her a ring as a pledge of his faith and a token of love:

> Now Alee partakes of the delicate feast,
> And then, as was fitting, to bar all reproach,
> With the blessing of Kunber, who acted as priest,
> He leads Bul Sheenwauree, a bride, to his couch. (p. 157)

The ring is a key element in our tale, for it is by means of the ring that Hanifah is able to prove his identity when he meets his father. But in this legend there is no mention of a son, and the poem ends with Hazrat Ali's departure from Afghanistan.

28. The Simurgh (AT 300, B30, F145)

In this brief tale Hazrat Ali kills the snake which eats the offspring of the mythical Simurgh (see the Glossary). No analogue was found.

29. The Woodcutter (H1263)

This is a humorous and philosophical tale about the nature of divine providence. As in the case of the first tale, 'Fate and Intelligence', it demonstrates that destiny is more important than intelligence and that hard work and generosity will be rewarded, even if one's motives are not altruistic. Compare this tale with 'The Man who Fought with God' (Kang, no. 1, pp. 1–3). A poor woodcutter hears that anyone who gives in charity will receive double in return. He gives alms every day, yet his savings never increase. So he says that he will fight with God. On the way he meets a king, a man, and a woman in a well, and then a withered tree. Each begs him to ask God a question, which he promises to do. In the end his charity is rewarded, for he marries the king's daughter and becomes exceedingly rich. Similarly, in the 'The Barber's Clever Wife' (Steel, pp. 149–55), the lazy and foolish barber is advised by his wife to beg the king to give him something, and the king gives him a piece of wasteland; some thieves who are deceived into thinking that there is buried treasure there dig it up; the thieves are outwitted and the king makes the barber his vizier. Another version of Tale 29 is 'The Man Who Went to Seek His Fortune' (Dracott, pp. 96–100).

The question, 'Where is the centre of the earth?' is central to a tale briefly narrated by Idries Shah's father Ikbal Ali Shah (I.A. Shah, pp. 149–51). Mahmud, the ruler of Ghazni, told a fakir that if he failed to answer this question, he would be put to death. Following his clever daughter's advice, the fakir touched one of the legs of the royal throne and said that the centre of the earth was beneath that leg, and that the King ruled in the centre of the earth. The King was very pleased with this reply and gave him an embroidered robe.

30. The Swindlers (AT 1525N, AT 1532, AT 1654, K301, K305, K306, K331, K335.1.2.2, K341.6, K451.5, K1974)

This is a version of a well-known tale, combining three types: The Two Thieves Trick Each Other (AT 1525N); The Voice from the Grave (AT 1532); and The Robbers in the Death Chamber (AT 1654). El-Shamy notes that AT 1654 is common in Egypt, where it sometimes includes elements of AT 1525N, involving a thief from Egypt and a thief from al-Sham (Syria); he also remarks that AT 1525N is 'recurrent in the Middle East, particularly among the Berbers of North Africa and in south Arabia' (el-Shamy, p. 298). AT 1532, on the other hand, belongs to the Indian subcontinent and is 'reported nowhere in European tale collections' (Beck, p. 274). It probably derives from Buddhistic literature. The usual plot is as follows: two rascals hear of a wealthy man who has recently died; one claims that the dead man owes him a large sum of money and asks his relatives to repay him; his confederate, concealed near the grave, answers that the debt must be repaid. This story has been found in Tibet (O'Connor, pp. 124–32), Kashmir (Knowles, pp. 297–300), Punjab (Swynnerton, *Indian Nights' Entertainment*, no. 21), and elsewhere. In many of these stories one finds the motif of shoes dropped separately to distract attention (K341.6) and that of robbers frightened from goods by a sham-dead man (K335.1.2.2).

The motifs of the master thief (K301), thieves stealing from each other (K306), and goods stolen while the owner sleeps (K331), which are usually incorporated into type AT 1525N, are found in many tales from Kashmir to Sri Lanka. In 'The Master Thief' (*NINQ*, vol. 3, no. 135), a king boasts that he is an expert at catching thieves. His son tests him by stealing his drinking-bowl (*kattora*). The king offers his son half his kingdom if he can steal a tray. He hangs the tray over his head and fills it with water, so it would spill and wake him up if anyone were to attempt to steal it. The prince puts sand in the tray to soak up the water and then successfully steals it. It is by much the same trick that the swindler from Kabul steals the silver drinking-bowl from his Hindustani rival: he fills it with ashes. But for a parallel to the hiding of the bowl in the river and the detective work used by the Hindustani swindler to recover it, one should read the southern Indian tale, 'How the Three Clever Men Outwitted the Demons' (Frere, pp. 203–10), about a pearlshooter, a wrestler, and a pundit who compete in swindling. At night the wrestler steals an enormous iron cauldron and hides it in the river. The pundit and his wife follow the wrestler's footsteps to the river, and the cunning pundit knows that the wrestler has been up to his neck in fresh water because, when he licks his body while asleep, there is no taste of salt on his skin. In 'Eesara and Caneesara' (Swynnerton, *Indian Nights' Entertainment*, no. 21) the brass plate hidden in the mud is discovered by the Hindu Eesara when he notices the solitary reed marking where it is hidden.

31. The Barber's Son (AT 1693, J1705, J2461.6)

This is the motif of the literal fool: fool told to follow his nose in journey, runs head against tree, climbs it. Strictly speaking it is a tale type, not a motif, although not a common one. Both the tree-climbing and oil-spilling incidents are found in 'Shaykh Chilli and the Camel Man', collected by Crooke and told by Farzand Ali of Bareilly (*NINQ*, vol. 5, 1895, no. 249). Another good example of the genre is 'A Simpleton who Followed His Instructions Too Literally' (Oakley and Gairola, pp. 213–16), which also, like Tale 35, belongs to Type 1685A (Stupid Son-in-Law). But the incidents recounted are entirely different.

32. The Shepherd (AT 1698A, X111.1)

This tale belongs to a universal type about deaf people, which has been studied by Antti Arne. Stith Thompson summarizes the story as follows: 'A inquires for his lost animals. – B talks about his work and makes a gesture. – A follows the directions of the gesture and happens to find the animals. He returns and offers an injured animal to B in thanks. – B thinks he is blamed for injuring the animal and a dispute arises which is taken to a deaf judge' (Thompson, *The Folktale*, p. 211). The tale has been found in Lapland, Greece, Turkey, Palestine, Morocco, and southern India. See 'The Story of the Three Deaf Men', translated from Tamil (Kingscote and Sastri, no. 1). It is curious that, as far as I am aware, there are no published examples of this tale from northern India or Pakistan.

33. The Weavers (AT 1321, J1705, J2600)

This tale belongs to the general category of tales about fools and numskulls. Several tales have been reported in northern India in which jokes are made at the expense of weavers. Since weaving has traditionally been considered a profession of the menial tribes, weavers are depicted as foolish and cowardly, as illustrated in the Kashmiri tale, 'Fatteh Khan, the Valiant Weaver' (*Indian Antiquary*, vol. 11, 1882, ed. F.A. Steel and R.C. Temple, pp. 282–85). The tale 'Of Certain Deluded Weavers' (Swynnerton, *Romantic Tales*, pp. 268–69) sheds some light on the alleged inferiority of weavers, for in this tale we learn that 'when the Duranis had subdued the country, there was a certain small village inhabited by weavers'. When government officials came to collect tax revenue, the weavers were unable to explain their grievances because they only knew Punjabi. It was therefore decided to dispatch 'two of their number to Kabul to purchase a supply of the language of Persia'. At every village they were hooted at with contempt until they reached Jalalabad, where a clever and cruel man sold them two jars full of black wasps, saying they were full of the most excellent Persian, which they should share among themselves when they are undressed at home with their friends. As a result the weavers were severely stung and decided in future not to meddle with Persian. This demonstrates that weavers were generally not of Pashtun stock. This also explains their ignorance of the pastoral life and their reluctance to fight.

34. Nasruddin, The Holy Man (K1956.2, K1961.1.5, K1970)

The most famous humorous anecdotes about a holy man are those concerning the legendary Turkish folk hero Khodja Nasruddin. These jests are widely known in the Muslim world and are used by Sufi sheikhs for teaching purposes (Idries Shah). This explains why the hero of this tale bears the name Nasruddin, even though he is a sham holy man.

35. The Barber and the Farmer's Wife (AT 1685A, AT 1691, D2176.3.1.1, J1705, J1786, J2541, P672.2)

This tale exemplifies two tale types: the Stupid Son-in-Law (AT 1685A) and Don't Eat Too Greedily (AT 1691). It contains the motifs of a man thought to be a devil or ghost (J1786), and the evil spirit exorcized by a religious ceremony (D2176.3.1.1). Swynnerton published a similar tale (*Indian Nights' Entertainment*, pp. 264–66), except that in our tale the foolish son-in-law is a barber, not a weaver, his companion is a woman in disguise, not the best man, he is not lowered down the chimney-hole, and the mullah is covered in yoghurt, not flour. Furthermore, our tale is set within the framework of an insult avenged, *cf.* 'Sheikh Chilli Goes to His In-Laws' (Bahadur, no. 21).

In another version of the tale, the stupid son-in-law eats little because he is afraid to be considered greedy and is then caught at night with his mouth stuffed with food. As he cannot speak, he makes a sign in dumb show and his in-laws believe that he is possessed by a *jinn*. They summon the barber, who cures him by means of a poultice (Thorburn, pp. 203–4). Entirely different, but equally entertaining, is a tale translated by A. K. Ramanujan in *Folktales from India* (pp. 96–99) about 'The Night-Blind Son-in-Law', one of whose misfortunes is to be butted by a ram like the foolish weaver in Tale 33.

Notes

Preface

1. The British used to call these tribal people Pathan. Journalists and anthropologists nowadays tend to favour the native pronunciation of the term: Pashtun, Pakhtun, or Pukhtun, a word that originally means modesty, shame, or integrity (Ahmed, *Pieces of Green,* p. 112). There are about 60 Pashtun tribes, with a total population of 19–20 million.
2. Report by Filippo Grandi, chief of the UNHCR mission to Afghanistan, cited in an article by Ron Synovitz, posted 27 February 2002, on Middle East News Online.
3. Caroe, pp. 3–103; Ahmed, *Pukhtun Economy and Society,* p. 128.
4. Ahmed, *Mataloona,* p. 11.
5. *Ibid.,* p. 47.
6. It could be argued that Osama bin Laden was able to take advantage of this code of hospitality when he was a 'guest' of the Taliban.
7. Ahmed, *Mataloona,* p. xviii; *cf.* Thorburn, proverbs on fate, pp. 269–71.
8. Folktale type numbers here and elsewhere are from Antti Aarne and Stith Thompson, *The Types of the Folktale*; see Bibliography.
9. Another example of a deceitful wife is found in 'The Dancing Dolls' (tale no. 20).
10. The clever peasant girl is listed by Aarne and Thompson as a universal type; see AT 875D.
11. This is a common motif (D2074.2.2), discussed in the notes to tale no. 26.
12. See the Glossary. The giant bird in 'The Greedy King' (tale no. 7) would seem to be inspired by the Roc of *The Arabian Nights,* not the Simurgh.
13. See tale no. 21. The same observation is made in a twelfth-century Latin bestiary: 'A parrot's beak is so hard that if you throw down the bird from a height on a rock, it saves itself by landing on its beak with its mouth tight shut, using the beak as a kind of foundation for the shock.' T.H. White, *The Book of Beasts,* (London: Jonathan Cape), 1954, p. 113.
14. 'Sex-Differential Mortality, Health and Family Planning: A Study of the Status of Women in the NWFP of Pakistan', London School of Hygiene and Tropical Medicine, University of London, 1979.

Tale 3

1. A Muslim should use this phrase, *insha Allah,* when expressing an intention to do something in the future.

Tale 4

1. In the North-West Frontier women rarely marry outside their clan, and it is the custom for cousins to marry.
2. The custom of demanding a bride-price is common among the Pashtun people, although it is not compatible with Islamic law.

Tale 5

1. According to the Qur'an (2: 77; 9: 60), travellers are among those with a special right to charity.

Tale 6

1. In the Pakistan Tribal Areas the mere suspicion of adultery can lead to the penalty of death for both men and women.
2. When they are performing their ablutions, Muslims resort to this practice, known as *tayammum,* when water is not available.

Tale 10

1. He was worried because he would have to provide each of his daughters with a suitable dowry.

Tale 11

1. The word used here, and in the title of the next tale, is *pir,* a Sufi Shaykh or spiritual master.

Tale 12

1. As his name Dhobi indicates, he is a washerman by profession.

Tale 18

1. See *ghusl* in the Glossary.
2. This is how Tam O'Shanter escaped from the witches in Robert Burns' famous poem; see Folkloristic Analysis.

Tale 19

1. Measure of weight which varies considerably. In Peshawar it is equivalent to two lb (0.9 kg).
2. See *tor* in the Glossary.

Tale 21

1. Muslims are expected to pray five times a day, if possible at the correct

time. See *namaz* in the Glossary.
2. In many parts of the Muslim world people visit the shrines of holy men to seek their help, although this custom (*ziyarat*) is frowned upon by the Wahhabis of Saudi Arabia and by those, such as the Taliban, who have been influenced by Wahhabi preaching.
3. See *tor* in the Glossary.

Tale 22
1. See *ghusl* in the Glossary.
2. See *tor* in the Glossary.
3. See Simurgh in the Glossary.

Tale 23
1. It is considered a grave sin in Islam to refuse anyone water.

Tale 24
1. In the North-West Frontier, as in most parts of the Indian subcontinent, marriages are arranged by the girl's parents or legal guardians, but, according to Islamic law, or the *shariah,* the marriage contract is not valid without the consent of both parties and the presence of two witnesses.
2. This is a common image in Persian and Pashto love-poetry.

Tale 25
1. See *ghusl* in the Glossary.
2. According to a saying of the Prophet Muhammad, reported by al-Bukhari, 'Whoever believes in God and the Last Day, let him entertain his guest; and his trouble is for one day and one night, and entertainment is for three nights, and what is after that is charity.'
3. Marriage between a father and daughter-in-law is forbidden in the Quran (4: 23).

Tale 26
1. The Pashto for 'exchange' in this context is *badal,* see the Glossary.

Tale 27
1. This refers to the four companions who, after the Prophet Muhammad's death, were to become rulers of the Islamic community: Abu Bakr, Umar ibn al-Khattab, Uthman ibn Affan, and Ali, the Prophet's cousin and son-in-law. They are known as the 'Rightly-Guided Caliphs'. Shia Muslims venerate Hazrat Ali as the Prophet's rightful successor.
2. These words give the false impression that the Islamic faith was spread by the sword, a popular misconception of orientalist literature. In the Quran it is written: 'There shall be no coercion in matters of faith' (2: 256). It is evident from the Quran that only self-defence, in the widest sense, and in

particular the defence of religious freedom, makes war permissible for Muslims.

3. See *shahadah* in the Glossary.

4. According to the Quran, a man may not marry more than four wives, and he may not take more than one wife unless he can provide for them and treat them equally: 'but if you have reason to fear that you might not be able to treat them with equal fairness, then [marry] only one' (4: 3).

5. The word *haram* in Arabic and the Muslim world means 'that which is forbidden,' a suitable name for the territory of an infidel king. His daughter's name means 'olive.'

6. The purpose of the veil is to protect the woman's honour. Zaytun does not wear a veil because she has lost her honour. She can only recover her honour if her husband is returned to her. Pashtun women are expected to have a male guardian, who may be a husband, a father, a brother, or son.

7. The duty to show hospitality to travellers is central to *Pakhtunwali,* the Pashtun code of honour. This duty is also stressed in the Quran, where it is written that travellers are among those special categories of people who deserve to receive charity (2: 215). The failure of these infidel kings to offer hospitality must be seen within this context.

8. This episode is inspired by a parable in the Quran about Moses and his quest for a fish that symbolizes divine knowledge or eternal life (18: 60–82). He meets a mysterious sage, usually identified as al-Khidr, who offers to guide him, but warns him not to question his actions. The sage scuttles a boat, slays a young man, and rebuilds a wall without receiving any payment. On each occasion Moses protests and is rebuked for doing so. The sage later explains that he scuttled the boat because it belonged to some needy people and would have been seized by a king; he slew the young man because he was wicked and would have harmed his parents, who were true believers; and he rebuilt the wall because it belonged to two orphan boys, and beneath it was some treasure that they would inherit when they came of age.

Tale 28

1. *Cf.* no. 22, 'Gul and Sanobar'; also see Simurgh in the Glossary.

Tale 30

1. The land of the Hindus, India.

Tale 34

1. One would not expect to find a hard earth floor in a palace bedroom. This is a point overlooked by the narrator.

2. It is customary for Muslims to uncover the anklebone during prayer, and this may be done by tucking in the *shalwar* at the waist.

Tale 35

1. The barber should have known that this is bad advice because yoghurt is considered a 'cold food'. By following this advice, he is again demonstrating his stupidity.

2. *Qissa lárra pa akhtar.*
   Za ti rakaz shúm pa nakhtar.
   Qissa lárra batt la,
   Zarlárama akpal katt la.

Glossary

anna	A unit of currency in India and Pakistan, the sixteenth part of a rupee.
badal	Exchange, substitution, retaliation, revenge. The term is applied to the obligation to take revenge for a wrong committed, which is of fundamental importance in the Pashtun code of honour, known as *Pakhtunwali*, the way of the Pashtuns. It has given rise to hereditary blood-feuds between certain tribes. The term is also applied to marriages in which a sister or cousin is given in marriage in exchange for the marriage of the other person's sister or cousin, often in order to settle a dispute between the two families.
Bahram	Bahram, the Persian word for the planet Mars, is the name of five kings of the Sassanian dynasty. Bahram V (r. 420–38) was known as Gur (wild ass), either on account of his great strength, or because he died while hunting a wild ass. He became a hero of Persian literature, renowned both for his military prowess and his love of poetry. In one of Nizami's works, the *Haft Paikar*, seven stories are related to Bahram Gur by seven princesses with whom he is in love.
chadur	Piece of cloth, serving as a turban-cloth, veil, sheet, or prayer mat.
charpoy	(Anglo-Indian): Light bedstead, made of hempen rope stretched over a wooden frame (Pashto *char-payi,* literally 'four-legs').
churi	Small pieces of dried fruit, with breadcrumbs or flour, fried in ghee. It is given to women when they are pregnant.
deodar	Himalayan cedar (Sanskrit *deva-dar,* divine tree, tree of the gods).
deo	Species of demon, not necessarily malevolent (Sanskrit *deva*), which may take the form of a human, a giant, or a monster.

	According to Ikbal Ali Shah, they have tails, horns, and thick skin like oxen; they wear no clothes, except a girdle round the waist; and their chief function seems to be to guard the fairies. Both *deos* (sometimes spelt *divs, deevs, dews,* or *dayoos*) and fairies, or *paries,* are attracted by human beauty. A pretty girl will be forbidden to sleep in the open for fear the 'shadow' may fall on her and she may be transported to the mountain of Qaf. It is also for this reason that mothers do not permit their daughters to wear bright colours (I.A. Shah, pp. 106–7).
Duldul	This is the name of the Prophet Muhammad's white she-mule, which he rode on many campaigns. She is said to have survived into Muawiya's reign. According to Shia legends, she retained so much vigour that Ali was able to ride her in his campaigns against the Kharijites.
fakir	Beggar, mendicant dervish (Arabic *faqir,* one in need of God).
Fatihah	This is the first *surah,* or chapter, of the Quran, which is repeated before every bow. The word means 'opening'. It is a prayer, similar to the Christian Lord's Prayer, praising God and appealing for His help and guidance.
ghee	Clarified butter, made of buffalo milk or vegetable oil.
ghusl	Washing of the whole body as a preparation for prayer, which must be performed by a person in a state of ritual impurity, e.g. after sexual intercourse.
halwa	Sweetmeat made of flour, ghee, and sugar.
Hazrat Ali	Cousin and son-in-law of the Prophet Muhammad. He was the fourth orthodox caliph, or ruler, of the Muslim community. During the Prophet's lifetime he played a leading part in almost all military expeditions. The courage that he displayed in battle became proverbial. He is especially venerated by Shia Muslims who believe that the Prophet chose him to be his immediate successor. Although only a small minority of Pashtun tribes are Shia, Ali figures as a hero in several Pashto legends.
hujra	Room or building where guests are fed and lodged, also serving as bachelors' quarters for young men of the tribe and a place of assembly where men of the village meet to talk, drink tea, or play cards. Each village has at least one *hujra,* or guest-house, and *Khans* generally have their own.
imam	Leader of the congregational prayers in the mosque, literally 'one whose example is followed'.
Izrail	Angel of death, one of the four archangels (next to Jibril, Mikhail, Israfil). It is related in one of the traditions of the

Prophet Muhammad that when God created Izrail, 'He veiled him from creatures with a million veils. The east and west of this world are like a table in his hands upon which everything has been placed, and then is set before man that he may eat; so he eats what he wants of it' (al-Qadi, p. 29).

jarib A land measure equivalent to about half an acre, a corn measure of 384 *maunds*, or as much land as will produce this amount.

jinn Intelligent beings, said by some to be composed of vapour or flame, intermediate between humans and angels, capable of appearing in the form of an animal or a human being. God created the *jinn* prior to His creation of mankind; they may be good or bad. A Pashtun mother with a new-born child remains indoors and may keep a knife at her side to ward off evil *jinn*. She may propitiate them by laying aside a portion of food for them. A person with epilepsy is considered to be possessed by *jinn*. The same is true of the mentally deranged. The Arabic *jinni* (pl. *jinn*) derives from *janna*, *yajannu*, 'to be covered or hidden', which means that *jinn* are invisible or hidden beings.

jirga Assembly or council of elders, who meet to prepare for war, to make peace, to arbitrate in private disputes, and to discuss matters of common interest.

Khan Lord, prince, important landowner; a title principally used by Afghans or Pashtuns.

Loe Akhtar 'The big feast, ' or *Id al-Adha*, on 10th *Dhu l-Hijja* when sheep are sacrificed and the meat is distributed to the poor in memory of Abraham's willingness to sacrifice his eldest son Ishmael. Muslims say that in the Torah the name Isaac was substituted for that of Ishmael.

maund (Anglo-Indian): Measure of weight which varies considerably, the Qandahar or Tabriz *maund* being only 8 lb (3.6 kg) whilst that of Peshawar is 80 lb (36 kg) (Pashto, Persian, and Urdu *mann*). The word is believed to be of Chaldean or Babylonian origin.

Mecca Town in Arabia where the Prophet Muhammad was born about the year 570 AD, to which every Muslim should attempt to make a pilgrimage before he or she dies.

Medina Town to which the Prophet Muhammad migrated in 622 AD. It was here that the first Islamic state was established.

mehr The *mehr* (Arabic *mahr*) is a gift which a man gives to a woman at the time of marriage. This gift, which may be in the

362

	form of money, jewellery, or land, gives the woman some financial security in case of a divorce because her husband is forbidden to touch it without her consent.
Muhammad Hanifah	Muhammad ibn al-Hanafiya, born 16 AH, youngest son of Ali by his second wife Khawla, a woman of the tribe of Banu Hanifah, who had been brought to Medina as a prisoner after the battle of Aqraba. Although not related to the Prophet by blood, many looked to him as his father's political and spiritual successor after the death of Hasan and Husayn. Some Shias still regard him as the hidden Imam or Mahdi.
mullah	Muslim divine, charged with looking after a mosque and leading the congregational prayer. He officiates at births, circumcisions, weddings, and funerals. He is generally not a member of the village clan.
namaz	The five daily prayers, *namaz* (Arabic *salat*), can be performed almost anywhere, in a mosque, at home, outside, or in any clean place, either individually or in congregation, although congregational prayer is preferable. The times of prayer are as follows: at the first light of dawn, *salat al-fajr*; just after high noon, *salat al-dhuhr*; in the middle of the afternoon, *salat al-asr*; just after sunset, *salat al-maghrib*; and at night, *salat al-isha*.
paisa	Unit of currency, one-twentieth of an *anna*.
paratha	Flat bread fried in butter, consisting of many layers of gossamer-thin dough, made with wheat flour.
pilau	Baked rice containing meat, raisins, spices etc. (Pashto *pulao*).
pir	Sufi spiritual master, or saint.
purdah	Veil *(pardah)*; the system whereby women are kept in seclusion and veiled except in the presence of servants and close relatives.
Qaf	The distant mountain of Qaf; a mountain range surrounding the earth, said to be composed of emerald, separated from the flat disk of the earth by a region impassable to human beings. In ancient Islamic cosmology this mountain forms the boundary between the visible and invisible world. It is the home of fairies and *deo*s, and it is here that the Simurgh, the fabulous bird of Persian mythology makes its nest. It is sometimes identified with the mountains of the Caucasus.
rakat	Plural of *rakah*, a bow in prayer, followed by two prostrations, or unit of prayer. Each of the five prescribed daily prayers consists of a fixed number of *rakat*, obligatory

	(*farz*), customary (*sunnat*), or in accordance with the Prophet Muhammad's example.
Rustam	A hero of Persian romance. There are many tales about him in Firdausi's epic poem *Shahnama* (Book of Kings). He was the son of Zal, Governor of Sistan, and his wife Rudaba, a princess of the royal family of Kabul. He extended Irani rule to the Oxus, twice freed his sovereign Kai Kaus (Cambyses I) from captivity, killed the Deo Safed, or White Demon (perhaps a Russian prince), repelled a Turani invasion, and drove the invaders under King Afrasiab across the Oxus. On this campaign he engaged in combat with his unknown son Sohrab. In the succeeding reign of Kai Khusrau (the Great Cyrus, d. 528 BC), the founder of the Persian empire, he waged many wars against Afrasiab, who at length fell into his hands and was put to death. When Samarkand and Bukhara were annexed to Iran, Kai Khusrau appointed Rustam hereditary governor of Kabul, Zabalistan, and Nimroz. In the reign of Gushtasp (Darius Hystaspes) he defeated and killed the heir-apparent Isfandiar, and at length he himself, in the reign of Ard-Shir Drazdast (Artaxerxes Longimanus), fell a victim to his own brother's treachery.
seer	(Anglo-Indian): Measure of weight which varies considerably. In Peshawar it is equivalent to 2 lb (0.9 kg) (Pashto *ser*).
shahadah	The Islamic profession of faith that a person is required to make if he or she intends to embrace Islam: 'There is no god but Allah. Muhammad is the Messenger of Allah.' This is the first of the five pillars of Islam.
shalwar	Pashtun trousers, baggy cotton trousers, worn by both men and women, held up and gathered at the waist by a cord; *shalwar kameez,* trousers and matching shirt, which is not tucked in, ideal for hot weather and for prayer.
shariah	Islamic law, or jurisprudence, based on the Quran and *hadith,* or sayings of the Prophet; literally the path to the watering-hole.
Simurgh	A bird of great size and wisdom, found in Persian mythology, which dwells in the Mountain of Qaf. In Firdausi's *Shahnama*, the Simurgh is the guardian of Sam and Zal, the grandfather and father of Rustam. The Persian mystic Fariduddin Attar, in his *Conference of the Birds,* makes the Simurgh on Mount Qaf a symbol of the Godhead, using a pun on *si murgh,* 'thirty birds'.

taweez Written charm or prayer, based on the text of the Quran, worn as a magical talisman to cure an illness, to evoke love, to destroy an enemy, etc. It may be tied in a handkerchief round the arm, or it may be sewn into a leather bag worn round the neck.

tor A woman accused of adultery is considered *tor,* literally black or impure. In the Tribal Areas death is still the usual punishment for adultery. The expression *sar tor* (literally 'black head') means uncovered, without a veil or *chadur,* hence debased or degraded. The association between the black lover and adultery is discussed in the Preface.

Zamzam Sacred well in Mecca, also called the well of Ishmael. According to Muslim tradition, the well was opened by the angel Gabriel to save Hagar and her son Ishmael, who were dying of thirst in the desert, after their departure from the household of Abraham. It has been regarded as sacred since pre-Islamic times, and since time immemorial the water has been renowned for its medicinal properties.

Bibliography

AARNE, Antti, and Stith THOMPSON. *The Types of the Folktale: A Classification and Bibliography.* 2nd revision (FF Communications, 184). Helsinki: Suomalainen Tiedeakatemia, 1961.

ABBAS, Zainab Ghulam. *Folktales of Pakistan.* Karachi: Pakistan Publications, 1957.

AHMAD, Aziz. *Studies in Islamic Culture in the Indian Environment.* Oxford: Clarendon Press, 1964.

AHMED, Akbar S., trans. *Mataloona: Pukhto Proverbs.* Karachi: Oxford University Press, 1975.

—— *Pieces of Green: The Sociology of Change in Pakistan (1964–1974).* Karachi: Royal Book Company, 1977.

—— *Pukhtun Economy and Society: Traditional Structure and Economic Development in a Tribal Society.* London: Routledge & Kegan Paul, 1980.

ANAND, Mulk Raj. *Folk Tales of Punjab* (Folk Tales of India Series, 18). New Delhi: Sterling Publishers, 1974.

ATKINSON, James. *Sketches in Afghanistan.* London: Henry Graves & Company, 1842.

BAHADUR, K. P. *Folk Tales of Uttar Pradesh* (Folk Tales of India Series, 10), 3rd edn. New Delhi: Sterling Publishers, 1983.

BECK, Brenda E. F., *et al.*, ed. *Folktales of India.* Chicago: University of Chicago Press, 1987.

BODDING, P.O., ed. *Santal Folktales.* 3 vols. Oslo: H. Aschehoug, 1925–29.

BOMPAS, Cecil Henry, trans. *Folklore of the Santal Parganas.* London: David Nutt, 1909.

BOWEN, John Charles Edward. *Plain Tales of the Afghan Border.* London: Springwood Books, 1982.

BRIGGS, Katherine M. *A Dictionary of British Folk-Tales in the English Language, Incorporating the F. J. Norton Collection,* 4 vols. London: Routledge & Kegan Paul, 1970.

BRODEUR, Arthur Gilchrist. 'The Grateful Lion', *Publications of the Modern Language Association of America,* 39 (1923), 485–524.

BROWN, W. Norman. 'Change of Sex as a Hindu Story Motif', *Journal of the American Oriental Society*, 47 (1927), 3–24.

BÜRGEL, Johann Christoph. *The Feather of Simurgh: The 'Licit Magic' of the Arts in Medieval Islam*. New York: New York University Press, 1988.

BUSHNAQ, Inea, trans. *Arab Folktales*. Harmondsworth: Penguin, 1987.

CALVINO, Italo. *Italian Folktales*, trans. George Martin. New York: Harcourt Brace Jovanovich, 1980.

CAMPBELL, A., trans. *Santal FolkTales*. Pokhuria: Santal Mission Press, 1891.

CAROE, Olaf. *The Pathans*. London: Macmillan, 1956.

CHILLI, Shaikh. *Folktales of Hindustan*, 2nd edn. Allahabad: Panini Office, [1913].

CHRISTENSEN, Arthur. *Persian Folktales*, trans. Alfred Kurti. London: G. Bell & Sons, 1971.

COSQUIN, Emmanuel. *Les Contes indiens et l'Occident*. Paris: Édouard Champion, 1922.

CROOKE, William. 'Folktales of Hindustan,' *Indian Antiquary*, 21–25 (1892–96) and 29 (1900).

CROUCH, Marcus. *The Ivory City and Other Stories from India and Pakistan*. London: Pelham, 1980.

DAMES, Longworth M. 'Balochi Tales,' *Folk-Lore*, 3 (1892); 4 (1893); 8 (1897).

DARMESTETER, J., ed. and trans. *Chants populaires des Afghans*, 2 vols. Paris: E. Leroux, 1888–90.

DAY, Lal Behari. *Folktales of Bengal*. London: Macmillan, 1883.

DHAR, Samnath. *Kashmir Folk Tales*. Bombay: Hind Kitabs, 1949.

DRACOTT, Alice Elizabeth. *Simla Village Tales, or Folk Tales from the Himalayas*. London: John Murray, 1906.

DUPREE, Louis. *Afghanistan*. Princeton: Princeton University Press, 1973.

EDEN, Emily. *Portraits of the Princes and People of India*. London: J. Dickinson, 1844.

EMENEAU, Murray B., ed. and trans. *Kota Texts* (Univ. of Cal. Pubns in Linguistics, 1–4), 4 vols. Berkeley: University of California Press, 1944–46.

ENTHOVEN, R. E. *The Folklore of Bombay*. Oxford: Clarendon Press, 1924.

FEINSTEIN, Alan S. *Folk Tales from Persia*. South Brunswick, N J: A. S. Barnes, 1971.

FONTANA, Maria Vittoria. *La leggenda di Bahram Gur e Azada: materiale per la storia di una topilogia figurativa dalle origini al XIV secolo* (Departimento di Studi Asiastici, Series minor., 24). Naples: Istituto Universitario Orientale, 1986.

FRERE, Mary. *Old Deccan Days, or Hindoo Fairy Legends Current in Southern India*. London: John Murray, 1898 (1st edn 1868).

Bibliography

GARCIN de TASSY. 'Gul o Sanaubar. Rose et Cyprès,' *Revue Orientale et Américaine*, 6 (1861), 69–130.

GRIERSON, G. A. *Linguistic Survey of India*, 9 vols. Calcutta: Office of the Superintendent of Government Printing, 1903–28.

HACKIN, Ria, and Ahmad Ali KOHZAD. *Légendes et coutumes afghanes*. Paris: Presses Universitaires de France, 1953.

HADDAWY, Husain, trans. *The Arabian Nights*. New York: W. W. Norton, 1990.

HANDOO, Jawaharlal. *A Bibliography of Indian Folk Literature*. Mysore: Central Institute of Indian Languages, 1977.

ISLAM, Mazharul. *A History of Folktale Collections in India and Pakistan*. Dacca: Bengali Academy, 1970.

JACOBS, Joseph, ed. *Indian Fairy Tales*. London: David Nutt, 1892; repr. New York: Dover, 1969.

KANG, Kanwarjit Singh, and Diljit Kaur KANG. *151 Folk Tales of India* [from NINQ, ed. William Crooke]. London: Asia Publishing House, 1988.

KING, L. W. 'Folktales from the Punjab'. *Folk-Lore*, 32, 33, 35, 36, 37, (1921–6).

KINGSCOTE, Mrs Howard, and Pandit Natesa SASTRI. *Tales of the Sun, or Folklore of Southern India*. London: W. H. Allen, 1890.

KIRKLAND, Edwin C. *A Bibliography of South Asian Folklore*. Bloomington: Indiana Univ. Research Center in Anthropology, Folklore, and Linguistics; The Hague: Mouton, 1966.

KNAPPERT, Jan. *Islamic Legends: Histories of the Heroes, Saints and Prophets of Islam*, 2 vols. Leiden: E. J. Brill, 1985.

KNOWLES, J. Hinton. *Folk-Tales of Kashmir*, 2nd edn. London: Kegan Paul, Trench, Trübner, 1893.

KOMAL, Laxman. *Folk Tales of Pakistan* (Folk Tales of the World, 3). New Delhi: Sterling Publishers, 1976.

LORIMER, D. L. R., and E. O. LORIMER, trans. *Persian Tales*. London: Macmillan, 1919.

McCULLOCH, William. *Bengali Household Tales*. London: Hodder and Stoughton, 1912.

MALYON, F. H. 'Some Current Pushto Folk Stories,' *Memoirs of the Asiatic Society of Bengal*, 3 (1913), 355–405.

MASSON, Charles. *Legends of the Afghan Countries*. London: J. Madden, 1848.

MUHAWI, Ibrahim and Sharif KANAANA, trans. *Speak Bird, Speak Again: Palestinian Arab Folktales*. Berkeley: University of California Press, 1989.

NAKHSHABI, Ziya al-Din. *The Cleveland Museum of Art's Tuti-Nama: Tales of a Parrot*, trans. and ed. Muhammad A. Simsar. Graz: Akademisch Druck u.Verlaganstalt, 1978.

NINQ. *North Indian Notes and Queries*, ed. William Crooke, vols. 1–6 (1891–96).

OAKLEY, E. S., and Tara Dutt GAIROLA. *Himalayan Folklore*. Allahabad: Superintendent, Printing and Stationary, United Provinces, 1935.

O'CONNOR, W. F., trans. *Folk Tales from Tibet*. London: Hurst and Blackett, 1906.

PARKER, H., trans. *Village Folk-Tales of Ceylon*. 3 vols. London: Luzac, 1910–14.

PENZER, N. M., ed. *The Ocean of Story, Being C. H. Tawney's Translation of Somadeva's 'Kathasaritsagara'*, 10 vols. London: C. J. Sawyer, 1924–28; repr. Delhi, Motilal Banarsidass, 1968.

PETRONIUS. *The Satyricon*, trans. J. M. Mitchell. 2nd edn. London: George Routledge and Sons, [1923].

PLOWDEN, Trevor Chichele. *Translation of the Kalid-i-Afghani: The Text Book for the Pakhto Examination*. Lahore: Central Jail Press, 1875.

al-QADI, 'Abd ar-Rahim ibn Ahmad. *Islamic Book of the Dead*. Norwich: Diwan Press, 1977.

ur-RAHMAN, Inayat. *Folk Tales of Swat* [Pashto text & trans.] (Istituto Italiano per il Medio ed Estremo Oriente. Centro Studi e Scavi Archeologici in Asia, Reports and memoirs 13 [pt 1]). Rome, 1968.

RALSTON, W. R. S. *Russian Folk-Tales*. London: Smith, Elder, 1873.

RAMANUJAN, A. K. *Folktales from India: A Selection of Oral Tales from Twenty-two Languages*. Delhi: Penguin Books, 1993.

RAMASWAMI, Raju. *Indian Fables*. London: Swann Sonnenschein, 1901 (1st edn, 1887).

RANELAGH, E. L. *The Past We Share: The Near Eastern Ancestry of Western Folk Literature*. London: Quartet Books, 1979.

RASHID, Talib. *Gul au Sanaubar* [Pushtu text in verse] (Peshawar Academy Publication Series, 13). Peshawar, [1960].

RATTRAY, James. *Costumes and Scenery of Afghaunistaun*. London: Hering & Remington, 1848.

RAVERTY, H. G. *Selections from the Poetry of the Afghans from the Sixteenth to the Nineteenth Century: Literally Translated from the Original Pushto*. London: Williams and Norgate, 1862.

SADHU, S. L. *Folk Tales from Kashmir*. London: Asia Publishing House, 1962.

SHAH, Amina. *Folk Tales of Central Asia*. London: Octagon Press, 1970.

SHAH, Idries. *Pleasantries of the Incredible Mulla Nasrudin*. London: Jonathan Cape, 1968.

SHAH, Sirdar Ikbal Ali. *Afghanistan of the Afghans*. London: The Diamond Press, 1928.

el-SHAMY, Hasan M., trans. and ed. *Folktales of Egypt*. Chicago: University of Chicago Press, 1980.

SINGER, André. *Guardians of the North–West Frontier: The Pathans*. Amsterdam: Time-Life Books, 1982.

—— *Lords of the Khyber: The Story of the North-West Frontier*. London: Faber & Faber, 1984.

SPAIN, James W. *The Way of the Pathans*, 2nd edn. Karachi: Oxford University Press, 1972.

STEEL, Flora Annie. *Tales of the Punjab: Told by the People*, Notes by R. C. Temple. London: Macmillan, 1894; new edn, London: Bodley Head, 1973.

STEVENS, E. S., trans. *Folk-Tales of Iraq*. New York: Benjamin Blom, 1971.

STOKES, Maive. *Indian Fairy Tales*. London: Ellis and White, 1880.

SWYNNERTON, Charles. 'Four Legends of King Rasulu of Sialkot', *Folk-Lore Journal*, 1 (1883), 129–52.

—— *Indian Nights' Entertainment; or Folk-Tales from the Upper Indus*. London: Elliot Stock, 1892.

—— *Romantic Tales from the Punjab with Indian Nights' Entertainment*, new edn. London: Constable, 1908.

TEMPLE, R. C. *The Legends of the Punjab*, 3 vols. Bombay: Education Society's Press, 1884–86.

THOMPSON, Stith. *The Folktale*. Berkeley: University of California Press, 1977.

—— *One Hundred Favorite Folktales*. Bloomington: Indiana University Press, 1968.

—— *Motif Index of Folk-Literature*, 2nd edn, 6 vols. Bloomington: Indiana University Press; Copenhagen: Rosenkilde and Bagger, 1955–58.

THOMPSON, Stith, and Jonas BALYS. *The Oral Tales of India* (Indiana Univ. Pubns, Folklore Series, 10). Bloomington: Indiana University Press, 1958.

THOMPSON, Stith, and Warren E. ROBERTS. *Types of Indic Oral Tales: India, Pakistan, and Ceylon* (FF Communications, 180). Helsinki: Suomalainen Tiedeakatemia, 1960.

THORBURN, S. S. *Bannu, or Our Afghan Frontier*. London: Trübner, 1876.

THORNHILL, Mark. *Indian Fairy Tales*. London: Hatchards, [1889].

VAN BUITENEN, J. A. B. *Tales of Ancient India, Translated from Sanskrit*. Chicago: University of Chicago Press, 1959.

WADIA, Putlibai D. H. 'The Artist's Stratagem; or the Princess who was resolved never to marry,' in 'Folklore in Western India,' *Indian Antiquary*, 17 (1888), at pp. 128–32.

WORTHAM, B. Hale. *The Enchanted Parrot: Being a Selection from the 'Suka Saptati,' or, The Seventy Tales of a Parrot, Translated from the Sanskrit Text*. London: Luzac, 1911.

Index of Tale Types

III. JOKES AND ANECDOTES

Index of Folk Motifs